T0258894

INFORMATION SYSTEMS *and* TECHNOLOGY
for the
NONINFORMATION SYSTEMS EXECUTIVE

An Integrated Resource Management
Guide for the 21st Century

The St. Lucie Press
Library of Executive Excellence Series

INFORMATION SYSTEMS *and* TECHNOLOGY

for the

NONINFORMATION SYSTEMS EXECUTIVE

An Integrated Resource Management Guide for the 21st Century

JAE K. SIIIM, Ph.D.

Professor of Business Administration
California State University at Long Beach, California

St. Lucie Press
Boca Raton   London   New York   Washington, D.C.

Library of Congress Cataloging-in-Publication Data

Shim, Jae K.
    Information systems and technology for the noninformation systems
executive : an integrated resource management guide for the 21st century / Jae K. Shim.
        p. cm.
    Includes index.
    ISBN 1-57444-285-6 (alk.)
    1. Information resources management. 2. Information storage and retrieval systems.
T58.64 .S53 2000
658.4′038—dc21   00-030347
                                                                 CIP

© 2000 by CRC Press LLC
St. Lucie Press is an imprint of CRC Press LLC

No claim to original U.S. Government works
International Standard Book Number 1-57444-285-6
Library of Congress Card Number 00-030347
Printed in the United States of America 1 2 3 4 5 6 7 8 9 0
Printed on acid-free paper

Preface

The book covers information systems in all phases of business and in all functional areas to analyze and solve business problems in the "real world." The practical and efficient use of computer technology, both software and hardware, is highlighted. All types of business applications are covered. The importance of databases, networking, and telecommunications is clearly presented. Popular accounting, tax, finance, management, manufacturing, and marketing software applications are explained for easy use. Software for decision support systems (DSSs), executive information systems (EISs), and artificial intelligence (AI)—such as financial modeling, budgeting, strategic planning and control, forecasting, data analysis, inventory planning, and optimization software—are covered with real-life examples. "What-if" analysis and the effects of changing assumptions are discussed.

The purpose of the book is to provide a wealth of current and essential information to managers in all types of organizations so they may make optimum decisions. It gives the business person sufficient information to perform in the computerized financial application and modeling environment. Emerging trends in information technology are anticipated and discussed. In other words, expected developments in computers are presented so as to properly plan ahead. The professional success of a business manager depends on keeping abreast to the latest thinking and applications in information technology. This surely gives a competitive edge.

The book is written for business professionals in a practical, reader-friendly manner, including clear illustrations. We have simplified difficult computer terminology and usage. Important topics include management information systems (MISs), selection of the best software and hardware for particular applications, business application software (e.g., accounting, finance, management, tax, marketing, and manufacturing), databases, telecommunications and online services (e.g., AOL, Prodigy, CompuServe, Dow Jones, Westlaw, AICPA), and computer security and auditing. The latest multimedia trends are covered. New developments in artificial intelligence and expert systems, decision support systems, and executive information systems are covered.

The audience for this book includes accountants, tax preparers, financial managers, general managers, marketing executives, production/operations managers, purchasing managers, personnel managers, business analysts, forecasters, budget analysts, chief financial officers (CFOs), chief executive officers (CEOs), chief operating officers (COOs), chief information officers (CIOs), project managers, consultants, systems analysts, and computer support staff. Managers in large, medium, and small companies will benefit. Private and nonprofit entities will find the material of equal value.

The following are some representative topics, among others discussed in the book, of vital interest to managers:

- Using software in planning and control
- The applications of telecommunication technologies and how digitized computer signals can take advantage of these technologies
- Accounting and information systems and packages showing how applications can be made to record keeping, reporting, and financial statement presentation
- An explanation of what a decision support system (DSS) is about and how it is useful to business decision makers to improve the quality of their analysis and evaluation (It improves problem solving.)
- The use of artificial intelligence and expert systems in making decisions
- Computerized security (e.g., protecting files, service contracts, backups, insurance coverage, and security devices) (It includes preventing fraud.)
- Database management involving organizing and managing information so it can be retrieved and utilized in an effective and efficient way
- What a management information system (MIS) is and what its applications and benefits are
- The use of online databases (e.g., World Wide Web, Dow Jones, Westlaw, Lexis) in making business decisions
- The use of an intranet within a company as an important information source
- Available accounting and financial software packages and how they improve financial reporting and analysis
- The use of networking to operate smarter and be more efficient in a computer environment
- The use of computer conferencing
- Financial modeling and "what-if" analysis in budgeting, forecasting, and general decision-making
- Manufacturing information systems packages to aid in inventory record keeping, inventory management and control, and production planning
- Expert systems (ESs) and executive information systems (EISs)
- Marketing information systems to aid in sales planning, sales forecasting, market research, and advertising effectiveness
- Selecting the best hardware for the particular application needs and to enhance productivity

Chapter 1 discusses what management information systems are about and presents MIS techniques. The different types of MISs are explained, including when each type would be most appropriate. Chapter 2 covers MISs in business decision making and explains decision models. Chapter 3 introduces basic hardware components and how to buy the "right" hardware combination for each user's requirements.

Chapter 4 presents systems software and explains the functions and terminology of different types of systems software. Chapter 5 covers application software and how such software can be used to improve profitability and enhance productivity. Chapter 6 discusses the use of database software, including query languages. Chapter 7 presents data communications. Chapter 8 discusses the different types of online databases and the information available on them. State-of-the-art communication technologies and popular network applications are also presented. Chapter 9 discusses how to use an intranet within the business. Chapter 10 covers information systems development. Chapter 11 presents accounting, audit, and tax software and related business applications. Chapter 12 shows how MISs can be applied to financial management to improve the management of assets and liabilities and to help plan the financing of debt and equity. The role of the MIS in forecasting is also explained. Chapter 13 discusses manufacturing information systems and packages. It includes applications to production planning so as to improve manufacturing activity and inventory management. Marketing information systems and packages are presented in Chapter 14. The chapter shows how software is used in marketing management, sales planning, and advertising effectiveness. The use of decision support systems (DSSs) to aid in management decision making by making it more accurate and reliable is the subject of Chapter 15. Chapter 16 deals with the use of artificial intelligence software to imitate the human mind process. It aids in managerial analysis and decision making. Chapter 17 is directed toward computer security and auditing. It presents protective data systems and information technology to safeguard the integrity of information. Ways to prevent misappropriation of resources and fraudulent transactions are enumerated.

A glossary of MIS terms is included. The presentation is generic in nature. The reader does not need to know programming. There are many checklists, charts, tables, and graphs. In the index, a specific area of interest may easily be found.

In conclusion, the book shows clearly how computers can aid business managers in efficiently performing their functions. Their success depends on being up to date in the computer environment and having all information immediately available to make successful decisions.

About the Author

Jae K. Shim is Professor of Business Administration at California State University, Long Beach. He received his M.B.A. and Ph.D. degrees from the University of California at Berkeley (Haas School of Business).

Dr. Shim is a coauthor of *Information Systems Management Handbook*, *The Handbook of Electronic Commerce*, *The Handbook of Computer Security*, *Handbook of Financial Analysis, Forecasting, and Modeling*, *Strategic Business Forecasting*, *The Vest-Pocket CFO*, and the best selling *Vest-Pocket MBA*. Dr. Shim has 50 other professional and college books to his credit.

Dr. Shim has also published numerous refereed articles in such journals *Decision Sciences*, *Management Science*, *Long Range Planning*, *OMEGA*, *Journal of Operational Research Society*, *Journal of Business Forecasting*, *Econometrica*, *Simulation and Games*, and *Journal of Systems Management*. He was a recipient of the 1982 *Credit Research Foundation Outstanding Paper Award* for his article on financial modeling.

Table of Contents

1 What Are Management Information Systems?

An information system is a computerized system that processes data (facts) and produces information. This process is defined as an *information processing cycle* (IPC). The information processing cycle consists of four operations. They are input, process, output, and storage. The retrieval of raw data from the environment and delivering it to the computer is called *input*. After the computer receives data from the input device, it will manipulate, refine, and process the data to produce useful information for users. This step is called *processing*. After data has been refined and manipulated into useful information, the information is displayed to the end users, and that is called *output*. Finally, the information needs to be saved for further use. That is the *storage* step. All four processes make up the information processing cycle. The input of the IPC is raw data. Raw data consists of raw facts, while information is a collection of facts organized or processed in such a way that they have additional value for further use.

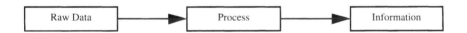

Information itself has value, and commerce often involves the exchange of information rather than tangible goods. Information is valuable and useful because it can help decision makers. For example, investors are using information to make multimillion-dollar decisions, financial institutions employ information to transfer millions of dollars. Retailers use information to control inventory and process orders. Information technologies are consistently changing our society, our ways of doing business, and our lives. To fully understand what an information system is and its concepts, the components of information systems first should be identified. A complete information system should contain the following elements.

COMPUTER HARDWARE

Computer hardware can be classified into five categories: personal computers, servers, minicomputers, mainframes, and supercomputers.

PERSONAL COMPUTERS

Personal computers are also called *microcomputers*. Each contains a microprocessor and is designed for individual or personal use. Classifications within this category include nonportable computers and portable computers.

Desktop Computers

These are the most popular type of microcomputer and are designed to fit on the top of a desk. With the same options in the system, desktop models are the least expensive.

Workstations

Workstations are the most high-end personal computers. They are more powerful and expensive than any other personal computers. They are used frequently as the file servers in a network environment. Many engineers also use workstations to aid in product design and testing. Workstations are very good in calculations and graphics.

Laptop Computers

These are the largest portable computers in this category. They weigh between 8 and 15 lb and have a hard drive, CD-ROM drive, and other equipment.

Notebook Computers

These are a smaller version of laptop computers. They weigh between four and eight pounds. The functions available for notebooks are very similar to those in laptop computers but with a more compact design and smaller screen.

Subnotebook Computers

These are even smaller than notebook computers. They weigh less than four pounds and carry fewer optional devices such as CD-ROM drives and regular hard drives.

Pen-Based Computers

These are the smallest computers and use a pen-like device to enter data. This pen-like device can be used to write directly on the screen or used as a pointing device to make selections on the menu displayed on screen. The unique feature about pen-based computers is the special software design to allow users to enter information by handwriting after several training sessions.

SERVERS

Server computers are designed to support a computer network that allows users to share files, applications, and hardware resources. A server computer is normally used to serve other computers in the network in terms of file storage and resources management, data communications, print management, and other computer functions. The characteristics of a server computer are as follows:

- It communicates with other networks.
- It enhances communication speed within the network.
- It offers high-end central processing unit (CPU) power with high capacity on the hard drive.
- Some offer parallel processing capabilities by employing more than one CPU.
- It has extensive memory capacity.

A server computer could be either a high-end microcomputer or a powerful microcomputer with minicomputer-like functions. The prices for server computers are in the $5,000 to $150,000 range.

MINICOMPUTERS

Minicomputers are more powerful than microcomputers in terms of the multiple user environment. In other words, a minicomputer can be used by many users simultaneously. Many businesses and other organizations use minicomputers for their information processing requirements. The cost of minicomputers can be from $15,000 up to several hundred thousand dollars. The most powerful minicomputers are called *superminicomputers*.

MAINFRAME COMPUTERS

Mainframe computers are large computer systems that can handle hundreds of users, store large amounts of data, and process transactions at a high speed. Mainframe computers use a very sophisticated computer operating system to manage and control the whole system. Mainframes usually require a specialized environment including air conditioning and raised flooring that allows computer cables to be installed underneath. The price range for mainframes is from several hundred thousand to several million dollars.

SUPERCOMPUTERS

Supercomputers constitute the most powerful category of computers. Typical applications are scientific calculations, engineering design, space exploration, and other tasks requiring complicated processing. Supercomputers cost several million dollars.

COMPUTER SOFTWARE

Computer *software* refers to instructions, called *programs,* written in programming languages by programmers. Software consists of sequences of operations the computer will follow. Before a program can run (be *executed*), the program must be loaded into the main memory of the computer. After that, programs can be executed to perform certain functions based on how they are designed. For example, a word processing program allows users to enter their typing and edit the contents. A graphic design program is used to perform graphic designs. Most computer programs are written by people with special training. These people, called *computer programmers,* write the necessary instructions.

SYSTEM SOFTWARE

System software consists of programs that are use to control and operate the computer hardware. There are three components in system software: the operating system, utility programs, and language processors. The operating system tells the computer how to perform functions such as how to load, store, and execute programs; how to transfer data between input/output devices; and how to manage resources available (CPU time). To operate a computer, the operating system must be loaded in the main memory first. Other application software can then be loaded into the computer with the help of the operating system. Utility programs are designed to perform functions that are not available in application software, such as formatting a diskette and creating a directory.

APPLICATION SOFTWARE

Application software consists of programs used to perform a specific user's task, such as preparing a document, designing a financial worksheet, and creating a useful database. When you think of the different ways people use computers to improve the efficiency in their workplace, you are usually thinking of application software. Most users do not write their own software programs (either system software or application software). They can buy ready-to-use programs known as software *packages.*

DATA

Data are usually the input of a management information system (MIS). After data are processed by the MIS, information will be generated. Users can then use information for decision making. Data are normally organized into files' tables, and files are organized into database. Users can retrieve data as input of application software and produce information as output. If data are not accurate, the information produced will not be useful. Therefore, the garbage-in, garbage-out (GIGO) syndrome should be avoided.

TRAINED PERSONNEL

People who operate MIS should be properly trained. MIS professionals and programmers are responsible for designing and programming MIS, while computer operators and users use them. With adequate training, users can achieve the desired functions designed by MIS professionals. An experienced user can also provide MIS professionals with valuable suggestions or be involved in MIS development.

PROCEDURES

MIS procedures are designed for users to achieve certain functions. Well designed procedures guarantee the quality and the security of information processing.

Information systems that are implemented on a computer can be classified into five different systems.

- Transaction processing systems
- Management reporting systems
- Executive information systems/executive support systems
- Decision support systems
- Office information systems

The following sections describe the above systems.

WHEN TO USE TRANSACTION PROCESSING SYSTEMS

Transaction information systems are designed to process the day-to-day transactions of an organization so that many labor-intensive business transactions can be replaced by automated processes. Theses transactions have characteristics of large numbers and routine processes. Each process has a very simple data transaction, and the transaction processing system (TPS) is expected to process each one in a very short period of time. Examples are supermarket/grocery checkout (billing systems) or bank transaction processes.

When computers were first used for processing business applications, TPS was the primary system implemented to replace the manual system. Typically, a successful TPS can improve transaction efficiency, customer service, and reduce transaction costs. The first TPS was a batch system. A TPS in batch processing implies that all transactions are collected first and processed later. The disadvantage of batch processing is that information cannot be updated immediately. A TPS with on-line processing updates information when the transaction is entered. In a business where immediate update is required, an on-line TPS is necessary. On-line TPS requires higher fees for operation than batch TPS. Today, most TPS use on-line processing to achieve better customer satisfaction and current information.

WHEN TO USE MANAGEMENT REPORTING (INFORMATION) SYSTEMS

After TPS had been implemented, some organizations realized that the results produced by TPS are not satisfiable for higher-level decision making and that the computer's capability to perform rapid calculations and logical functions could be used to produce meaningful information for management. As the result, management reporting systems (MRSs) began to be develop so that managerial reports and summarized data could be produced. Theses reports helped managers perform their duties and provided middle management with statistical or summarized data for tactical-level decision making.

In general, MRS is usually used with TPS. TPS processes daily transactions, updates inventory, and keeps customer information while MRS uses the data from TPS to produce daily total sales, inventory ordering lists, and customer lists with different criteria. The output from MRS provides middle management with printed reports and inquiry capabilities to help maintain operations and management control of the enterprise. The concept of management reporting systems evolved as managers realized that computer processing could be used for more than just day-to-day transaction processing; it could also be used to produce meaningful information for management.

Frequently, an MRS is integrated with a TPS, and the input source of MRS is usually the result of TPS. For example, a sales transaction can be processed by using a TPS to record the sales total and customer's information. An MRS can further process these data to generate reports on average sales daily or fast moving items.

WHEN TO USE DECISION SUPPORT SYSTEMS

Decision support systems (DSSs) are designed to help managers reach a decision by summarizing or comparing data from different resources. They are suitable for semi-structured and unstructured problems. Decision support systems often include query languages, statistical analysis capabilities, spreadsheets, and graphics to help decision makers evaluate their decisions. DSSs are a type of MIS expressly developed to support the decision-making process. DSSs facilitate a dialogue between the user, who is considering alternative problem solutions, and the system, with its built-in models and access able database. A typical DSS process involves retrieving a model from the model base and allocating proper data from the database.

With a model, users can ask if-then questions by changing one or several variables as the input, and the combination of data and model generates the recommendations from a DSS. The database is managed by a data base management system (DBMS), whereas a model base is managed by a model base management system (MBMS). Some DSSs allow users to create models for better evaluation. For example, the vice president of marketing may want to know the net effect on company profit if the advertising budget decreases. TPSs and MRSs usually do not provide this type of information.

WHEN TO USE OFFICE INFORMATION SYSTEMS

Office information systems (OISs) are designed to support office tasks with information technology. Voice mail, multimedia system, electronic mail, video conferencing, file transfer, and even group decisions can be achieved by office information systems. The final goal for an OIS is to have an office environment where no paper need be used *(paperless environment)*.

WHEN TO USE EXECUTIVE INFORMATION SYSTEMS

An executive information system (EIS) is designed to generate information that is abstract enough to present the whole company operation in a simplified version to satisfy senior management. Characteristically, senior managers employ a great variety of informal sources of information, so computerized information systems are able to provide only limited assistance. However, the CEO, senior and executive vice presidents, and the board of directors also need to track the performance of their company and of its various units, assess the business environment, and develop strategic directions for the company's future.

In particular, these executives need a great diversity of external information to compare their company's performance to that of its competition and to investigate the general trends of the economies in the many countries where the company may be doing business. EIS is therefore designed to address the information needs for senior management who may not be familiar working with computer systems. An EIS also provides features that make it easier for executives to use. An EIS provides a graphical user interface that can be mouse or touch screen oriented. EIS relies heavily on graphic presentation of both the menu options and data.

WHY DO YOU NEED AN MIS TO SOLVE YOUR BUSINESS PROBLEMS?

The business environment is changing on a daily basis. The competition is everywhere, from cost cutting to marketing strategies. To maintain competitiveness, management must improve the efficiency of operation without sacrificing the quality of products and services. To achieve this task, making timely and correct decisions is the key to success. Since good decision making requires quality data and timely information, an MIS is specifically designed to provide information on a timely basis. An MIS also provides different types of information based on users' need to improve effectiveness and efficiency.

WHAT COMPUTER TECHNOLOGIES ARE AVAILABLE FOR BUSINESS?

Information systems are used in all business domains. For example, finance uses information to forecast revenues and maximize investment, make selections on stocks, and even predict bankruptcies. Accounting uses information systems to record transactions, prepare financial statements, manage cash flow, and predict profit or loss. In marketing, information systems are used to develop new merchandise and services, for customer segmentation, to determine the locations for production and distribution facilities (so that the cost can be reduced and more customers will be attracted), to develop formulate price strategies (so they can maximize total profits), and even to develop the promotion policies (so that advertising will be more efficient). In manufacturing, information systems are used to process customer orders, develop production schedules, design new products, and test product quality.

In addition, network technologies allow users to share information and other resources. As a result, information retrieval can be more efficient and readily available. Current Internet technology provides businesses with a variety of external business information. requires. Multimedia information transmissions (text, graphics, image, and video) are also available in the Internet. With the impact of Internet, *intranet* becomes another new technology popular for businesses. An intranet is a small version of Internet in one organization. It provides almost the same services as the Internet but with better security and privacy. *Artificial intelligence* technologies are also applied to business functions. *Neural networks* have been used to predict the stock and bond markets. *Expert systems* are used to help managers with financial decisions. In the future, more intelligent agents will be used in the business environment to improve the quality of services and products.

HOW TO MANAGE YOUR INFORMATION RESOURCES

Managing information resources can be a very complicated task, due to rapid changes in this field. Generally speaking, there are two options available to managers.

In-house operation
Outsourcing

In-house operation requires your own data processing facilities and personnel. This approach allows users to receive MIS services faster and easier. However, it requires the company to use the equipment and employ MIS personnel to ensure that the facility is fully functional.

Outsourcing deals with subcontracting MIS tasks to professional MIS companies. With professional help, the task can be achieved more efficiently and effectively. However, the response time to acquire services might be a little longer and, very often, the communication channels between subcontractors and users might not be well established. Different MISs are designed for different management functions. To understand which MIS will serve specific management needs, we categorize management into three levels (see Figure 1.1).

- *First level.* Strategic management is the highest level of management. This level contains fewer decision makers but controls much power over the whole organization. Therefore, EIS becomes the most appropriate information system available at this level.
- *Second level.* Tactical management is the middle level of management. Managers in this level very often use MRS for summarized information and to generate management reports for decision making.
- *Third level.* Operational is the lowest level of management. Foremen and supervisors are in this level. TPS with large routine transaction processing capability is usually used for this management level.

DSSs and OISs are not specifically designed for any management level. They are appropriate for all three levels of management.

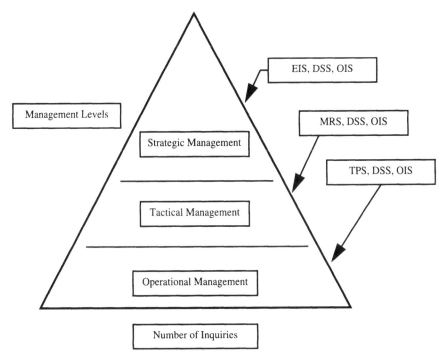

FIGURE 1.1 Management Task Hierarchy

2 Management Information Systems and Decision-Making Models

A management information system (MIS) comprises computer-based processing and/or manual procedures that provide useful, complete, and timely information. This information must support management decision making in a rapidly changing business environment. The MIS system must supply managers with information quickly, accurately, and completely.

Information systems are not new; only computerization of them is new. Before computers, information system techniques existed to supply information for functional purposes.

The scope and purpose of MIS is better understood if each part of the term is defined. See Figure 2.1.

MANAGEMENT

Management has been defined in a variety of ways, but for our purposes it comprises the processes or activities that describe what managers do in the operation of their

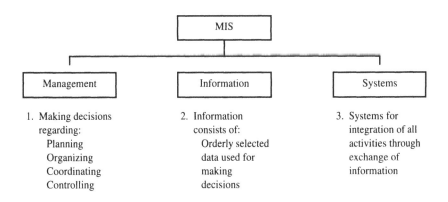

FIGURE 2.1 The meaning of a management information system (MIS).

organization: plan, organize, coordinate, and control operations. They plan by setting strategies and goals and selecting the best course of action to achieve the plan. They organize the tasks necessary for the operational plan, set these tasks up into homogeneous groups, and assign authority delegation. They control the performance of the work by setting performance standards and avoiding deviations from standard.

Because decision making is such a fundamental prerequisite to each of the foregoing processes, the job of an MIS becomes that of facilitating decisions necessary for planning, organizing, and controlling the work and the functions of the business. In general, the work that management performs can be classified as (a) planning, (b) organization and coordination, (c) controlling, and (d) decision making.

PLANNING

The planning function of management involves the selection of long- and short-term objectives and the drawing up of strategic plans to achieve those objectives. For example, the vice president of marketing must consider numerous factors when planing short-term ad campaigns and promotional activities aimed at opening up new long-term markets.

ORGANIZING AND COORDINATING

In performing the organization and coordination function, management must decide how best to put together the firm's resources to carry out established plans. For example, top management must decide on the type and number of divisions and departments in the company and evaluate the effectiveness of the organizational structure. Furthermore, managers must identify the personnel needs of the company and select the personnel as well as training staff.

CONTROLLING

Controlling entails the implementation of a decision method and the use of feedback so that the firm's goals and specific strategic plans are optimally obtained. This includes supervising, guiding, and counseling employees as necessary to keep them motivated and working productively toward the accomplishment of organization objectives.

DECISION MAKING

Decision making is the purposeful selection from a set of alternatives in light of a given objective. Each primary management function involves making decisions, and information is required to make sound decisions. Decisions may be classified as short-term or long-term. Depending on the level of management, decisions can be operational, tactical, or strategic.

INFORMATION

Data must be distinguished from information, and this distinction is clear and important for our purposes. Data are facts and figures that are not currently being used in a decision process, and they usually take the form of historical records that are recorded and filed without immediate intent to retrieve for decision making. An example would be supporting documents, ledgers, and so on that constitute the source material for profit-and-loss statements. Such material would only be of historical interest to an external auditor.

Information consists of data that have been retrieved, processed, or otherwise used for informative or inference purposes, arguments, or as a basis for forecasting or decision making. An example would be any one of the supporting documents mentioned above, but in this case the data could be used by an internal auditor, the management services department of an external auditor, or by internal management for decisions-making purposes such as profit planning and control.

SYSTEMS

A *system* can be described simply as a set of elements joined for a common objective. A *subsystem* is part of a larger system. All systems are parts of larger systems. For our purposes, the organization is the system, and the parts (divisions, departments, functions, units, etc.) are the subsystems. While we have achieved a very high degree of automation and joining together of subsystems in scientific, mechanical, and factory manufacturing operations, we have barely scratched the surface of applying systems principles for organizational or business systems. The concept of synergism has not generally been applied to business organizations, particularly as it applies to the integration of the subsystems through information interchange. Marketing, production/operations, and finance are frequently on diverse paths and working at cross purposes. The systems concept of MIS is therefore one of optimizing the output of the organization by connecting the operating subsystems through the medium of information exchange.

CLASSIFYING MANAGEMENT INFORMATION SYSTEMS IN TERMS OF THE TYPE OF OUTPUT PROVIDED

Another way of classifying MISs depends on the format of the output desired by the users of the management information system. Here, three distinctions are made.

1. MISs that Generate Reports

These reports can be income statements, balance sheets, cash flow reports, accounts receivable statements, inventory status reports, production efficiency reports, or any report on the status of a situation of interest to the decision maker. The reports can be historical or refer to the current status of the situation.

2. MISs that Answer "What-If" Kinds of Questions Asked by Management

These information systems take the information stored in the data base and reply to questions asked by management. These questions are in the form of "what would happen if this or that happened?" The information system thus uses its stored information, its comparison and calculation capabilities, and a set of programs especially written for this situation to provide management with the consequences of an action they are considering.

It works like this. The vice-president for human resources of an airline wonders what pilot recruiting levels would be necessary if the company changed its retirement age from 65 to 62.

The vice president uses a "what-if" information system approach to answer the question. The computer indicates that monthly recruiting levels would have to be increased from 110 to 185 pilots to meet these two conditions. The vice president realizes that is not feasible and now "asks" the system the "what-if" question with the retirement age changed to 63. The reply is now 142 pilots per month recruited. This appears to be an attainable recruiting target. Some "what-if" systems print out entire financial statements reflecting the financial consequences of actions that are being contemplated. Figure 2.2 depicts a "what-if" scheme.

"What-if" management information systems combine models (to be discussed later), software that enables the decision maker to make various inputs to those models and receive the outputs, and report-generating capability. These are generally run on a real-time system, which can be online and which can also run on a time-sharing basis. In Figure 2.2, we have illustrated a "what-if" MIS.

3. MISs THAT SUPPORT DECISION MAKING (DECISION SUPPORT SYSTEMS)

These advanced systems attempt to integrate the decision maker, the data base, and the models being used. A decision support system (DSS) requires a very comprehensive data base plus the ability to manage that data base, to provide outputs to

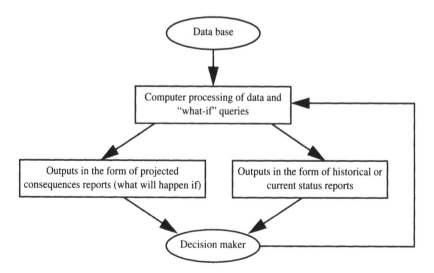

FIGURE 2.2   "What-If" MIS.

the decision maker, and to update whatever permanent models are stored in the system. It requires extensive hardware and software. Two features distinguish DSS from other information systems: (1) they actually make a recommended decision instead of merely supplying additional information to the decision maker, and (2) they "build in" the decision maker as an integral part of the system (the software accommodates the person as part of the decision process). Figure 2.3 illustrates a DSS management information system.

AN MIS AND ORGANIZATIONAL LEVELS

An MIS should produce useful, accurate, and timely information to management on three levels: low-level (operational), middle (tactical), and top (strategic). Lower management makes day-to-day operational decisions that affect a relatively narrow time frame and that involve details. These decisions are structured. Middle management is involved on more tactical decisions that cover a broader range of time and involve more experience. Middle managers use summary reports, exception reports, periodic reports, on-demand reports, and event-initiated reports to make semistructured decisions. Top management deals with decisions that are strategic and long-term in nature.

The primary objective of the MIS is to satisfy the needs at the various levels. Generally, the information needs to be (1) more summarized and relevant to the specific decisions that need to be made than the information normally produced in an organization and (2) available soon enough to be of value in the decision-making process. The information flows up and down through the three levels of management and is made available in various types of reports.

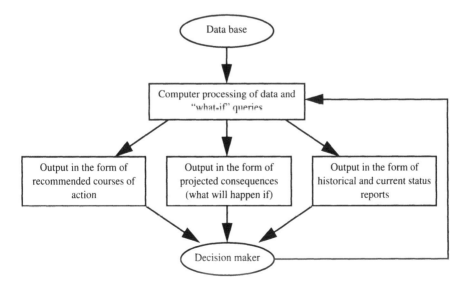

FIGURE 2.3   Decision maker's "what-if" questions.

LEVELS OF MANAGEMENT: WHAT KINDS OF DECISIONS ARE MADE?

Each level of management can be differentiated by the types of decisions made, the time frame considered in the decisions, and the types of report information needed to make decisions (see Table 2.1).

TABLE 2.1
A Comparison of the MISs at the Operational, Tactical, and Strategic Levels

Characteristic	Operational	Tactical	Strategic
Frequency	Regular, repetitive	Mostly regular	Often ad hoc (as needed)
Dependability of results	Expected results	Some surprises may occur	Results often contain surprises
Time period covered	Past	Comparative	Future
Level of data	Very detailed	Summaries of data	Summaries of data
Source of data	Internal	Internal and external	Internal and external
Nature of data	Highly structured	Some unstructured data	Highly unstructured (semistructured)
Accuracy	Highly accurate data	Some subjective data	Highly subjective data
Typical user	First-line supervisors	Middle managers	Top management
Level of decision	Task-oriented	Control and resource allocation oriented	Goal-oriented

LOWER MANAGEMENT

The largest level of management, lower (operational) management, deals mostly with decisions that cover a relatively narrow time frame. Lower management, also called *supervisory management,* actualizes the plans of middle management and controls daily operations—the day-to-day activities that keep the organization humming. Examples of a lower-level manager are the warehouse manager in charge of inventory restocking and the materials manager responsible for seeing that all necessary materials are on hand in manufacturing to meet production needs.

Most decisions at this level require easily defined information about current status and activities within the basic business functions—for example, the information needed to decide whether to restock inventory. This information is generally given in detail reports that contain specific information about routine activities. These reports are structured, so their form can usually be predetermined. Daily business operations data is readily available, and its processing can be easily computerized. Managers at this level typically make structured decisions. A structured decision is a predictable decision that can be made by following a well defined set of predetermined, routine procedures. For example, a clothing store floor manager's decision to accept your credit card to pay for some new clothes is a structured decision based on several well defined criteria:

1. Does the customer have satisfactory identification?
2. Is the card current or expired?
3. Is the card number 011 on the store's list of stolen or lost cards?
4. Is the amount of purchase under the cardholder's credit limit?

MIDDLE MANAGEMENT

The middle level of management deals with decisions that cover a somewhat broader range of time and involve more experience. Some common titles of middle managers are plant manager, division manager, sales manager, branch manager, and director of personnel.

The information that middle managers need involves review, summarization, and analysis of historical data to help plan and control operations and implement policy that has been formulated by upper management. This information is usually given to middle managers in two forms: (1) summary reports, which show totals and trends— for example, total sales by office, by product, by salesperson, and total overall sales—and (2) exception reports, which show out-of-the-ordinary data—for example, inventory reports that list only those items that number fewer than 10 in stock. These reports may be regularly scheduled (periodic reports), requested on a case-by-case basis (on-demand reports), or generated only when certain conditions exist (event-initiated reports).

Periodic reports are produced at predetermined times: daily, weekly, monthly, quarterly, or annually. These reports commonly include payroll reports, inventory status reports, sales reports, income statements, and balance sheets. On-demand reports are usually requested by a manager when information is needed for a particular problem. For example, if a customer wants to establish a large charge account, a manager might request a special report on the customer's payment and order history. Event-initiated reports usually clear with a change in conditions that requires immediate attention, such as an out-of-stock report or a report on an equipment breakdown.

Managers at the middle level of management are often referred to as *tactical* decision makers who generally deal with semistructured decisions. A *semistructured decision* is a decision that includes some structure procedures and some procedures that do not follow a predetermined set of procedures. In most cases, a semistructured decision is complex, requiring detailed analysis and extensive computations. Examples of semistructured decisions include deciding how many units of a specific product should be kept in inventory, whether to purchase a larger computer system, from what source to purchase personal computers, and whether to purchase a multiuser minicomputer system. At least some of the information requirements at this level can be met through computer-based data processing.

TOP MANAGEMENT

The top level of management deals with decisions that are the broadest in scope and cover the widest time frame. Typical titles of managers at this level are chief executive officer (CEO), chief operating officer (COO), chief financial officer (CFO), treasurer, controller, chief information officer (CIO), executive vice president, and senior partner. Top managers include only a few powerful people who are in charge of the four basic functions of a business—marketing, accounting and finance, production, and research and development. Decisions made at this level are unpredictable, long-range, and related to the future, not just past and/or current activities. Therefore, they demand the most experience and judgment.

A company's MIS must be able to supply information to top management as needed in periodic reports, event-initiated reports, and on-demand reports. The information must show how all the company's operations and departments are related to and affected by one another. The major decisions made at this level tend to be directed toward (1) strategic planning—for example, how growth should be financed and which new markets should be tackled first; (2) allocation of resources, such as deciding whether to build or lease office space and whether to spend more money on advertising or the hiring of new staff members; and (3) policy formulation, such as determining the company's policy on hiring minorities and providing employee incentives. Managers at this level are often called *strategic* decision makers. Examples of unstructured decisions include deciding five-year goals for the company, evaluating future financial resources, and deciding how to react to the actions of competitors.

At the higher levels of management, much of the data required to make decisions come from outside the organization (for example, financial information about other competitors). Table 2.2 shows the decision areas that the three levels of management would deal with in (a) a consumer product business and (b) a bank.

MODELING A REAL-LIFE SYSTEM

Many MISs are model based. The real world is complex, dynamic, and expensive to deal with. For this reason, we use models instead of real-life systems. A model is an abstraction of a real-life system that is used to simulate reality. Especially in the computing environment we live in, managers and decision makers find the use of models to be less expensive and easier to understand, allowing them to make better decisions.

There are several different types of models, as follows:

1. Narrative
2. Physical
3. Graphical
4. Mathematical

NARRATIVE MODELS

A narrative model is either written or oral. The narrative represents a topic or subject. In an organization, reports, documents, and conversations concerning a system are all important narratives. Examples include a salesperson verbally describing a product's competition to a sales manager, and a written report describing the function of a new piece of manufacturing equipment.

TABLE 2.2
Three Levels of Management and Information Needs

Consumer Product Business	
Strategic	Competitive
Planning	Industry statistics
Tactical	Sales analysis by customer
	Reorder analysis of new products
	Sales analysis by product line
	Production planning
Operational	Bill of materials
	Manufacturing specifications
	Product specifications
	Order processing
	On-line order inquiry
	Finished goods inventory
	Accounts receivable
	General ledger
Bank	
Strategic	Market forecast
Planning	New product development
	Financial forecast
Tactical	Branch profitability
	Product profitability
Operational	Loan billing
	Accounting systems
	Policy issuance and maintenance

PHYSICAL MODELS

The fashion model is an example of a physical model, as are dolls and model airplanes. Many physical models are computer designed or constructed. An aero space engineer may develop a physical model of a shuttle to gain important information about how a large-scale shuttle might perform in space. A marketing department may develop a prototype of a new product.

GRAPHICAL MODELS

A graphical model is a pictorial representation of reality. Lines, charts, figures, diagrams, illustrations, and pictures are all types of graphical models. These are used often in developing computer programs. *Flowcharts* show how computer programs are to be developed. A graph that shows budget and financial projections and a break-even chart are good examples of graphic models. The break-even chart depicts the point at which sales revenues and costs are equal, as shown in Figure 2.4.

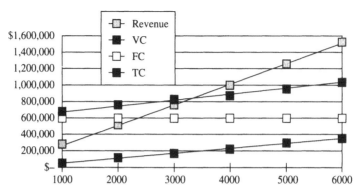

FIGURE 2.4   Break-Even Chart

MATHEMATICAL MODELS

A mathematical model is an quantitative representation of reality. These models are most popular for decision making in all areas of business. Any mathematical formula or equation is a model that can be used for simulation or "what-if" analysis purposes. Once properly constructed, management can experiment with them just as physical scientists do with a controlled experiment in their laboratory. In a sense, mathematical models are the managers' laboratory. For example, the break-even formula used to compute the break-even point in Figure 2.4 is simply

$$X_{be} = \frac{FC}{(P - V)}$$

where X_{be} = break-even point, P = price or average revenue per unit, V = unit variable cost, and FC = total fixed costs.

THE MODEL BASE

The purpose of the model base in a MIS is to give decision makers access to a variety of models and to assist them in the decision-making process. The model base can include model management software (MMS) that coordinates the use of models in a MIS. Depending on the needs of the decision maker, one or more of these models can be used.

FINANCIAL MODELS

Financial models provide cash flow, internal rate of return, and other investment analysis. Spreadsheet programs such as Excel® are often used for this purpose. In addition, more sophisticated financial planning and modeling programs, such as Comshare's Interactive Financial Planning System (IFPS), can be employed. Some organizations develop customized financial models to handle the unique situations and problems faced by the organization. However, as spreadsheet packages continue to increase in power, the need for sophisticated financial modeling packages may decrease.

STATISTICAL MODELS

Statistical models can provide summary statistics, trend projections, hypothesis testing, and more. Many software packages, including Statistical Packages for Social Scientists (SPSS), Statistical Analysis System (SAS), and MINITAB, provide outstanding statistical analysis for organizations of all sizes. These statistical programs can calculate means, variances, and correlation coefficients; perform regression analysis; do hypotheses testing; etc. Many packages also have graphics output capability.

The following illustrates the use of SPSS for Windows for regression analysis and the sample output.

Example 1

Cypress Consumer Products Corporation wishes to develop a forecasting model for its dryer sales by using multiple regression analysis. The marketing department prepared the following sample data.

Month	Sales of Washers (x_1)	Disposable Income (x_2)	Savings (x_3)	Sales of Dryers (y)
January	$45,000	$16,000	$71,000	$29,000
February	42,000	14,000	70,000	24,000
March	44,000	15,000	72,000	27,000
April	45,000	13,000	71,000	25,000
May	43,000	13,000	75,000	26,000
June	46,000	14,000	74,000	28,000
July	44,000	16,000	76,000	30,000
August	45,000	16,000	69,000	28,000
September	44,000	15,000	74,000	28,000
October	43,000	15,000	73,000	27,000

SPSS for Windows was employed to develop the regression model. Figure 4.5 presents the regression output results using three explanatory variables.

OPTIMIZATION MODELS

The term *optimization models* refers to techniques for establishing complex sets of mathematical equations and inequalities that represent objectives and constraints. These models are "prescriptive" in that they try to provide the best possible solution to the problem at hand. They include mathematical programming such as linear programming (LP) and goal programming (GP) models.

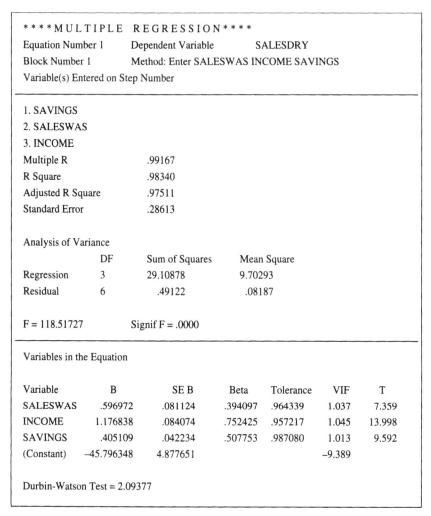

****MULTIPLE REGRESSION****

Equation Number 1   Dependent Variable   SALESDRY

Block Number 1   Method: Enter SALESWAS INCOME SAVINGS

Variable(s) Entered on Step Number

---

1. SAVINGS
2. SALESWAS
3. INCOME

Multiple R	.99167
R Square	.98340
Adjusted R Square	.97511
Standard Error	.28613

Analysis of Variance

	DF	Sum of Squares	Mean Square
Regression	3	29.10878	9.70293
Residual	6	.49122	.08187

F = 118.51727   Signif F = .0000

Variables in the Equation

Variable	B	SE B	Beta	Tolerance	VIF	T
SALESWAS	.596972	.081124	.394097	.964339	1.037	7.359
INCOME	1.176838	.084074	.752425	.957217	1.045	13.998
SAVINGS	.405109	.042234	.507753	.987080	1.013	9.592
(Constant)	−45.796348	4.877651				−9.389

Durbin-Watson Test = 2.09377

FIGURE 2.5   SPSS for Windows.

Linear programming (LP) is a mathematical technique designed to determine an optimal decision (or an optimal plan) chosen from a large number of possible decisions. The optimal decision is the one that meets the specified objective of the company, subject to various restrictions or constraints. It concerns itself with the problem of allocating scarce resources among competing activities in an optimal manner. The optimal decision yields the highest profit, contribution margin (CM), or revenue, or the lowest cost. A linear programming model consists of two important ingredients:

1. *Objective function.* The company must define the specific objective to be achieved.
2. *Constraints.* Constraints are in the form of restrictions on availability of resources or meeting minimum requirements. As the name *linear pro-*

gramming indicates, both the objective function and constraints must be in linear form.

A firm wishes to find an optimal product mix. The optimal mix would be the one that maximizes its total CM within the allowed budget and production capacity. Or the firm may want to determine a least-cost combination of input materials while meeting production requirements, employing production capacities, and using available employees.

Applications of LP are numerous. They include:

1. Selecting least-cost mix of ingredients for manufactured products
2. Developing an optimal budget
3. Determining an optimal investment portfolio (or asset allocation)
4. Allocating an advertising budget to a variety of media
5. Scheduling jobs to machines
6. Determining a least-cost shipping pattern
7. Scheduling flights
8. Gasoline blending
9. Optimal manpower allocation
10. Selecting the best warehouse location to minimize shipping costs

FORMULATION OF LP

To formulate an LP problem, certain steps are followed. They are:

1. Define the *decision variables* that enter into the solution.
2. Express the objective function and constraints in terms of these decision variables. All the expressions must be in linear form.

In the following example, we will use this technique to find the optimal product mix.

Example 2

The JKS Furniture Manufacturing Company produces two products: desks and tables. Both products require time in two processing departments, the Assembly Department and the Finishing Department. Data on the two products are as follows:

	Products		
Processing	Desk	Table	Available Hours
Assembly	2	4	100
Finishing	3	2	90
Contribution margin per unit	$25	$40	

The company wants to find the most profitable mix of these two products.

Step 1

Define the decision variables as follows:

A = Number of units of desk to be produced
B = Number of units of table to be produced

Step 2

The objective function to maximize total contribution margin (CM) is expressed as

$$\text{Total CM} = 25A + 40B$$

Then, formulate the constraints as inequalities.

2A + 4B ≤ 100 (assembly constraint)
3A + 2B ≤ 90 (finishing constraint)

In addition, implicit in any LP formulation are the constraints that restrict A and B to be nonnegative, i.e.,

$$A, B \geq 0$$

Our LP model is:

Maximize:	Total CM = 25A + 40B
Subject to:	2A + 4B ≤ 100
	3A + 2B ≤ 90
	A, B ≥ 0

USE OF COMPUTER LP SOFTWARE

We can use a computer LP software package such as LINDO (Linear Interactive and Discrete Optimization) and What's Best! to quickly solve an LP problem.

Figure 2.6 shows a LINDO output by an LP program for our LP model set up in Example 2. *Note:* The printout shows the following optimal solution:

A = 20 units
B = 15 units
CM = $1,100

Shadow prices are:

Assembly capacity = $8.75
Finishing capacity = $2.50

DECISION ANALYSIS MODELS

Decisions are made under certainty or under uncertainty. Decision making under certainty means that for each decision there is only one event and therefore only

*** INFORMATION ENTERED ***

NUMBER OF CONSTRAINTS	2
NUMBER OF VARIABLES	2
NUMBER OF <= CONSTRAINTS	2
NUMBER OF = CONSTRAINTS	0
NUMBER OF >= CONSTRAINTS	0

MAXIMIZATION PROBLEM

   $25 A + 40 B$

SUBJECT TO

   $2 A + 4 B <= 100$
   $3 A + 2 B <= 90$

*** RESULTS ***

VARIABLE	VALUE	ORIGINAL COEFF.	COEFF. SENS.	
				Solution:
				A = 20
A	20	25	0	B = 15
B	15	40	0	

CONSTRAINT NUMBER	ORIGINAL RHS	SLACK OR SURPLUS	SHADOW PRICE
1	100	0	8.75

(shadow price of the assembly capacity)

OBJECTIVE FUNCTION VALUE: 1100 = CM

SENSITIVITY ANALYSIS

OBJECTIVE FUNCTION COEFFICIENTS

VARIABLE	LOWER LIMIT	ORIGINAL COEFFICIENT	UPPER LIMIT
A	20	25	60
B	16.67	40	50

RIGHT HAND SIDE

CONSTRAINT NUMBER	LOWER LIMIT	ORIGINAL VALUE	UPPER LIMIT
1	60	100	180
2	50	90	150

FIGURE 2.6   Computer printout for LP.

one outcome for each action. Decision making under uncertainty, which is more common in reality, involves several events for each action with its probability of occurrence. When decisions are made in a world of uncertainty, it is often helpful to make the computations of (1) expected value, (2) standard deviation, and (3) coefficient of variation.

Standard Deviation

The standard deviation measures the tendency of data to be spread out. Cost analysts and managerial accountants can make important inferences from past data with this measure. The standard deviation, denoted with the Greek letter σ, read as *sigma*, is defined as follows:

$$\sigma = \sqrt{\frac{\sum (x - \bar{x})^2}{n - 1}}$$

where $\bar{x}$ is the mean (arithmetic average).

The standard deviation can be used to measure the variation of such items as the expected contribution margin (CM) or expected variable manufacturing costs. It can also be used to assess the risk associated with investment projects.

Example 3

One and one-half years of quarterly returns are listed below for United Motors stock.

Time Period	x	$(x - \bar{x})$	$(x - \bar{x})^2$
1	10%	0	0
2	15	5	25
3	20	10	100
4	5	-5	25
5	-10	-20	400
6	20	10	100
	60		650

From the above table, note that

$$\sigma = \sqrt{\frac{\sum (x - \bar{x})^2}{n - 1}} = \sqrt{\frac{650}{(6 - 1)}} = \sqrt{130} = 11.40\%$$

The United Motors stock has returned on the average 10 percent over the last six quarters, and the variability about its average return was 11.40%. The high standard deviation (11.40%) relative to the average return of 10% indicates that the stock is very risky.

Although statistics such as expected value and standard deviation are essential for choosing the best course of action under uncertainty, the decision problem can best be approached using what is called *decision theory*. Decision theory is a systematic approach to making decisions especially under uncertainty. Decision theory utilizes an organized approach such as a decision matrix (or payoff table).

DECISION MATRIX

A decision matrix is characterized by

1. the row, representing a set of alternative courses of action available to the decision maker,
2. the column, representing the state of nature or conditions that are likely to occur and the decision maker has no control over, and
3. the entries in the body of the table, representing the outcome of the decision, known as *payoffs,* which may be in the form of costs, revenues, profits or cash flows. By computing expected value of each action, we will be able to pick the best one.

Example 4

Assume the following probability distribution of daily demand for a product:

Daily demand	0	1	2	3
Probability	.2	.3	.3	.2

Also assume that unit cost equals $3, selling price equals $5 (i.e., profit on sold unit equals $2), and salvage value on unsold units equals $2 (i.e., loss on unsold unit equals $1). We can stock either 0, 1, 2, or 3 units. The question is, *how many units should be stocked each day?* Assume that units from one day cannot be sold the next day. Then the payoff table can be constructed as follows:

	State of Nature				
Demand	0	1	2	3	Expected value
Stock (probability)	(.2)	(.3)	(.3)	(.2)	
	0	0	0	0	0
Actions 1	−1	2	2	2	1.40
2	−2	1[a]	4	4	1.90[b]
3	−3	0	3	6	1.50

a. Profit for (stock 2, demand) equals (no. of units sold)(profit per unit) − (no. of units unsold)(loss per unit) = (1)($5 − 3) − (1)($3 − 2) = $1.

b. Expected value for (stock 2) is: −2(.2) + 1(.3) + 4(.2) = $1.90.

The optimal stock action is the one with the highest expected monetary value i.e., stock 2 units.

Decision Tree

A decision tree is another approach used in discussions of decision making under uncertainty. It is a pictorial representation of a decision situation.

As in the case of the decision matrix approach previously discussed, it shows decision alternatives, states of nature, probabilities attached to the state of nature, and conditional benefits and losses. The decision tree approach is most useful in a sequential decision situation.

Example 5

Assume that XYZ Corporation wishes to introduce one of two products to the market this year. The probabilities and present values (PV) of projected cash inflows are given below.

Product	Initial investment	PV of cash inflows	Probabilities
A	$225,000		1.00
		$450,000	0.40
		200,000	0.50
		−100,000	0.10
B	80,000		1.00
		320,000	0.20
		100,000	0.60
		−150,000	0.20

A decision tree analyzing the two products is given in Figure 2.7.

Graphical Models

Graphical modeling programs are software packages that assist decision makers in designing, developing, and using graphic displays of data and information. Numerous personal computer programs that can perform this type of analysis are available on the market. In addition, sophisticated graphic design and analysis such as computer-assisted design (CAD) is widely available.

Project Planning and Management Models

Project planning and management models are used to navigate and coordinate large projects, and to discover critical paths that could delay or jeopardize an entire project if they are not completed in a timely and cost-effective fashion. Some of these programs can determine the best way to speed up a project by effectively using additional resources, including cash, labor, and equipment. Project management allows decision makers to keep tight control over projects of all sizes and types.

Program evaluation and review technique (PERT) is a useful management tool for planning, scheduling, costing, coordinating, and controlling complex projects such as

		Initial Investment (1)	Probability (2)	PV of Cash Inflows (3)	PV of Cash Inflows (2) × (3) = (4)
			0.40	$450,000	$180,000
		$225,000	0.50	200,000	100,000
Product A			0.10	−100,000	−10,000
			Expected PV of cash inflows		$270,000
Choice A or B					
Product B			0.20	$320,000	$64,000
		$80,000	0.60	100,000	60,000
			0.20	−150,000	−30,000
			Expected PV of cash inflows		$94,000

For product A:

Expected NPV = expected PV − I = $270,000 − $255,000 = $45,000

For product B:

Expected NPV = $94,000 − $80,000 = $14,000

Based on the expected NPV, choose product A over product B; however, this analysis fails to recognize the risk factor in project analysis.

FIGURE 2.7 Decision tree.

- Formulation of a master budget
- Construction of buildings
- Installation of computers
- Scheduling the closing of books
- Assembly of a machine
- Research and development activities

Questions to be answered by PERT include

- When will the project be finished?
- What is the probability that the project will be completed by any given time?

SIMULATION MODELS

The primary use of a simulation model is to respond to "what if...?" questions. These descriptive models can produce large amounts of detailed output, because they work by mimicking many parts of the real-world system. One major weakness is that no automatic searching or optimizing is done by the model. (Any such features must be built on top of the simulation model and must be used as a submodel.) In such cases, the simulation may have to be performed many, many times while a search for the best decision parameters is under way. This can be quite expensive, if the simulation is complex.

Two major issues in simulation modeling are how long a simulation run must proceed to achieve *steady state* (typical behavior) and how many different runs must be performed to achieve statistical significance. Inside most simulation models is a pseudo-random number generator. This is a mathematical subroutine that produces numbers that appear to be random. These random numbers are manipulated further to represent parts of the model that are not deterministic. Examples might include the arrival of customers at a ticket counter or the time of failure of an electronic circuit component. These random number generators can be "seeded" with special input parameters to make them produce different streams of random values. Repeating runs with different seed values provides a set of outputs that has a statistical distribution to be analyzed.

Many commercial software packages are available that can be used to build simulation models. Some of these are general-purpose simulation languages that have general but powerful features, such as waiting lines and resource pools that ease the modeling task. At the other extreme are tailored simulation models (such as oil refinery models) that are already built but afford the user the ability to specify input parameters to describe the precise configuration under study. In between these extremes are simulation languages that are suited for a large class of models, such as networks, that are a formalism in which many problems can be represented.

Example 6

During lunch hour, customers arrive at a fast-food restaurant at a rate of three per minute. They require 1.5 minutes to place an order and pay the bill before going to pick up the food. How many cash register stations are needed to ensure that the number of customers waiting in line does not exceed 6 and that this waiting time does not occur more than 30% of the time during the lunch hour rush?

A simulation language such as the SLAM II can be used to simulate the sequence of the operation in this problem. The language consists of symbols that can be composed on a computer terminal screen into a diagram like the one shown. The first circle represents customer arrivals. The second circle represents the queue, or waiting line. The last circle represents departures from the system.

A random normal probability distribution was chosen to model the customer arrivals. The mean, or average, time between arrivals is set at 20 seconds, and the standard deviation is set to 5 seconds. The simulation model was run for 3,600 seconds for each experiment. The number of servers was changed between runs. The service time was represented by an exponential distribution with a mean of 90 seconds.

The simulation software generates random numbers using mathematical formulas and then computes when customers arrive, how long they require service, and so forth. A clock is simulated to keep track of what should happen next. These performance statistics are collected and reported.

Statistics describing the queue are produced automatically by the simulation software package. Table 2.3 shows that 5 servers are needed to ensure that the queue will be no longer than 6 persons for 70 percent of the time. A thorough analysis would involve making more runs to confirm that the above statistics still hold true when different random numbers are used and longer periods of simulation are tried.

Table 2.3 would serve as a tool for establishing optimal staffing levels for a fast-food restaurant.

TABLE 2.3
Percentage of the Time that Queue Length Is No More than Number Indicated

Number of Servers	0	1	2	3	4	5	6	7
4	14	20	24	27	27	28	31	36
5	46	55	60	63	64	68	73	76

3 How to Select the Best Microcomputer System

Generally speaking, computers can be classified into five categories: microcomputers, network servers, minicomputers, mainframe computers, and supercomputers.

MICROCOMPUTERS

Microcomputers are designed for a single-user environment and small business applications. However, more and more business people are using microcomputers for both multi-user networks and business applications. For example, a business person can use a microcomputer to organize financial transactions, prepare the corporate tax return (Form 1120 or 1120S), or to update the inventory of several supermarkets on a network. Today's microcomputers can be so powerful that they provide solutions for most business applications.

A microcomputer uses a microprocessor as the central processing unit. Microprocessors can be very powerful despite their small size. Currently, there are two major microcomputer systems available on the market. They are the IBM-compatible system and the Apple system. Both systems use different platforms (operating systems) to control the hardware. The IBM-compatible system uses a Windows operating system developed by Microsoft. The Windows operating system provides a graphical user interface (GUI) and a multitasking environment. The Windows operating system including Windows 3.1, Windows 95, Windows 98, Windows 2000, and Windows NT workstation dominate most of the microcomputer operating system market. Apple's Macintosh uses a totally different operating system developed by Apple Computer. Newer Apple operating systems are able to run Windows-based applications. However, due to poor marketing strategy, the Apple system has lost significant market share. It is suggested that the average business person use the IBM system because of greater compatibility, wider program availability, and a more open platform.

LARGE-SYSTEM COMPUTING

Large systems consist of mainframe computers, minicomputers, and supercomputers. They are typically multi-user computer systems in which many users share the same computing resources at the same time (time sharing). The computing power of minicomputers or mainframe computers is usually more than microcomputers, and so the cost is greater. Mainframe computers and supercomputers can be very expensive to purchase and maintain, so only large corporations can afford them. The computing power of mainframe computers is usually shared by many users. That means that the operating system of a mainframe computer allows many computer users to participate simultaneously. Mainframe computers are typically used for business applications where a large number of transactions are processed. They are fast in processing speed and have large storage capacity. Supercomputers have the most processing power of computers available. They are primarily designed for high-speed computation, especially for scientific research or the defense industry, but their use is growing rapidly in business as supercomputer prices decrease.

Supercomputers are also very valuable for large model simulation and complex mathematical calculations. Weather forecasting agents use supercomputer to model the world's weather system to improve weather predictions in a very short period of time. The computer performance and speed required to achieve the above goal needs enormous speed and processing power. To increase the speed of supercomputers, some companies are linking together individual or serial processors into multiple processors or parallel processing systems.

NETWORK SERVERS

Network servers are used to manage and control computer networks. A network server needs to have larger storage capacity to store network programs and a high-performance CPU to provide timely network functions. Computer networks can be localized or worldwide scale. Therefore, computer servers can be designed to manage as few as several microcomputers in a local area network (LAN) or several hundred computers in a wide area network (WAN).

COMPUTER SYSTEM UNITS

The system unit is made up of components that include system board (mother board), central processing unit (CPU), main memory (including registers, cache memory, RAM, and ROM), system clock, power supply, expansion slots, ports, and bus lines.

SYSTEM BOARD

The system board (or mother board) consists of a flat board that contains the CPU, memory chips, and other devices. A chip has many tiny circuit boards etched on a small square of crystalline material called *silicon*. Chips are mounted on carrier packages, which then plug into sockets on the system board.

CPU

The central processing unit (CPU) is the center of all computer processing activities. It is here that all processing is controlled, all data are manipulated, and arithmetic/logic computations are performed.

The CPU takes data from the input device (such as the keyboard) and processes them to generate information so that output devices (such as the monitor) can display it. Inside the CPU, there are the arithmetic/logic unit (ALU) and the control unit (CU). The ALU is used to perform the four basic arithmetic operations, addition, subtraction, multiplication, and division. Logic functions are used to compare values. They are >=, <=, =, <, >, and <>. All computer applications from typing a document to supercomputer simulation are achieved through these simple operations.

The control unit is responsible for managing the traffic of the CPU. It interprets and carries out computer operations contained in computer programs. It moves instructions from the memory to the registers in the control unit. The control unit executes only one instruction at a time and executes it so quickly that the control unit appears to do many different things simultaneously. The CPU capacity is often described in word sizes. A *word* is the number of bits (such as 16, 32, or 64) that can be processed at one time by the CPU. Therefore, the more bits of the word size, the more powerful is the CPU.

MAIN MEMORY (OR PRIMARY STORAGE)

The main memory consists of registers, cache memory, random access memory (RAM), and read only memory (ROM). Registers are located in the control unit and arithmetic/logic unit of a CPU. Registers are special high-speed staging areas that hold data and instructions temporarily during processing. Because the registers are located inside the CPU, their contents can be handled much faster than data in other main memory.

CACHE MEMORY

Cache memory, pronounced as "cash," is located between RAM and CPU for faster access. It is a special high-speed memory area that the CPU can access quickly. The most frequently used routines are stored in the cache memory to improve performance.

RAM

RAM is the memory used to store temporary data or programs when the computer power is on.

ROM

ROM usually stores very essential information permanently.

SYSTEM CLOCK

Part of the computer performance is determined by the speed of system clocks. The system clock controls how often an operation will take place within a computer. The system clock uses fixed vibrations from a quartz crystal to deliver a steady stream of digital pulses to the CPU. The faster the clock (measured in megahertz, MHz), the faster the processing, all other factors being equal. For example, the high-end Macintosh G4 uses a PowerPC microprocessor running at 500 MHz. The most recent Intel Pentium III, used in workstations, run at speeds substantially higher than 500 MHz. Both Intel and Motorola have announced new processors that can operate at 1 gigahertz (GHz) or faster. It should be noted, however, that newer processors are capable of executing more than one operation per clock "tick," so clock rate is becoming less revealing as a performance benchmark.

POWER SUPPLY

A computer runs on direct current (dc), but the available electricity from a standard outlet is alternating current (ac). The power supply is a device that converts ac to dc to run the computer. Because the power supply can generate lots of heat, a fan in the computer is necessary to keep other devices from becoming too hot. In addition, electrical power drawn from a standard ac outlet can be quite uneven. For example, a sudden electrical surge can burn out the dc circuitry in your computer. Instead of plugging your computer directly into the wall electrical outlet, it is better to plug it into a power protection device. The two principal types are surge protectors and uninterruptible power supply (UPS) units. The surge protector is a device that protects a computer from being damaged by a high voltage. A computer can be plugged in a surge protector, which in turn is plugged into a standard electrical outlet.

EXPANSION SLOTS AND BOARDS

Most microcomputers are expandable. Expandability refers to a computer's capacity to accept more functions such as more memory or a fax modem. In other words, when you buy a PC, you can later add devices to enhance its computing power. Expansion slots are sockets on the motherboard into which you can plug expansion cards. Expansion cards (add-on boards) are circuit boards that provide more memory or control of peripheral devices. The following are examples of expansion cards:

Controller cards. Control cards allow your PC to work with the computer's various peripheral devices such as a floppy drive or a hard drive.
Graphics cards. These cards allow you to adapt different kinds of color monitors for your computer, such as super VGA cards.

BUS LINES

A bus line is an electrical pathway through which bits are transmitted between the CPU and other devices. There are different types of buses. The bus between the CPU and the expansion slots is called a local bus. The bus between RAM and the expansion slots is called an expansion bus. The old 8-bit bus can only transfer 8 bits at a time, while a 32-bit bus can transmit 32 bits at one time.

PORTS

A port is a socket on the outside of the system unit that is connected to a board on the inside of the system unit. A port allows you to plug in a cable to connect other devices such as a monitor, a keyboard, or a printer. In general, ports are categorized into two types:

Parallel ports. A parallel port allows a line to be connected that allows many bits to be transmitted at one time. Since many bits can be transmitted, the transmission speed is higher. Printers, monitors, and keyboards use parallel ports.

Serial ports. A serial [for example, RS-232] port enables a line to be connected that will send one bit at a time. The serial port is usually used for data communication purposes.

HOW TO SELECT A MICROCOMPUTER SYSTEM UNIT

Before you decide to buy a microcomputer, you have to know what kind of work you want to achieve. IBM-compatible computers have more application software, while the Apple Mac has better graphical capabilities. If you just want to do word processing, an IBM-compatible with a high-end Pentium processor may be a waste. However, if you decide to use your computer with many multimedia functions, a Pentium processor is a must. A brand name computer such as IBM, Hewlett Packard, Dell, Toshiba (very good in notebook computers), or Compaq will probably cost you several hundred dollars more than other brands with the same configuration. In addition, an IBM-compatible computer with an Intel processor inside may also cost you more than a system with a non-Intel processor. The best way to select your microcomputer is to follow the recommendations below.

BECOME COMPUTER LITERATE

You can become much more knowledgeable, in terms of computer configurations, by talking to your friends or reading computer-related magazines. For example, a 1-gigabyte hard drive has a higher storage capacity than a 200-megabyte one. An IBM-compatible Pentium CPU is faster than an 80486 CPU. A multimedia system requires CD-ROM drives, speakers, and sound cards and a modem to connect to the Internet. Without basic computer knowledge, it would be very difficult to make good business decisions.

DECIDE WHAT TASKS YOU PLAN TO PERFORM ON YOUR COMPUTER

This step will let you better understand how your computer power can match your job requirement. Define your needs in writing and prioritize them. You should make your list as practical as possible. A job that requires special computer hardware support will cost you more. You can also consult with business associates to understand what kinds of jobs can be done by a personal computer. Beware that you must satisfy the minimum hardware requirements to run different applications software. Each software has a different hardware requirement. In addition, two computers with different configurations may be able to run the same job. The difference would be how fast you need the job to be done. If you are a manager mostly doing word processing for your department's projects, an IBM-compatible Pentium III would be too much power for your work. However, if you are a professional editor, a Pentium II is just what you need.

DETERMINE WHICH SOFTWARE IS AVAILABLE FOR YOUR JOB

You should consider the reputation of a software company, the functionality available, the reliability (i.e., any known bugs), and the upgrade capacity of the software. Good software should be able to expand when needed, be compatible with other software as much as possible, and be compatible with other different types of hardware. An expensive piece of software with millions of functions may not be as good as easy-to-use software with a few useful functions and a small price. Remember to choose the software you really need and not one that is too powerful and costly to be useful. You are just wasting your time and money by buying more sophisticated software than you need to perform your job responsibilities.

DECIDE WHICH SYSTEM YOU ARE GOING TO USE (IBM-COMPATIBLE OR APPLE MAC)

Both IBM-compatible and Mac can deliver good results for most users. Apple Mac used to have an advanced user interface as compared to IBM-compatibles. However, this advantage no longer exists since the Microsoft Windows system was introduced for IBM-compatibles. In addition, IBM-compatibles have more application software available than Apple Mac. For users with heavy usage of multimedia applications, Mac has a good reputation. Some products from Apple, such as PowerPC/Mac, which can run both IBM-compatible and Apple Mac applications software, would be a good choice for users who would like to take advantage of both systems.

PROJECT HOW MANY YEARS OF SERVICE YOU ARE GOING TO PUT ON THIS COMPUTER

A high-end computer is expected to provide a longer service. The life span of a PC is getting shorter and shorter. You may have to replace your system every two years if you want to keep up to date. To keep your system in service for a longer time, you need to buy a high-end model instead of a less powerful system.

SELECT THE VENDOR WITH THE LOWEST PRICE AND BEST PERFORMANCE IN THAT CLASS

This information normally can be obtained from computer professional magazines. A computer system can normally be purchased from a computer retail store, discount store, or by mail order. Generally speaking, mail order has the lowest price (and savings on sales tax) but the poorest service. Computer retail stores have better quality service for a higher price. If you are an experienced computer buyer and know what you want in your system, mail order is a good way to find bargains. Without any previous computer background, it would be better to go to computer retail stores and ask for help. Pay attention to new product announcements—that means the price of old models will be reduced. Brand name computers are normally more reliable and more expensive than others. Avoid brands that have a bad reputation for quality of products and services. A portable or note book computer will cost you $500 to $1000 more than a desktop model of the same configuration. With a smaller screen and a smaller keyboard, a notebook model would not be very convenient for you. If you do not travel frequently, you do not really need a notebook model. All this information can be easily found in computer magazines.

Computer Hardware Rarely Breaks, as Long as You Don't Abuse It

Generally speaking, most computers are replaced because they are obsolete functionally, not because they are broken. The life span of a PC is about two years. However, you should still observe the following instructions for hardware protection.

- Use screen savers to protect your monitor from being damaged.
- Do not use any broken diskettes in your floppy drive.
- Keep your computer from any dusty area or too much heat.
- Clean your mouse once in a while and use reset buttons or software boot-up instead of turning the power off and on. In addition, you should always turn off the computer when you are not using it.

If you follow the above recommendations, the chance of failure is really very small. Therefore, any repair insurance or extended services warranty would be a waste of money. It is also not worthwhile to upgrade peripherals if your computer mother board is obsolete.

Just like buying any other merchandise, you should always shop around, collect as much information as you can, and use your own judgment to make the best deal.

How Does the CPU Affect Computing Power?

The CPU is the "brain" of a computer system. It contains the control unit (CU) and the arithmetic/logic unit (ALU). The power of CPU can very much determine the performance of the whole system. The CPU is measured by its processing capacity, speed in terms of speed in megahertz (MHz), word size, and million instructions per second (MIPS). The megahertz (million of cycles per second) is the measurement for computer execution frequency. This frequency is controlled by the system clock. Word size is the number of bits the CPU can process at a time. The larger the word size, the faster the computer can process data. MIPS is used to measure how many millions of instructions can be processed within a second. For microcomputers, CPU can be classified into two categories: Apple Mac system (developed by Motorola) and IBM-compatible system (manufactured by Intel).

There are many microprocessors available in the market. Not knowing the differences can be quite frustrating—especially when it means saving or spending a couple hundred dollars. Table 3.1 is a chart that compares and contrasts important features found on some of the more popular chips in the market today. It provides a handy guide for microcomputer CPU comparison.

TABLE 3.1
Microprocessor Comparison Chart

	Celeron	Pentium II	Pentium III	Pentium III Xeon	AMD K6-III	Athlon (K7)	PowerPC G3	PowerPC G4
CPU speed	333 MHz– 500 MHz	300 MHz– 450 MHz	450 MHz– 600 MHz	500 MHz– 550 MHz	400 MHz– 450 MHz	500 MHz– 600 MHz	233 MHz– 333 MHz	400 MHz– 450 MHz
Cache	128 kB, full speed	512 kB, half speed	512 kB, full speed	512 kB, 1 MB, full speed	256 kB, full speed	512 kB, half speed	512 kB, 1 MB, half speed	1 MB, half speed
Front-side bus speed	66 MHz	100 MHz	133 MHz	100 MHz	100 MHz	200 MHz	66 MHz	100 MHz
Floating point	strong	strong	strong	strong	weak	very strong	very strong	very strong
Integer	strong	strong	strong	strong	excellent	very strong	NA	NA

INPUT TECHNOLOGIES

Input devices are used to collect data (information) from the environment. The data source could be a document, picture, speech, movie, or even the temperature of a certain location. Most current input technologies are designed to capture data and send it to the computer system. The following are some of the input technologies available.

KEYBOARD

Keyboards are conventional input devices. Microcomputer keyboards have all the keys that typewriter keyboards have, plus others unique to computers. People who always thought typing was an overrated skill will find themselves slightly behind in the digital age, since learning to use a keyboard is still probably the most important way of interacting with a computer. Users who have to use the hunt-and-peck method waste a lot of time. Fortunately, there are software programs available that can help you learn typing skills or improve your existing ones.

You are probably already familiar with a computer keyboard. As the use of computer keyboards has become widespread, so has the incidence of various hand and wrist injuries. Accordingly, keyboard manufacturers have been giving a lot of attention to *ergonomics*. Ergonomics is the study of the physical relationships between people and their work environment. Various attempts are being made to make keyboards more ergonomically sound to prevent injuries. One interesting variation is a $99 device that substitutes foot-driven pedals for the Shift, Alt, and Ctrl keys.

MOUSE

A mouse is a device that is rolled about on a desktop and directs a pointer on the computer's display screen. The pointer sometimes may be, but is not necessarily the same as, the cursor. The mouse pointer is the symbol that indicates the position of the mouse on the display screen. It may be an arrow, a rectangle, or even a representation of a person's pointing finger. The pointer may change to the shape of an I-beam to indicate that it is a cursor and show the place where text may be entered. The mouse has a cable that is connected to the microcomputer's system unit by being plugged into a special port. The tail-like cable and the rounded "head" of the instrument are what suggested the name *mouse*. On the bottom side of the mouse is a ball (trackball) that translates the mouse movement into digital signals. On the top side are one, two, or three buttons. Depending on the software, these buttons are used for such functions as selecting, dropping, and dragging. Gently holding the mouse with one hand, you can move it in all directions on the desktop (or on a mouse pad, which may provide additional traction). This will produce a corresponding movement of the mouse pointer on the screen.

TRACKBALL

Another form of pointing device, the trackball, is a variant of the mouse. A trackball is movable ball, on top of a stationary device, that is rotated with the fingers or palm of the hand. In fact, the trackball looks like the mouse turned upside down. Instead of moving the mouse around on the desktop, you move the trackball with the tips of your fingers. Trackballs are especially suited to portable computers, which are often used in confined places, such as on airline tray tables. Trackballs may appear on the keyboard centered below the space bar, as on the Apple Powerbook, or built into the right side of the screen. On some portables, the trackball is a separate device that is clipped to the side of the keyboard.

Bar Code Readers

Bar code readers are designed to read Universal Product Code (UPC) or similar bar codes. You can find this type of device in the supermarket or in the library when you check out a book.

Pen-Based Input

This type of device uses handwriting as the input. Human handwriting can be converted into typed letters for further processing. This technology makes the keyboard an optional device and reduces the computer size a great deal.

Image Scanner

This device allows users to store a picture as a computer file. Images can be modified by the computer software after they are digitized and saved as a computer file.

Voice-Recognition Device

Users can use voice to issue a command, and typing or mouse input can be optional. A training session may be required to let the computer understand and recognize your voice.

Video Capture

A video recording can be digitized as a computer file. This file can be further modified or edited for special effects.

Touch Screens

A touch screen is a video display screen that has been sensitized to receive input from the touch of a finger. Because touch screens are easy to use, they can convey information quickly. You'll find touch screens in automated teller machines and tourist directories in airports. Touch screens are also available for personal computers, consisting of an overlay that mounts with adhesive to the front of a monitor.

What Input Devices Do You Need?

A keyboard and a mouse may be the most useful input devices to use most software. However, if you need to use multimedia software or have a variety of information sources stored in different media, you might need devices such as image scanners, a microphone for your voice input, or a digital camera. Digitized sound and image files require lots of disk space for storage. Before you upgrade your system with advanced input devices such as video and audio input, ample secondary storage devices will be needed.

OUTPUT TECHNOLOGIES

The types of output generated by the computer depends on the needs of users and the hardware software equipment. In general, output can be classified into two categories, based on how output is displayed.

- *Hard copy.* Printed output by printers or plotters.
- *Soft copy.* Output displayed by monitors or other devices.

Output can also be classified based on the way output is presented, as outlined below.

TEXT FORMAT

Text format is the original output, used when computers were first created. Text output can be numeric, alphabetic, or in the form of other symbols on the keyboard. It has a great limitation in terms of presenting charts and images. Today, very few computer systems use text format as the only output display.

GRAPHIC FORMAT

Graphic format allows users to view output as graphic images. By using a graphic format, computer user interfaces have been dramatically improved.

VIDEO FORMAT

Video output is designed to display movies that have been digitized. This type of output provides a movie-like image to the user. However, digitized movies require lots of capacity to store and transmit digital signals. This limitation keeps the video format from being widely used.

AUDIO FORMAT

Voice can also be digitized into computer files. An audio file can be stored or transferred just like a regular computer data file. With a sound card, speakers, and a microphone, users can use voice to communicate with another party.

The above output formats constitute *multimedia,* which will be the major computer output in the future.

WHAT OUTPUT TECHNOLOGIES DO YOU NEED?

Depending on the task you would like to address, the output devices you need will vary.

GENERAL COMPUTER USERS

A computer with a multimedia system can provide you with many ways of presenting information. This system should include speakers, a video capture board, a digital camera, and a microphone. With the necessary software, the user is able to create a picture, a movie, or a voice message.

RETAILERS

A retailer requires inventory update and pricing display when merchandise is checked out. A bar code reader allows cashiers to scan the Universal Product Code (UPC) and retrieve current price as well as update the inventory.

CARTOON/MOVIE MAKERS

For the ability to modify videos or animation, special software for graphics is needed. This type of software allows users to create special effects and modify videos as desired.

INFORMATION HELP CENTER

The information center is designed to provide users with a self-guided information guide. For example, a supermarket may have information centers with touch- screen monitors that allow shoppers to touch the screen for menu selection and receive information.

PUBLISHERS

Desktop publishing software allows users to edit magazines, newspapers, or other publication on a computer. This can dramatically improve the efficiency of publication.

VIDEO CONFERENCES

A meeting can be held without all participants attending the meeting physically. Users can use the video conferencing technology to conduct a meeting through the network and still see other participants.

ARCHITECTS

By using computer aided design (CAD) software, users are able to generate architectural drawings more efficiently. Some CAD software provides three-dimensional capability, which allows users to create a 3-D image design.

SECONDARY STORAGE

In comparison to the primary storage devices, secondary storage devices are generally less expensive and slower in terms of data retrieval speed. Information stored on secondary storage devices is also static (i.e., is not lost when the computer is powered off). We classify secondary storage devices into three categories: magnetic tape, magnetic disk, and optical disk.

Magnetic Tape

Magnetic tape is thin, plastic tape that has been coated with a substance that can be magnetized; data is represented by the magnetized or nonmagnetized spots. Magnetic tapes are the original secondary storage device of computer systems. Since the sequential access method is used, magnetic tape drives are slow in data retrieval but are the least expensive secondary devices. For large storage and low-performance requirements, such as backup or duplication, magnetic tapes are the ideal choice. The two principal forms of tape storage of interest to us are magnetic tape units used with mainframes and minicomputers and cartridge tape units used on micro-computers.

Magnetic Disks

There are two types of magnetic disk devices: hard disks and floppy disks. They both are random access devices. Therefore, they are faster and more expensive.

Floppy Disks

A floppy disk is a device that holds, spin, and reads data from and writes data to a diskette. A diskette is inserted into a slot, called the *drive gate* or *drive door,* in front of the disk drive. On a diskette, data is recorded in rings called *tracks*. Each track is divided into eight or nine *sectors*. Sectors are invisible wedge-shaped sections used for storage. Unformatted disks are manufactured without tracks and sectors in place. The operating system writes tracks and sectors on the diskette to make formatted disks. All contemporary diskettes are double sided, capable of storing data on both sides. A disk's capacity also depends on its recording density. A 3.5-inch double-sided, double-density disk can store 720 kilobytes. A 3.5-inch high-density disk can store 1.44 megabytes.

Zip Disks

Zip disks are slightly larger than conventional floppy disks, and about twice as thick. They can hold 100 MB of data. Because they're relatively inexpensive and durable, they have become a popular medium for backing up hard disks and for transporting large files. The Zip drive for this high-capacity floppy disk drive was developed by Iomega Corporation.

SuperDisks

The SuperDisk is a new disk storage technology developed by Imation Corporation that supports very high-density diskettes. SuperDisk diskettes are etched with a servo pattern at the factory. This pattern is then read by the SuperDisk drive to precisely align the read/write head. The result is that a SuperDisk diskette can have 2,490 tracks, as opposed to the 135 tracks that conventional 3.5-inch 1.44 MB diskettes use. This higher density translates into 120 MB capacity per diskette.

Unlike other removable disk storage solutions, such as the Zip drive, SuperDisk is backward compatible with older diskettes. This means that you can use the same SuperDisk drive to read and write to older 1.44 MB diskettes as well as the new 120 MB SuperDisk diskettes. Imation's current SuperDisk drive is called the LS-120.

Hard Disks

A hard disk is a disk made out of metal and covered with a magnetic recording surface. Hard disk drives read and write in much the same way that diskette drives do. However, hard drives can handle thousands times more data than diskettes. In addition, they are faster than floppy disk drive in terms of reading and writing data. Hard disks are one or more platters sealed inside a hard-disk drive that are built into the system unit and cannot be removed.

The operation speed and the capacity of a hard drive is much more than a floppy disk because a hard disk can store data 30 to 2000 times and spins several times faster than a diskette. For example, a 2.1 gigabyte hard disk will spin at 7800 revolutions per minute compared to 360 rpm for a diskette drive. The disadvantage of a hard drive is that the read/write head rides on a cushion of air about 0.000001 inch thick over the disk surface. A head crash happens when the surface of the read/write head or particles on its surface come into contact with the disk surface, causing the loss of some or all of the data on the disk.

Optical Disks

Optical disks are removable disks on which data is written and read through the use of laser beams. A single optical disk of the type called CD-ROM can hold up to 700 megabytes of data. This is equivalent to about 270,000 pages of text. Other optical devices are CD-RW; write-once, read-many (WORM); and erasable optical disks.

CD-ROMs

Compact disk read only memory (CD-ROM) is an optical-disk format used for prerecorded text, graphics, and sound. Since CD-ROM is a read-only disk, CD-ROM can not be written or erased by the user. CD-RW is a rewritable version of CD-ROM. A CD-RW drive can write about 650 megabytes of data to CD-RW media an unlimited number of times. Most CD-RW drives can also write once to CD-R media. CD-RW media cannot be read by CD-ROM drives built prior to 1997, due to the reduced reflectivity (15% compared to 70%) of CD-RW media. CD-RW drives and media are currently (2000) more expensive than CD-R drives and media. CD-R is sometimes considered a better technology for archival purposes, as the data cannot be accidentally modified or tampered with, which encourages better archival practices.

WORM Drives

WORM stands for *write once, read many*. A WORM disk can be written to just once and then used as a CD-ROM. WORM technology is useful for storing data for backup and archival purposes. A mainframe based WORM disk may hold 200 gigabits of data; a microcomputer-based WORM disk can hold about 600 megabytes.

Erasable Optical Disks

Erasable optical disks allow users to erase data so that the disk can be used over and over again. The most common erasable disk is the magneto-optical disk, which uses aspects of both magnetic-disk and optical-disk technologies. A typical erasable optical disk can hold 4.6 gigabits of data.

SUMMARY

No matter how complex a computer system is, it all consists of input, output, processing, and secondary devices. New technologies make computer hardware and software so advanced that end-users can operate or program the computer without professional training. Computers are an essential part of our business life. The key to buying a computer is to understand what you want and need in the business, and shop around for the best price. It may not be necessary to buy state-of-the-art equipment to do your job effectively and efficiently.

4 What Is System Software?

THE OPERATING SYSTEM, UTILITY PROGRAMS, AND LANGUAGE TRANSLATORS

System software is used to control the computer hardware so that all computer devices can interact with application software smoothly. System software creates a layer of insulation between the computer hardware and application software. System software can greatly help and simplify the design of application software. Generally speaking, system software consists of three components: operating systems, utility programs, and programming language processors (language translators).

THE OPERATING SYSTEM

The operating system (OS) consists of the master system of programs that manage the basic operations of the computer. These programs provide the control and use of hardware resources, including disk space, memory, CPU time allocation, and peripheral devices. They are also the interface between computer hardware and application programs, allowing end users can concentrate on their own tasks or applications rather than on the complexities of managing the computer. To be more specific, the operating system is used to control the hardware memory, schedule the execution of programs, and schedule input output traffic between the CPU and other devices.

A good operating system can dramatically improve the effectiveness and the efficiency of program execution performance. Many different operating systems are available for computers. For example, Cray supercomputers use UNICOS and COS, IBM mainframes use MVS and VM, Data General minicomputers use AOS and DG, and DEC minicomputers use VAX/VMS. Most IBM-compatible microcomputers use Microsoft Windows 95 and 98. Most Apple computers use Macintosh System 7 or 8. UNIX is a very popular OS, which can be on microcomputers or mainframe computers.

Some operating systems are designed for a microcomputer single-user environment, and others are for multiple users. The complexity of OS is much higher in a multiple-user OS due to the management of computer memory and CPU time shared by many users. Today, many computers use what is called an *operating environment,* which provides end users with a user friendly interface to use. Some operating systems have a graphical user interface (GUI) that provides visual clues such as icons and objects the help the users. Each icon represents a folder, an application package, or a file. By clicking icons, users can open a folder or use an application package.

Windows 98 is the latest version of the IBM-compatible operating system that has been widely used by most IBM compatible microcomputers. Common features of Windows operating systems include support for the use of a mouse, icons, pull-down menus, and the capability to open several applications at the same time. Windows NT is a more sophisticated version of the Windows operating system. There are some unique features available in Windows NT:

- The ability to run 32-bit application programs
- Support of most networking communication protocols
- Monitoring of the performance and management of the system, such as users' account creation and update

The hardware requirement of Windows NT is greater than that of Windows 95, 98, and 2000. It requires 12 to 16 MB of RAM and 75 to 100 MB of disk space.

Since 1994, Apple Computer has successfully implemented multi-tasking operating systems with graphical user interfaces. It has set the standard for operating system in terms of ease of use (user friendly environment). In the latest version of Apple Macintosh OS, System 9.0, special features such as built-in networking support, a step-by-step help system, and expanded Internet utilities are included.

Major functions provided by OS are the following:

BOOTING

Booting refers to the process of loading an operating system into a computer's main memory from the hard disk. This loading is accomplished by a program that is stored permanently in ROM.

HOUSEKEEPING TASKS

Housekeeping tasks provide end users with functions that can be engaged without starting application programs. One example is the Format command.

USER INTERFACE

This function allows users to communicate or interact with the OS. Three types of user interfaces are common: command, menu-driven, and graphical user interface (GUI).

MANAGING COMPUTER RESOURCES

Computer resources include the CPU, main memory, the printer, the monitor, and other peripheral devices. This activity manages and controls the resources available to the user so that each user's task can be accomplished.

MANAGING FILES

This function allows users to find, copy, erase, and manipulate computer files from the hard disk and the floppy disk. For example, you can copy files from one disk to another, back up files, make a duplicate copy of a disk, or erase a file from a disk.

MANAGING TASKS

Operating systems are designed to run user tasks more efficiently. They can be classified into three types.

1. *Multi-tasking* is the concurrent execution of two or more programs by one user on the same computer with one CPU.
2. *Multiprogramming* is the execution of two or more programs on a multi-user operating system. The CPU time is shared by many users who are in the management of the OS.
3. *Multiprocessing* uses multiple CPUs to perform work simultaneously. In other words, tasks can be decomposed into several subtasks, and each subtask is assigned to a CPU for processing.

UTILITY PROGRAMS

The utility programs are used to provide end users with a tool box to fine tune hardware components or modify system software functions. Utility programs are normally associated with the operating system. The utility programs for large computer systems (such as mainframe computers and supercomputers) are designed for professional system programmers to either modify or repair the system software. However, the utility programs for microcomputers are very often used by end users. They are user friendly and designed for end users to, for example, format a diskette, change the monitor's background pattern, or install a computer hardware. Some vendors provide utility programs that can enhance the performance of the computer, such as RAM disk, virtual memory, and virus protection. Some of the principal utility programs are as follows:

- *Data recovery.* A data recovery utility is used to "undelete" a file or information that has been accidentally deleted. With this function, users are able to undo the last delete operation that has taken place.
- *Screen saver.* A screen saver prevents a monitor's display screen from being etched by an unchanging image (burned in).
- *Backup.* The backup utility allows users to make a backup (duplicate) copy of the information on the hard disk.
- *Data compression.* Data compression removes redundant elements, gaps, and unnecessary data from a computer's storage space, so less space is required to store or transmit data.
- *Virus protection.* A virus consists of hidden programming instructions that are buried within an applications or system program. They can reproduce themselves and cause damage to computer programs.

PROGRAMMING LANGUAGE PROCESSORS

A program language processor can be either a *compiler* or an *interpreter*. A compiler translates programming codes into machine code all at once so that an executable file will be created for further execution. An interpreter translates a program line by line for each execution. Interpreters are usually used by business researchers or software developers who frequently modify their software and make lots of changes. It is easier to diagnose the programming errors line by line after the execution. An example is the BASIC interpreter.

A compiler has the advantage of being able to generate an executable file for later operation. This file, called the *object code,* is represented in binary code (machine code). The original program is called the *source code.* Users only need the object code to execute the program. Therefore, they do not have to compile the program every time they need to run it. The drawback is that, if there are any programming errors in the program, it is very hard for the program designers to tell what went wrong. Therefore, compilers are best used for programs that are fully developed and ready for the user.

IBM-COMPATIBLE OPERATING SYSTEMS

The original IBM personal computer, and most IBM-compatible computers, used an OS sold by Microsoft called the Personal Computer Disk Operating System (PC-DOS) and Microsoft Disk Operating System (MS-DOS). Since the 1980s, these operating systems have been the most popular operating systems for IBM PC and compatible systems. In 1988, IBM announced an operating system for personal computers called Operating System 2 (OS/2). This operating system, designed to run on more powerful personal computers, requires a minimum of 2 MB of memory, at least 5 MB of hard disk storage, and a powerful CPU. OS/2 has the ability to run applications written for OS/2, DOS, and Windows.

More recently, IBM introduced OS/2 Warp. This operating system has excellent multi-tasking and memory management capabilities and is backed by strong technical support. Microsoft also introduced Windows to provide a graphical user interface when used with DOS. Newer versions of Windows, including Windows 95, 98, 2000, and Windows NT, which is a local network operating system, are fully functional operating systems that do not require DOS. There are many operating systems for IBM compatibles on the market (such as DOS, OS/2, and so on).

WINDOWS

Windows, in its various versions, is expected to remain the most popular OS over the next several years. Windows 95 and up allow users to have a graphical user interface, and they create a single-user and multi-tasking work environment. Several tasks can be performed simultaneously if the hardware has enough capacity to accommodate them. Windows 98's most visible feature is the *Active Desktop*, which integrates the Web browser (*Internet Explorer*) with the operating system.

WINDOWS NT

Windows NT is an operating system intended to support network computing. It consists of a Windows NT workstation and a Windows NT server. The Windows NT workstation is designed to support a 32-bit hardware platform so it can run Windows software more efficiently. The Windows NT server supports a client/server environment and provides network management and monitoring for a local area network.

IBM OS/2 AND OS/2 WARP

OS/2, which stands for Operating System 2, is designed to run on IBM and IBM-compatible computers. Like Windows, it has a graphical user interface, called Workplace Shell (WPS), that uses icons resembling documents, folders, printers, and the like. OS/2 can also run applications for DOS and Microsoft Windows. Because of management and marketing disasters, IBM slipped far behind Microsoft. By mid-1994, an estimated 50 million Windows packages had been sold versus 5 million of OS/2. In late 1994, IBM launched a souped-up version of OS/2 called WARP. Despite spending $2 billion on OS/2 in its long struggle against Windows, the company failed to increase its market share. It is expected that IBM will eventually abandon OS/2.

MACINTOSH OPERATING SYSTEMS

While IBM system platforms traditionally use microprocessors made by Intel and use DOS or Windows for the OS, Apple computers typically use Motorola processors and the proprietary Mac Operating System. Macintosh had a very successful experience in designing graphical user interfaces in the 1980s. A multi-tasking environment was also available in the 1980s. However, at the time, IBM-compatible computers only used DOS operating systems, which have very poor user interfaces. However, this advantage was eliminated after Microsoft launched a Windows serial operating system, which has a similar graphical user interface and multi-tasking environment.

The Macintosh OS has an important program call the Finder, which manages the desktop screen and its icons. Later versions include "Sherlock," which can search not only the computer's internal storage devices but the Internet as well. The Mac OS also enables users to read MS-DOS and Windows files. It has a feature called Apple Guide, which offers "active assistance" to accomplish different tasks on the computer. Although Macintosh is easier to use, not as many application programs are written for Macintosh (about 6,900). In contrast, there are more than 29,400 application programs written for IBM-compatible systems. However, its graphics capabilities make the Macintosh a popular choice for people working in commercial art, desktop publishing, multimedia, and CAD/CAM applications.

OTHER OPERATING SYSTEMS

Other operating systems, such as UNIX, are designed for minicomputers or mainframe computers.

UNIX

UNIX is a powerful operating system developed by AT&T for minicomputers. At the time of UNIX development in the 1970s, AT&T was not permitted to market the operating system due to federal regulations that prohibited the company from competing in the computer marketplace. In 1980s, when AT&T was decomposed into many small companies, many federal regulations were removed. Since then, UNIX has increased in popularity. Today, UNIX is the leading portable OS. It can be used on many computer system types and platforms from personal computers to mainframe systems, because it is compatible with different types of hardware. Users have to learn only one system.

LINUX

Linux is a freeware variant of the Unix operating system. Since the source code for Linux is freely distributed, problems can be fixed and updates developed very rapidly. Pronounced *lee-nucks,* it runs on a number of hardware platforms, including Intel and Motorola microprocessors. It was developed mainly by Linus Torvalds. Because it's free, and because it runs on many platforms—including PCs, Macintoshes, and Amigas—Linux has become extremely popular over the last couple years.

NETWARE

Novell's Netware has become the most popular operating system for coordinating microcomputer-based local area networks (LAN) within an organization. In 1994, Netware controlled 43% of the market for computer network operating systems. However, another competitor, Microsoft Windows NT, is moving toward this growing market. Since Windows NT is designed to support all Microsoft application software, more users are moving from Novell to Windows NT to ensure the compatibility.

SINGLE-USER VS. MULTI-USER SYSTEMS

Single-user operating systems allow only one user to work at a time. This kind of OS has a relatively simple design and usually has fewer graphic user interfaces. Most microcomputers have a single-user OS. DOS and Windows are good examples. A multi-user OS allows many users to share the same computer—normally a mini or a mainframe. A multi-user OS has a more complicated design, since many users have to access the same resources at the same time. This creates tremendous traffic and management problems among different users. UNIX is a good multi-user system.

SINGLE-TASKING SYSTEMS VS. MULTI-TASKING
SYSTEMS

SINGLE TASKING

Single tasking implies that only one job or task can be executed at one time. DOS is a typical example of a single-tasking system, since only one job can be executed at once. However, a multi-tasking system allows more than one job (task) to be executed at the same time. For example, you can work on your word processing program while your print manager software is running the functions that control the printer. This is usually conducted by opening several windows. Microsoft Windows and Macintosh OS are good examples.

MULTI-TASKING

The multi-tasking environment allows users to perform several computer tasks at one time. Each task occupies a window. By swapping between windows, users are able to use different packages as they wish.

EVOLUTION OF PROGRAMMING LANGUAGES

Programming languages can be classified into five generations in terms of the history of development.

FIRST-GENERATION PROGRAMMING LANGUAGE

Machine code is represented in binary representation. All numbers are represented by 1s and 0s, since inside the computer, only 1 or 0 can be represented by circuits. To see how hard this is to understand, image having to read this:

0001010100111011110011100000111110100001111

Machine languages also vary according to the make of the computer. This is another characteristic that makes for difficulty. However, machine codes are very efficient from a hardware point of view, because no additional processing procedures are required.

SECOND-GENERATION PROGRAMMING LANGUAGE

Assembly language is designed to simplify the coding process for machine codes. Instead of binary code, all addresses are coded in a hexadecimal system, and all operators are represented in English abbreviation. For example,

ADD 43(9, 2), B4(10, A)

is a piece of assembly code, which is still pretty obscure. Therefore, assembly language is also considered to be a low-level language. Both first- and second-generation programming languages are "hardware dependent." That means programmers must know the hardware structure and configuration to write codes properly.

THIRD-GENERATION PROGRAMMING LANGUAGE

Third-generation languages are designed to let programmers develop codes without any knowledge of computer memory configuration. Examples are COBOL, Pascal,

FORTRAN, and many popular languages. One drawback of a third-generation language is that it may be complicated to code. A good programmer usually requires a couple of years of training and experience.

BASIC

An acronym for Beginner's All-purpose Symbolic Instruction Code, BASIC is a popular microcomputer language. It is widely used on microcomputers and easy to learn. It is suited to both beginning and experienced programmers. It is also interactive, i.e., users and computers communicate with each other directly during the waiting and running of programs.

Another version, created by the Microsoft Corporation, is Visual Basic, which has been hailed as a programming breakthrough. Visual BASIC makes it easier for novice programmers, as well as professionals, to develop customized applications for Windows. The new language is expected to become quite popular for corporate, in-house development.

PASCAL

Another language that is widely used on microcomputers and easy to learn is Pascal. It is named after Blaise Pascal, a seventeenth-century French mathematician. Pascal has become quite popular in computer science programs. One advantage is that it encourages programmers to follow structured coding procedures. It also works well for graphics.

C/C++

C is a general-purpose language that also works well with microcomputers. It is useful for writing operating systems, spreadsheet programs, database programs, and some scientific applications. Programs are portable: they can be run without change on a variety of computers. C++ is a version of C that incorporates object-oriented technologies. It is popular with some software developers and promises to increase programmer productivity.

COBOL

COBOL, which stands for Common Business-Oriented Language, is one of the most frequently used programming languages in business. Although harder to learn than BASIC, its logic is easier to understand for a person who is not a trained programmer. Writing a COBOL program is sort of like writing the outline for a business research analysis. The program is divided into four divisions. The divisions, in turn, are divided into sections, which are divided into paragraphs, then into statements.

FORTRAN

Short for FORmula TRANslation, FORTRAN is a widely used scientific and mathematical language. It is very useful for processing complex formulas. Thus, many scientific and engineering programs have been written in this language.

Ada

Ada is named after Augusta Ada, the English Countess of Lovelace, who is regarded as the first programmer. Ada was developed under the sponsorship of the U.S. Department of Defense. Originally designed for weapons systems, it has commercial uses as well. Because of its structured design, modules (sections) of a large program can be written, compiled, and tested separately—before the entire program is put together.

FOURTH-GENERATION LANGUAGE

Fourth-generation languages are designed for people who need a simplified and powerful tool to conduct programming processes. The equivalent of many lines of third-generation language codes can usually be compacted into several lines. However, this language requires lots of hardware power to translate into machine code and perform the execution.

Query Languages

Query languages enable nonprogrammers to use certain easily understood commands to search and generate reports from a database.

Application Generators

An application generator contains a number of modules—logically related program statements—that have been preprogrammed to accomplish various tasks. An example would be a module that calculates overtime pay. The programmer can simply state which task is needed for a particular application. The application generator creates the program code by selecting the appropriate modules.

FIFTH-GENERATION PROGRAMMING LANGUAGE (NATURAL LANGUAGE)

Natural language programs are designed to give people a more human connection with computers. The language used to communicate is basically the language we use on a daily basis, such as English, Chinese, and French. This kind of language allows users to speak or type in a human language command to execute the function. This type of language provides a computer novice with a handy tool.

Generation	Sample Statement
First	1000011101110011
Second	ADD 32(4, B), 8AB(5, 9)
Third	Counter: = 20
Fourth	Select name FROM Executive
Fifth	Update the inventory file by transaction file

WHAT ARE OBJECT-ORIENTED LANGUAGES AND COMPUTER AIDED SOFTWARE ENGINEERING TOOLS?

Object-oriented languages have a different way to code. They allow the interaction of programming objects. This approach to programming is called *object-oriented programming (OOP)*. In OOP, data, instructions, and other programming procedures are grouped together. The items in a group are called an *object*. The process of grouping items into an object is called *encapsulation*. Encapsulation means that functions or tasks are captured into each object, which keeps them safer from changes, because access is protected. Objects often have properties of *polymorphism* and *inheritance*. Polymorphism allows the programmer to develop one routine that will operate or work with multiple objects. Inheritance means that objects in a group can take on or inherit characteristics of other objects in the same group or class of objects. This helps programmers select objects with certain characteristics for other programming tasks or projects. Professional MIS programmers are consistently looking for ways to make the programming development process easier, faster, and more reliable. A CASE tool provide some automation and assistance in program design, coding and testing. Some CASE tools can even convert your design into real codes.

SUMMARY

In the future, more powerful and easier-to-use versions will keep evolving. These new systems will be created with OOP, which can create a series of interchangeable software objects or modules. By using OOP, new operating systems can be developed faster and more efficiently.

5 A Practical Guide to Application Software

FINDING OUT WHAT IS AVAILABLE: AN INTRODUCTION

Before you decide to buy a piece of software, you should decide what functions are to be achieved. For example, if you just want to have a simple word processing system for resume preparation, a simple word processing package would be enough. However, if you need to edit magazines for publication, professional desktop publication software is required. If the required computer functions are generally common ones, packaged software will be easier to find on the market. If, however, your requested function is rare or on such a large scale so that no existing packaged software is available, you may have to develop your own from scratch. This is called "customized software." In general, customized software is more time consuming and costs more money to develop, but it's more efficient in operation due to the special design of functions. You can buy packaged software from many computer software stores or through mail order. However, if you decide to design from scratch, you then have to choose a programming language to do the coding. This design processes is known as the *system analysis and design* cycle.

VERSIONS

A *version* is a major upgrade in a software product. Version are usually represented by numbers such as 1.0, 2.0, 3.0 and so forth. The higher the number, the more recent the version.

RELEASE

A *release* is a minor upgrade. The number indicates releases after the decimal point. For example, 3.1, 3.12, 3.121, and so on.

YEARLY VERSION

Microsoft uses "Windows 98" instead of "Windows 95" for its new operating system, since it was launched in 1998. Most software is *upward compatible (forward compatible)*. That means a document created under earlier version or release can be processed using a later version or release. *Downward compatible* means that a document created using a later version can be run on older versions or releases. Software can be categorized in terms of software copyrights.

Proprietary Software

With proprietary software, the rights are owned by an individual or business. Therefore, the ownership of the software is protected by the copyright. There are two types of licenses offered.

- *Single-user licenses.* Users can buy one copy of the software license and use this software in a single machine.
- *Site licenses.* Users can buy multiple usage in a certain areas such as a campus or a company.

Public Domain Software

Public domain software is software that is not protected by copyright law and may be duplicated by anyone. Examples include a government-developed program for the general public and a program donated by the original creator. Public domain software can normally be downloaded from the Internet or from the bulletin board of network service providers such as America on Line, CompuServe, etc.

Freeware

Freeware is software that is available free of charge through the Internet or computer users group. Sometimes software developers promote their product by giving away free software for trial. This trial might be a 30-day trial or an unlimited time period. To create a standard for software on which people are apt to agree, the developers want to see how users respond, so they can make improvements in a later version. This is one of the reasons why there is no need to pay for it. The software distributed is free of charge, but it usually offers limited functions. Freeware developers often retain all rights to their programs so that, technically, you are not supposed to duplicate and distribute it. An example of freeware is Mosaic.

SEVEN MAIN TYPES OF SOFTWARE AND HOW THEY OPERATE

There are seven major types of application software on the market. They are presentation software, word processors, spreadsheets, database programs, communication software, desktop publishing programs, graphics software, and personal management applications.

PRESENTATION SOFTWARE

Presentation software is designed to generate graphical presentation slides used to communicate or make a presentation of data to others. Good presentation software provides users with graphical user interface and lots of utilities to make transparencies. Some presentation graphics packages provide artwork, drawing function, and even multimedia utilities to make the presentation more attractive.

WORD PROCESSING SOFTWARE

Word processing software allows users to create, edit, format, save, and print documents such as letters, memos, reports, and manuscripts. Some word processing software also includes artwork, drawing functions, spreadsheet utilities, and graphics. Others provide users with a spelling checker, grammar checker, or thesaurus functions.

SPREADSHEETS

A spreadsheet allows users to create tables and financial schedules with mathematical functions by entering data in prepared tables; spreadsheets can calculate entered data and provide solutions. In the late 1970s, Daniel Bricklin was a student at the Harvard Business School. One day, he was staring at columns of numbers on a blackboard when he got the idea for computerizing the spreadsheet. VisiCalc was the first product resulting from his idea. Today, the principal spreadsheets are Microsoft Excel, Lotus 1-2-3, and Quattro Pro.

A spreadsheet contains many cells, each of which can be used to store a number (such as 34), a formula (such as =A4+B4), or a label (1996 Sales Report). A cell is where a row and a column intersect. For example, C4 is the address of the cell, where column C and row 4 intersect. A cell pointer indicates where data is to be entered. The cell pointer can be moved around like a cursor in a word processing program. The cell pointer moves to activate that cell and allows user to input or update the content of that cell.

Since a cell contains numbers, labels, and formulas, users can design a template with formulas and labels so that other users will type in collected data and receive the answer. Today's spreadsheets are more sophisticated than earlier versions. They very often have drawing facilities, an artwork library, a database interface, and a very nice graphics generator. Therefore, spreadsheets have become the most popular small-business program.

DATABASE SOFTWARE

Database software is a program that controls the structure of a database and access to the data. In other words, a database is any electronically stored collection of data in a computer system. These computer-based files are organized according to their common elements so that data can be retrieved easily. The following is a description of database elements.

File	A collection of related records
Record	A collection of related fields
Field	A unit of data consisting of one or more characters

A database management system (DBMS) is software that controls and manipulates the structure of a database. Major database software is dBase, Oracle, Paradox, and Access. Recently, newer DBMS has undergone dramatic improvement in that not just data but images, voices, and even motion pictures can be included. Principal features of database software are as follows:

1. *Database creation.* Users can create a database by creating files (or tables). Each table has several *fields.* A field is a string of one or more characters. A field can have the attribute of text, data, number, or even object. After the format of a table is created, users can input *records* into the database. A record is collection of related fields. An example is a person's name, address, and phone number.
2. *File or report selection and display.* After a database (consisting of several files) is created, users can manipulate this database by issuing queries. The function of a query is to screen all records by defined criteria.
3. *Database update.* Users can delete, add, or change a record in a data file.
4. *Database calculation and formatting.* Some DBMS contains built-in mathematical formulas. This feature can be used, for example, to find the average number of a selected group, as to find the average age of all customers who live in California.

Major database manipulation languages are Structured Query Language (SQL) and Query By Examples (QBE). Generally speaking, SQL is more powerful than QBE. Most professional database administrators are required to know SQL. Generally speaking, database software is much better than the old file managers, because it can access several files at one time (also can be known as flat-file management systems).

COMMUNICATION SOFTWARE

Computers are often networked so that information can be shared. To transfer information between different computers, communication software is required. Communication software allows computers to exchange data over private network such as a local area network or over a public network such as a wide area network (WAN). When proper communication software exists in both the sending and receiving units, computers are able to establish and share electronic links, code and decode data transmissions, verify transmission errors, compress data streams for more efficient transmission, and manage the transmission of documents. Communication software provides functionality far beyond numeric computation, textual editing, and graphics. It provides access to a virtually unlimited amount of information from anywhere on Earth.

DESKTOP PUBLISHING

Desktop publishing involves using a microcomputer and peripherals to mix text and graphics to produce high-quality printed output. Magazines or newspapers usually use the final product of desktop publishing. Major desktop publishing programs are Adobe PageMaker, Quark Xpress, and Ventura Publisher.

This type of program presents pictorial descriptions.

PACKAGED, CUSTOMIZED, OR SEMI-CUSTOMIZED SOFTWARE

There are three approaches to acquire software, depending on its intended use and the cost and the duration of development.

- Large software corporations (such as Microsoft) target their products for a large number of end users and for general purposes, so they usually design packaged software. In other words, the software functions available are common and popular to the general public. This enables a large population to share the development cost and pay a smaller price for well designed software. However, these programs may not fit every user's particular needs. Since packaged software is developed to satisfy most end users, the user interface and software documentation are very well prepared. The cost of development is shared by many users and therefore can be dramatically reduced for any individual purchaser.
- Customized software requires intensive development efforts. It usually takes longer time and more money to develop. Typically, only a large corporation can afford the development costs. The major reason to acquire customized software is if suitable commercial software is not available, which usually is the situation if the potential user group is so small that it would not be worthwhile for any software company to develop products for it. Customized software requires more time and effort to develop, but it can be tailored to customer's needs. In other words, the functions available in customized software are more flexible and powerful. Two system development methodologies are available: *system analysis and design life cycle,* and *prototyping.*
  - *System analysis and design life cycle.* The system development life cycle consists of seven steps:
    1. Identify problems and opportunities
    2. Analyze and document existing systems
    3. Determine information requirements
    4. Design technology and personal requirements
    5. Develop, test, and validate the system
    6. Implement the system
    7. Evaluate and maintain the system
  - *Prototyping.* This method involves building a working model and modifying it to fit our requirement. A working model (system) may cover only a subset of the whole system or only some functions among others. A complete system can then be built by including more functions or by expanding to other subsystems.

- Semi-customized software represents a trade-off between customized software and packaged software is to have software. I provides a general structure, and customers can modify this software and customized the functions. For example, most of database software provides a general database structure. Based on different individual needs, users can develop different applications for different environments.

WHERE TO GET SOFTWARE ASSISTANCE

You can receive software assistance from several sources.

1. *Software vendors.* Software producers usually provide buyers with telephone assistance. Users can call technology support department for help.
2. *Software on-line help.* Most software programs come with on-line help. On-line help contains functions or explanations that can be retrieved right from the program. Users can get an immediate response from the *help* menu. One drawback to on-line help is that users may not be able to get all the answers they are looking for.
3. *Networks.* On the Internet, and other networks, there are many software users' bulletin boards. Many ideas and problems are posted on these bulletin boards. Users can certainly exchange ideas or answers through these places.
4. *Professional consulting firms.* Most software consulting firms provide software assistance by a fee. However, services provided by consulting firms can be very expensive.
5. *Software training facilities.* Schools or training institutes give seminars and courses for different types of software.
6. *Vendor's seminars.* Most vendors provide seminars for new software releases. Users (or buyers) can attend these seminars for more information and help. Most seminars are free to users.

PRESENTATION SOFTWARE

Presentation software offers users a wide choice of presentation effects. These include three-dimensional displays, background patterns, multiple text fonts, and image libraries that contain illustrations of objects such as people, birds, cars, and others. Using graphics software as a presentation tool allows you to effectively create professional quality graphics that can help you communicate information more effectively. Persuasion, Harvard Graphics, and PowerPoint are popular presentation graphics packages.

WORD PROCESSING SOFTWARE

Word processing is the most widely used general application. If you need to create a document, such as a letter or memo, you can make the process much easier using a word processing tool. Some of the most popular word processor packages are

Microsoft Word, Word Perfect, and WordStar. Word processing software allows you to enter text on the computer keyboard in the same manner as you create document on a typewriter. As you enter the characters, they are displayed on the screen and stored in the computer's main memory. You can then edit this document electronically. Editing includes such functions as the ability to delete, insert, move, or copy words or sentences. You can also use format function to specify the margin and page length, and to select character size and font. Most word processing software also includes a spelling checker, thesaurus, and grammar checker.

GUIDELINES FOR PREPARING SPREADSHEET SOFTWARE

This software allows you to organize numeric data in a worksheet or table format called a *spreadsheet*. Within a spreadsheet, data is organized horizontally in rows and vertically in columns. The intersection point where a row and column meet is called a *cell*. Cells are named by their location in the spreadsheet. Each cell may contain three types of data: labels (text), values (numbers), and formulas. The text (label) identifies the data and documents the spreadsheet. The numbers are values, which can be calculated. The formulas perform calculations on data in the spreadsheet and display the resulting value in the cell containing the formula.

DATABASE SOFTWARE

A *database* refers to a collection of data that is stored in files. Database software allows you to create a database and to retrieve, manipulate, and update the data that you store in it. In a manual system, data might be recorded on paper and stored in a filing cabinet. In a database on the computer, data will be stored in an electronic format on an auxiliary storage device such as a hard disk. There are several terms you should understand. A *file* is defined as a collection of related data that are organized in records. Each *record* contains a collection of related facts called *fields*. For example:

Student File		
Name	Social Security No.	Phone No.
Robert Jones	365-98-6509	909-675-9842
Mary Smith	876-92-1425	818-837-2897
Jim Lee	987-26-3833	909-824-2225
John Doe	873-22-2998	818-827-9988

This student file contains four records, and each record has three fields.

Database software can organize data in a certain way that allows users to retrieve, update, delete, or create data at a very high speed. Users can therefore improve productivity by using database software.

DATA COMMUNICATION SOFTWARE

Data communication software is used to transmit data from one computer to another. It gives users access to databases such as stock prices and airline schedules. There are two kinds of data communication software: *network operating systems* and *network browsers*. A network operating system is the software used to manage network communications. A network OS can be very powerful, allowing it to manage several hundred workstations or even many network servers in a wide area network. A network OS can also be designed to manage only a handful of PCs in a local area network.

A network browser is used to access the network. Network users can access the network and retrieve information from the network through the network browser. For example, Novel and Windows NT are two popular local networks OS. Netscape Navigator and Mosaic are popular network browsers.

WHEN TO USE INTEGRATED SOFTWARE PACKAGES

Integrated software packages combine the features of several popular applications such as word processing software, spreadsheet software, database software, presentation software, and data communication software. Since different software is combined in a single package, users do not have to pay the full price of each individual program. In addition, the functions available for each different software package are more consistent than with individual programs. Three major integrated software packages are Microsoft Office, Lotus SmartSuite, and Corel PerfectOffice.

SUMMARY

Application software is designed to accomplish managers' tasks. The major efforts to improve application software are aimed at achieving better usability and an improved user interface. A better interface indicates that the user can perform a user's task in a more efficient way so that productivity and efficiency can be improved. In the future, the user interface of application software is going to be so natural that it will take little effort for users to communicate with a computer.

One of the challenges of application software is file exchangeability. The information used for different applications may not be exchangeable. However, this has been dramatically improved with the "open system" architecture. This enables end users to exchange information between different application software and to communicate more effectively.

6 Data and Databases

WHAT IS A DATABASE?

A database is a system in which data are organized in a certain way so that accurate and timely information can be retrieved. The information system used to manage databases is called a database management system (DBMS). A database management system is software that allows managers to create, maintain, and report the data and file relationships. A file management system is software that allows users to manipulate one file at a time. Database management systems offer many advantages over file management systems, as discussed below.

- *Reduced data redundancy.* Data redundancy means that the same data field appears in different tables, sometimes in a different format. For example, a customer's name, address, and phone number can be stored in both the checking account file and the receivables account file. This would cause problems in terms of maintenance and update. It requires more time and money to maintain files with redundant records.
- *Improved data integrity.* Data integrity means that data are accurate, consistent, and up-to-date. If the same data are store in different files, data updating may not cover all data elements in different files. Some reports will be produced with erroneous information.
- *Improved data security.* Database management systems allow users to establish different levels of security over information in the database. This guarantees that data will be retrieved or updated only by authorized users. For example, the sales manager can only read employee payroll information, not modify it. A non-management employee probably has no access privilege to the payroll data and can neither inquire nor modify the data.
- *Reduced development time.* Since database management systems organize data in a better way, this enables the data base administrator (DBA) to improve the efficiency and productivity of database development. For example, instead of creating a new file, the DBA can add new fields to existing files and still maintain data integrity.

WHAT IS A DATABASE FILE (TABLE)?

A database file is a collection of related records that describe a subject using a set of fields. Figure 6.1 shows a file with three records used to describe a student by using fields of "Name," "GPA," and "Major."

Name	GPA	Major
Robert Smith	3.2	IS
Mary Lee	3.5	ACCT
Jim Shaw	2.9	IS

FIGURE 6.1   A typical data file.

Most organizations have many files which have the numbers of records from hundreds to hundreds of thousands. Files that are stored on secondary storage devices can be organized in several different ways, and there are advantages and disadvantages to each of these types of file organizations.

TYPES OF FILE ORGANIZATION

Three types of file organization are used on secondary storage devices. They are *sequential, indexed-sequential,* and *direct* files. Files stored on tape are processed as sequential files. Files on disk are usually direct or indexed-sequential files.

SEQUENTIAL FILE

Sequential files can be stored on a sequential access device such as tapes or on a random access device such as a disk. In a sequential file, records are arranged one after another, in a predetermined order. For example, an employee file can be organized by employee ID number. If this file is stored on a disk or tape, the employee record with the smallest ID number would be the first record in the file.

INDEXED-SEQUENTIAL FILE

An indexed-sequential file allows both sequential and direct access to data records. Thus, files must be on a direct access storage device such as a disk. In indexed-sequential files, records are usually physically arranged on a storage medium by their primary key, just as they are with sequential files. The difference is that an index also exists for the file; it can be used to look up and directly access individual records. Files set up to allow this type of access are called indexed sequential access method (ISAM) files. Many database management systems (DBMSs) use ISAM files because of their relative flexibility and simplicity. This is often the best type of file for business applications that demand both batch updating and on-line processing.

DIRECT FILE

A direct file provides the fastest possible access to records. ISAM also provides users with direct access to individual records. A direct file is typically the best when access time is critical and when batch processing is not necessary. A direct file uses a formula to transfer the primary key to the location of each record. This formula is called a Hashing algorithm. Therefore, no index is needed to locate individual records. Many hashing algorithms have been developed. One popular procedure is to use prime numbers in the formula process. In general, the primary key value is divided by a prime number, which corresponds to the maximum number of storage locations allocated for the records of this file. The reminder obtained in this division is then used as the relative address of a record, but relative address can be translated into physical locations on the storage medium.

DATA MODELS (RELATIONAL, HIERARCHICAL, AND NETWORK)

RELATIONAL DATABASES

The relational database relates or connects data in different files through the use of a key field, or common data element. (See Figure 6.2.) In this arrangement, data elements are stored in different tables or files made up of rows and columns. In database terminology, tables are called "relations," rows are called "tuples," and columns are called "attributes." In a table, a row resembles a record—for example, a student's GPA record has a field of "student name," a field of "GPA," a field of "address," and a filed of "phone number." In this table, a student is described by a record or a combination of fields. The advantage of a relational database is that the manager does not have to be aware of any data structure or data pointer. Managers can easily add, update, delete, or create records using simple logic. However, a disadvantage is that some search commands in a relational database require more time to process compared with other database models.

HIERARCHICAL DATABASES

In a hierarchical database, fields and records are arranged in a family tree, with lower-level records subordinate to higher-level records. (See Figure 6.3.) In a hierarchical database, a parent record may have more than one child, but a child always has only one parent. This is called a one-to-many relationship. To locate a particular record, you have to start at the top of the tree with a parent record and trace down the tree to the child. Hierarchical databases are the oldest of the four data models and are still used in some reservation systems. In addition, accessing or updating records is very fast, since the relationships have been predefined. The drawback of hierarchical data models is that the structure is quite rigid, and adding new records to the database may require that the entire database be redefined.

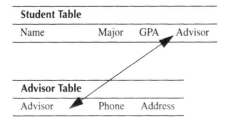

FIGURE 6.2   A relational database.

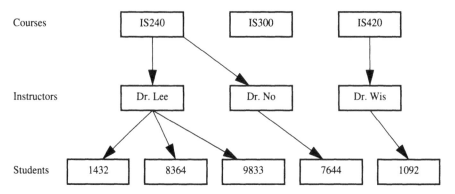

FIGURE 6.3   A hierarchical database.

NETWORK DATABASES

A network database (See Figure 6.4) is similar to a hierarchical database except that each child can have more than one parent record. In other words, a child record is referred to as a "member" and a parent record is referred to as an "owner." The advantage of the network database is its ability to establish relationships between different branches of data records and thus offer increased access capability for the manager. However, like the hierarchical database, the data record relationships must be predefined prior to the use of the database and must be redefined if records are added or updated.

OBJECT-ORIENTED DATABASES

An object-oriented database uses *objects* as elements within database files. An object consists of text, sound, images and instructions on the action to be taken on the data. For example, traditional data models such as hierarchical, network, and relational data models can contain only numeric and text data of an instructor. An object-oriented database might also contain the instructor's picture and video. Moreover,

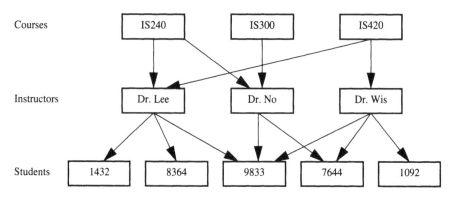

FIGURE 6.4   A network database.

the object would store operations, called *methods*, that perform actions on the data—for example how to calculate this person's pension fund based on age and contributions.

PRIMARY KEYS, SECONDARY KEYS, AND FOREIGN KEYS

In a database, data records are organized and identified by using the key field. A key field contains unique data used to identify a record so that it can be easily retrieved and processed. There are three types of key fields used for database management.

PRIMARY KEYS

The primary key can be a single field or a combination of several fields. It is the most important identifier for retrieving records. It is unique, and there can be only one in each table. For example, the social security number is a good primary key to identify each person, whereas age may not be useful, since many people may have the same age.

SECONDARY KEYS

Secondary keys can be any field or the combination of several fields. A secondary key does not have to be unique, and there can be many of them in a table. For example, we can use *major* as a secondary key to locate students majoring in information systems.

FOREIGN KEYS

The foreign key is the field or a combination of several fields that can be used to relate two tables. A foreign key must be a primary key in one table. This primary key can thus be connected to another table. For example, a student table contains social security number, major, and advisor's name. The advisor table has advisor's name, phone number, and address. The *advisor's name* is the foreign key to connect the student table with the advisor table. (See Figure 6.5.)

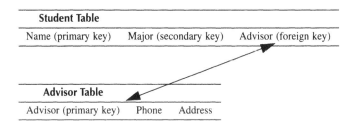

FIGURE 6.5 Key fields.

DATABASE DESIGN

Database design is an intuitive and artistic process. There is no strict algorithm for it. Typically, database design is an interactive process; during each iteration, the goal is to get closer to an acceptable design. Thus, a design will be developed and then reviewed. Defects in the design will be identified, and the design will be redone. This process is repeated until the development team and users are satisfied with what is available. A well designed database enables managers to perform efficient and useful tasks. In other words, a poorly designed database may cost lots of money and time without making a significant contribution to a company's operation. Database design procedures are therefore crucial to the success of a database system. Procedures for database design are listed below.

CURRENT SYSTEM ANALYSIS AND SURVEY

This process involves surveying and observing current manual data processes and potential benefits from computerized database systems. Usually, both decision-makers and process operators are interviewed to collect information of potential problems and opportunities. After the system analysis has been conducted, a feasibility report is prepared for evaluation. The suggestion of the feasibility report can be either positive or negative. The main reason for a suggestion of infeasible is mainly because of financial or managerial problems.

LOGICAL DATABASE DESIGN

A logical database design specifies the logical format of the database. The records to be maintained, their contents, and relationships among those records are specified. It is sometimes called the *conceptual schema,* or the *logical schema.* There is a technique called *normalization* developed for relational databases to improve the structure of files in a relational database. By using this method, data can be organized into the most efficient and logical file relationships.

PHYSICAL DATABASE DESIGN

The logical schema is transformed into the particular data constructs that are available with the DBMS to be used. Whereas the logical design is DBMS-independent, the physical design is DBMS-dependent. Logical schema specifies general database design, which can be implemented in any database management software, while physical schema is designed based on a real database management software and cannot be transferred from one to another.

IMPLEMENTATION

After the physical schema is designed, the database implementation will be conducted. This process involves lots of coding and programming. This process can be done with a DBMS such as ORACLE, FOXBase, Microsoft SQL Server, and a front-end tool for user interface development such as Visual Basic or Power Builder.

Testing and Debugging

This process involves testing the system and making sure that it is ready to operate. In this stage, both program developers and end users should get involved in the process.

Training, Evaluation and Documentation

If both the end-user group and development team are satisfied with the system, the training session should proceed. The purpose of the training session is to teach managers how to use this new system and perform simple troubleshooting functions. The development team should also prepare system documentation for the managers for reference purposes.

OTHER FEATURES IN A DATABASE MANAGEMENT SYSTEM

Data Dictionary

The data dictionary stores the data definitions or a description of the structure of data used in the database. This information could be stored in a dictionary-like document or on a text file. Managers can check the data dictionary and retrieve necessary information about the properties and nature of the database. Some data dictionaries can also monitor the data being entered into the database management system to make sure it conforms to the definition, such as field name, field size, and type of data (text, numeric, date, logic, and so on). The data dictionary can also help the database administrator (DBA) and other database designers with security concerns such as who has the right to access what kind of information.

Database Utilities

The database needs to undergo certain maintenance to ensure that the data are properly organized. Database utility programs provide the DBA with functions that can fine tune the database functionality such as remove redundant or non-used records, assign priorities to different users, and monitor resource allocation. A good database utility program can improve the productivity and efficiency of a DBA.

Database Recovery

Situations such as systems failure, computer malfunction, disk head crash, programs containing bugs, and so on will cause a database management system crash. Unfortunately, when systems fail, business does not stop. Customers continue to buy and pay, return merchandise, and obtain service. Therefore, the system must recover from a failure as quickly as possible. Furthermore, business requirements dictate that transactions that were being processed when the failure occurred be recoverable. In other words, any effects that the failure had on data should be evident. Recovering from a database system failure is becoming more difficult, due to the complexity of modern database management systems. It is often impossible to simply fix the problem and resume program processing where it was interrupted. Even if no data is lost during a failure, the timing and scheduling of computer processing is too complex to be accurately recreated. Some techniques have been developed to recover from a system failure:

- Recovery via reprocessing
- Recovery via rollback/rollforward
- Transaction logging
- Write-ahead log

The details of these techniques are beyond the scope of this book. Readers can check database books for more information.

THE DATABASE ADMINISTRATOR (DBA)

WHAT IS A DATABASE ADMINISTRATOR?

The DBA is the person who manages all activities related to the database. A qualified DBA should be able to understand the hardware configuration (such as the client server environment) and take advantage of existing hardware capability to improve the performance of the database management system. This individual should have expertise in terms of database engine (such as SQL) and front-end tools (such as Visual Basic and Power Builder) to create a good user interface. A DBA should be able to do limited troubleshooting in both the application area and system level, since a database crash may involve both application and system software.

MAJOR FUNCTIONS OF A DATABASE ADMINISTRATOR

The responsibilities of a DBA are as outlined below.

DATABASE DESIGN

The database administrator helps determine the design of the database, including fields, tables, and key fields. Later the DBA determines how resources are used on secondary storage devices, how files and records may be added and deleted, and how losses may be detected and remedied.

SYSTEM BACKUP AND RECOVERY

Because loss of data or a crash in the database could vitally affect the organization, a database system must be able to recover if the system crashes. The DBA needs to make sure that the system is regularly backed up and must develop plans for recovering data should a failure occur.

End-User Service and Coordination

A DBA should determine user access privileges and arrange resource allocation for different user groups. If different users conflict, the DBA should be able to coordinate to make sure that an optimal arrangement is performed.

Database Security

The DBA can specify different access privileges for different users of a database management system to protect the database from unauthorized access and sabotage. For example, one kind of user is allowed to retrieve data, whereas another might have the right to update data and delete records.

Performance Monitoring

The database base system should maintain a certain standard of services for all users. The DBA monitors the system and uses different database tools to make sure that the system is set up to satisfy managers performance requirements.

QUERY LANGUAGES

What is a Query Language?

A query language is a simple English-like language that allows managers to specify what data they are looking for, either on a printed report or on screen. Generally speaking, there are two types of query languages: *Structured Query Language* and *Query by Examples.*

Structured Query Language

Structured Query Language (SQL) is the most widely used database query language. In 1985, the American National Standards Institute formed a committee to develop industry standards for SQL. Today, most database management system support this standard. Figure 6.6 shows an example of the SQL statements.

Query by Example

Query by Example (QBE) helps the manager construct a query by displaying a list of fields that are available in the files from which the query will be made.

> SELECT name, gpa
> FROM student
> WHERE gpa >=3.0
> ORDER BY name

FIGURE 6.6   Structured Query Language.

SUMMARY

Information is the most valuable asset in a company, and the database management system is one of the most important MIS tools available to manipulate the company's information. Understanding the way that data is organized and represented in database management systems becomes one of the most important concepts an executive should have in mind. By applying information technology properly, including database management systems, the manager can dramatically maximize productivity and reduce corporate costs and risks.

7 Data Communications

Data communication has become more and more important in business. The ability to instantly communicate information is changing the way people do business and interact with each other. New data communication technologies also allow voice, image, and even video to be transmitted through the network. Many business applications are available because of new data communication technologies. Examples are electronic mail, voice mail, teleconferencing, fax, electronic data interchange (EDI), online services, and others. As a matter of fact, more and more new services will become available through the network because of the "information superhighway."

DIGITAL VS. ANALOG SIGNALS

Digital signals are individual voltage pulses that represent data bits, which are grouped together to form characters. This type of signal is usually used inside the computer to transmit data between electronic components and nearby devices. Digital signals have the limitation of short-range transmission (at most several hundred feet) and are represented by on/off binary systems. Local area networks (LANs) usually use digital signals for transmission. This transmission is normally restricted to a certain area such as a room or a building.

Analog signals are continuous electromagnetic waves. They are able to travel a long distance, and most long distance transmissions are carried out as analog signals. For example, voice transmission through the telephone lines and data transmission between computers rely on analog signals.

DIGITAL VS. ANALOG DATA

Data can be defined as *raw facts.* To transfer data between devices, data must be represented in a certain format. There are generally two types of data representations. One is called *digital data,* the other is *analog data.* Digital data representation uses a binary system (i.e., 1s and 0s) to represent anything. A number, a letter, an image, or even a video can be represented in a binary system. Analog data representation uses continuous signals. Voice, pictures, and video are normally represented in analog data representation. A videotape stores video in analog signals, and a cassette holds audio signals in analog form.

The same data or information can be represented by both digital and analog representations. For example, audiocassettes use analog representation to record voice, while compact disks have digital representation. In general, digital data representation is more accurate and durable for repetitive usage than analog data representation. However, digital data representations require more storage space for voice and video than do analog representations.

DIGITAL VS. ANALOG TRANSMISSION

Digital transmission can be used for both digital and analog signals. However, all analog data or information must be converted into digital form prior to transmission. For example, an image can be converted into digital file, and this digital file will be transmitted by analog signals, which carry this digital representation to the destination. Digital transmission uses repeaters instead of amplifiers for long-distance transmission. This is considered to be the best way to transmit information. Analog transmission uses analog data represented by analog signals. For example, a telephone conversation can be transmitted in analog form and will use analog transmission techniques.

	Digital Representation	Analog Representation
Digital transmission	Integrated Services Digital Network (ISDN)	Not available
Analog transmission	Using MODEM to transmit computer files	Traditional telephone calls

TYPES OF WIRED COMMUNICATION MEDIA

There are three basic types of wired transmission media, as described below.

TWISTED PAIR WIRE

Most telephone lines consist of cables made up of hundreds of copper strands called *twisted pair wire (TPW)*. TPW has been the standard transmission medium for years, for both voice and data. However, they are now being phased out by more technically advanced and reliable media such as fiber optical cables. Twisted-pair wire consists of two or more strands of insulated copper wire twisted around each other in pairs. They are then covered with another layer of plastic insulation. Since so much of the world is already served by twisted-pair wire, it will no doubt continue to be used for years, both for voice messages and for modern-transmitted computer data. However, it is relatively slow and does not protect well against electrical interference.

COAXIAL CABLE

Coaxial cable, commonly called *coax,* consists of insulated copper wire wrapped in a solid or braided metal shield, then in an external cover. Coaxial cable has a wider *bandwidth* as compared with TPW. Bandwidth refers to the number of communications can be transmitted at one time. A coaxial cable has about 80 times the transmission capacity of TPW. Coaxial cable is often used to link parts of a computer system in one building. In addition, coaxial cable is much better at resisting electromagnetic noise than is twisted-pair wiring.

FIBER OPTICAL CABLE

A fiber-optic cable (FOC) consists of hundreds of thin strands of glass that transmit not electricity but, rather, pulses of light. These strands, each as thin as a human hair, can transmit billions of pulses per second, with each "on" pulse representing one bit. When bundled together, fiber optic strands in a cable 0.12-inch thick can support 250,000 to 500,000 conversations at the same time. In other words, fiber optic cable has the widest bandwidth. In fiber optical cable, signals in the form of light waves are transmitted through tubes of glass. In general, FOC has 26,000 times the transmission capacity of TPW. In addition, FOC has several advantages over both TPW and CC. Such cables are immune to electronic interference, which makes them more secure. They are also lighter and less expensive that coaxial cable and are more reliable at transmitting data.

WIRELESS COMMUNICATION MEDIA

The major wireless transmission media are microwave systems and satellite systems. These are embodied in the global positioning system (GPS), pagers, and mobile phone systems.

MICROWAVE SYSTEMS

Microwaves are high-frequency radio waves that travel in straight lines through the air. Because of the curvature of the Earth, they must be relayed through amplifiers or repeaters to regenerate signals. Relays can be installed on towers, high buildings, and mountaintops. Satellites can be used as microwave relay stations (see Figure 7.1). Many of these orbit at a precise point and speed above the Earth, making them stationary with regard to the Earth's surface, and they can transmit signals as a relay station in the sky. The drawback is that bad weather can affect transmission quality.

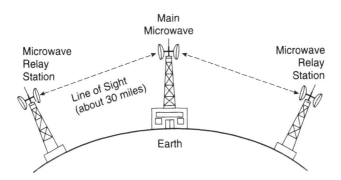

FIGURE 7.1   A microwave system.

SATELLITE SYSTEMS

Satellite systems use a *sky station* to transmit signals between two locations on Earth. Communication satellites are microwave relay stations in orbit around the Earth. Typically, the orbit is 22,300 miles above the surface. Since a satellite travels at the same speed that the Earth rotates, it appears to be stationary in space from (see Figure 7.2).

Satellites generate their power from the sun. When a satellite receives signals from a station on Earth, it will relay them to another ground-based station. Each satellite contains many communication channels and receives both analog and digital signals from Earth stations. Sometimes, it can take more than one satellite to deliver a message.

GLOBAL POSITIONING SYSTEM

The original design of the global positioning system (GPS) was for military purposes. The initial implementation cost about 10 billion dollars and consisted of 24 Earth orbiting satellites that constantly transmit navigation signals. A GPS receiver can pick up the signals from four satellites, calculate the directional origin of the signals, and generate the longitude, latitude, and altitude information with an accuracy to within a few feet. Although the system was designed for military use, business applications have been implemented. Examples are tracking a delivery truck or a salesperson's automobile. In addition, GPS systems have been certified for general and commercial aircraft navigation and are used extensively in ships.

PAGERS AND CELLULAR PHONES

Pagers, or *beepers,* are designed to receive another party's phone number so the owner of a pager can call back immediately. This is a one-way communication device

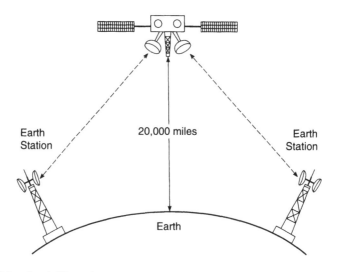

Earth
Station

20,000 miles

Earth
Station

Earth

FIGURE 7.2   A satellite system.

that does not provide response to the calling party. Paging services include SkyTel, PageNet, and EMBARC. Some pagers can transmit full-blown alphanumeric text and other data. Cellular phones are designed primarily for communicating by voice through a system of cells. Each cell is hexagonal in shape, usually eight miles or less in diameter, and is served by a transmitter-receiving tower. Calls are directly transmitted to a mobile telephone switching office (MTSO) and then connected to the regular telephone network. If a caller moves from one cell to another, the ongoing call will be "handed off" to another MTSO. Newer technologies allow digital signals to be transmitted by cellular phones.

MODEMS AND OTHER DEVICES

Current communication networks use voice-graded media. Digital signals, being voltage pulses, cannot travel a long distance. To send digital signals from the computer into the networks, a special device is needed to convert digital signals into analog signals so that analog signals can carry the information of digital signals and travel a long distance. A *modem* (modulator/demodulator) is used for this purpose. A modem converts digital signals into analog signals when transmitting them and converts analog signals to digital signals when receiving. With this device, computer digital signals can be converted into analog signals and transmitted through contemporary telephone networks.

LOCAL AREA NETWORKS AND APPLICATIONS

A local area network (LAN) is a communications network that covers a limited geographic area, such as a company computer laboratory, an executive's office, a single building, or a group of buildings in close proximity. Usually, they are privately owned. The maximum range is typically within a mile or so. Typical topologies of LANs are *star, ring, bus,* and *hybrid* (described later).

COMPONENTS OF A LAN

MICROCOMPUTER (WORKSTATION)

A LAN consists of a few or many workstations, each of which can be used as a server, a terminal, or a microcomputer. A server in a LAN stores network management software and performs management functions. Different types of LAN servers are in use, depending on the major functions assigned in a client/server environment. A print server provides printing services to other workstations, while a file server stores network and application software for the network. Other devices that may be networked include fax machines, scanners, and printers.

NETWORK INTERFACE CARD

A network interface card provides the interface between the network and the computer. This card provides the communication protocol recognized by the network architecture. For example, an Ethernet card is used to connect a PC with the network in a bus network.

NETWORK OPERATING SYSTEM

A network operating system (NOS) is software that allows a user to manage the resources of a computer network. The NOS runs on the server computer in addition to the client operating systems, such as Windows or OS/2. The functions provided by NOS follow:

- *Administration.* To add, delete, or organize client users and perform maintenance tasks such as backup.
- *File management.* To store and transfer software to client computers.
- *Printer management.* To prioritize printing jobs and direct reports to specific printers on the network.
- *Network security.* To control access to and use of the network.

TYPES OF LANS

- *Peer to peer.* All workstations on the network have the same priority and equal status. Workstations can exchange data or information through the network.
- *Client server.* Server computers are used to provide certain functions for other client computers. Each server computer is dedicated to a specific function.

WIDE AREA NETWORKS AND APPLICATIONS

Wide area networks (WANs) are communication networks covering a large geographical area. A WAN uses telephone lines, microwaves, satellites, or a combination of communication channels to transmit signals. A WAN that is limited to the area surrounding a city is referred to a *metropolitan area network* (MAN).

INTEGRATED SERVICES DIGITAL NETWORKS

An integrated services digital network (ISDN) is based on international standards for the digital transmission of both voice and data. Using ISDN lines, data can be transmitted over one or more separate channels at up to 64,000 bits per second (2.2 billion bits per second if fiber optical cables are used). The higher speed of this transmission system allows full-motion video images to be transmitted.

INTERNET

The Internet is the largest and best known wide area network in the world. As early as 1994, it was estimated to have 40 million users worldwide, in more than 120 countries. Growth has been rapid in recent years. Because of its tremendous size and the number of users, most businesses have taken advantage of the Internet's powerful and convenient features for many business applications and opportunities. Often called *electronic commerce,* business transactions can be made electronically. Consumers can browse the Internet virtual shopping mall and place orders for the company's merchandise. Investors can trade securities over the Internet. Telephone calls can also be connected via the Internet. Other services available on the Internet include the following:

- *Electronic mail.* E-mail can be sent anywhere in the world to users with an Internet address.
- *File transfer and software downloads.* The Internet can transfer files all over the world. Software can also be downloaded from Internet.
- *Database search.* The Internet can also be used to access different databases.
- *Discussion and news groups.* Thousands of discussion topics can be discussed in the bulletin boards that exist on the Internet. Information can be shared within a business group.

NETWORK TOPOLOGIES

Generally speaking, three basic LAN topologies, and a hybrid topology, are recognized.

- *Star.* A star network is one in which all microcomputers and other communication devices are connected to a central server. Electrical messages are routed through the central node to their destinations. The central node monitors the flow of traffic.
- *Ring.* A ring network is a network in which all workstations are connected in a continuous loop. Ring network uses a broadcast topology. Messages pass from node to node in one direction. The computer scans the message from the proceeding node for an address that it recognizes. If the message contains the proper address, it is read. Otherwise, it is sent ahead to the next node.
- *Bus.* The bus topology is a linear channel with many nodes connected. There is no central server. Each node transmits messages to all other devices. If a node receives a message that was not addressed to it, this message will be discarded; otherwise it is read. Advantages of a bus are that it may be organized as a client/server or peer-to-peer network, and it is easier to maintain than other networks. The bus topology is often called a *broadcast* topology, since every message or set of data sent on the bus goes to every node.
- *Hybrid.* Hybrid networks are combinations of star, ring, and bus networks. For example, a bus network may connect with a ring topology, which communicates with another star network.

Selection of the proper topology configuration depends on three primary criteria: the distance between points, the amount of time permissible for transmissions, and the amount of data to be transmitted from one point to another.

INTERNET

The Internet is an international network connecting approximately 36,000 smaller networks that link computers commercial institutions and businesses. At the end of 1999, there were an estimated 300 million Internet users worldwide. The Internet is becoming more popular because of its power and practicality. The potential and utilization of the Internet for business is unlimited.

ELECTRONIC COMMERCE

The term *electronic commerce (e-commerce)* emerged only several years ago, when business people started to understand the powerful tool that is the Internet. The basic idea of electronic commerce is to let business people conduct business transactions over the Internet. For example, a corporate buyer can browse the Internet, look at merchandise, and place an order. This transaction can be completed by sending a company's purchase order number to the vendor and receiving a confirmation number. The advantage of electronic commerce is that business transactions can be very efficient and fast through the Internet. Entrepreneurs can use the Internet as their marketplace rather than going through huge retail channels. However, some issues need to be researched, such as how to police the transactions over the network, how to certify the accuracy of each transaction, and how to prevent any transaction fraud.

INTERNET DEVELOPMENT TOOLS

To design an Internet application, proper tools are required. Hypertext Markup Language (HTML), which is the language of the World Wide Web, is designed to implement home page design. This language requires training in certain programming techniques, and many people may not like to learn a new language. Recently, more Internet development tools have been developed. Microsoft FrontPage is a tool that provide users with a graphical user interface (GUI) and a word processing type of user friendliness. Netscape Navigator 3.0 also provides an Internet development tool. In addition, JAVA by Sun Microcomputers provides sophisticated functions for Internet application development, and PageMill is available from Adobe.

INFORMATION SUPERHIGHWAY

The term *information superhighway* has roared into the business world's consciousness in recent years. It is, in fact, a vision or a metaphor for a fusion of the two-way wired and wireless capabilities of telephone and networked computers with cable TV's capability to transit hundreds of programs, images, multimedia, and other information in any other format. This information superhighway, after its completion, will link all businesses around the globe. Today, this information superhighway remains a vision, much like today's interstate highway system was a vision in the 1950s. However, it is believed that, in the next 15 to 20 years, most of the country will be linked by the information superhighway.

INTRANETS

Intranets are internal corporate networks that use the infrastructure and standards of the Internet and the World Wide Web. In other words, an intranet is a small version of the Internet that is basically developed and used by a corporation. Customers and employees can access the database or information in a company through web browsers to reduce operating costs. One of the greatest concerns regarding an intranet is security. There are worries that unauthorized people may access a company's data by intruding through the Internet. To prevent this, security software (called a *firewall*) has been developed. It blocks unauthorized traffic from accessing the intranet.

NETWORK SOFTWARE

NETWORK SYSTEM SOFTWARE

Popular network system software for LANs are Novell's NetWare, Microsoft's Windows NT Server, and Apple's AppleTalk. Most network system software for WANs is custom made and usually requires mainframe computers to operate.

NETWORK APPLICATION SOFTWARE

Most application software for individual computers has a network version. To share the same software on the network, a side license is required.

COMPUTER CONFERENCING

Another application, based on telecommunication technologies, is the computer conference. Conferences can consist of either voice communication through the network or voice plus video communications. This technology is also available on LAN, WAN, and even on the Internet. The benefit of the computer conference is to reduce travel cost and improve efficiency.

MULTIMEDIA

Multimedia refers to technology that presents information in more than one medium, including text, graphics, animation, video, music, and voice.

MULTIMEDIA COMPONENTS

To configure a multimedia computer that is able to deliver sound, video, image, and voice, a sound card is required (an add-on for some PCs, standard equipment in a

Macintosh and some others). The function of a sound card is to digitize voice or sound into a computer data file. This data file can then be transmitted and converted back to sound or voice. In addition, a video capture card is also needed to convert a video from a regular video device such as a VCR to a digital file. This file can be converted back to a regular video.

A digital camera can be useful you want to take a picture and store is directly into a digital file. This can also be accomplished by scanning a photo with a digital scanner. Since multimedia information (such as video) requires lots of storage space, a device called CD-ROM is generally used. CD-ROM (compact disk-read-only memory) is an optical disk format that is used to hold prerecorded text, graphics, and sound. Like a music CD, the standard CD-ROM is a read-only disk. *Read-only* means that the disk cannot be written to or erased by the user. A CD-ROM drive allows users to receive input information from a CD-ROM, which typically can store up to 650 megabytes of memory. At one time, a CD-ROM drive was only a single-speed drive. Now, speeds up to 24× are available. Typically, a single-speed CD-ROM drive can access data at the speed of 150 kilobytes (kB) per second. That is to say, a 12× speed drive can deliver data at the speed of 150 kilobytes × 12 = 1.8 MB per second. Erasable CD-ROMs are now available as well, but the price is considerably higher.

Other storage devices, such as the erasable magneto-optical disk, Easy drive, Zip drive, and Jaz drive are all designed to store large amounts of information.

MULTIMEDIA APPLICATIONS

Multimedia provides business people with a better way of communicating. Managers can deliver a better presentation or lecture by including animation and voice. Productivity can therefore be improved by using multimedia. Some applications are discussed below.

ENCYCLOPEDIAS, LARGE DATABASES

A large database, if it is not time sensitive, can be stored in a CD-ROM for later retrieval. For example, an encyclopedia and business article collections can be stored on a CD-ROM.

TRAINING

A lecture can be given by interactive multimedia systems over the Internet. As a result, employees can attend virtual educational classes in corporate business areas.

PRESENTATIONS

Various presentation software applications are designed to include animation, voice, and pictures. By using these tools, presenters can very effectively deliver important messages in forms that transcend presentations.

ANIMATION

Corporate visual presentations can employ multimedia techniques to produce special effects that aid corporate employee learning. For business presentations, it can be valuable to use lots of multimedia techniques to enhance the business education process.

SUMMARY

Data communications will continue to affect business life. Businesses are no longer limited to local information. With the help of data communication technologies, business managers are able to access information from any corner of the world. With communication technologies rapidly changing, today's businesses are being challenged to find ways to adapt the technology to provide better products and services. In addition, new business opportunities have been created. For executives, the new technology offers increased access to worldwide information services and provides new business opportunities.

8 Telecommunications

WHAT IS TELECOMMUNICATION?

Telecommunication refers to communication over a distance—in the context of this book, using computers. To communicate properly, two computers must use the same standard transmission procedures (protocols). Telecommunications is a popular application of personal computers. The future trend is toward increased use of telecommunications. Several types of online systems are used for this purpose.

Commercial online services offer both general-interest services that appeal to a wide variety of people and specialized services that address special interests such as stock market research and marketing research.

Bulletin board systems (BBSs) are often set up by special interest groups to provide the public with specialized services. Many BBSs have nothing more than a single telephone input line and a large hard disk. One may be managed by only a single owner or "system operator."

Direct connection is another common use of telecommunications in which you dial another computer directly. For example, you can connect directly to the computer of a customer or supplier. To connect, you only need the permission of the operator of the remote computer and its modem number. You incur no charges, except perhaps for any long distance calling charges. With specialized software, it is possible for you to control a computer from a remote location.

GOING ONLINE

To access any online service, you will need an access number and a password. You will also need a modem and communication software. Most service providers have their own communication software, and it is generally provided to subscribers for free. To access other online services, you will need your own communication software.

MODEM

You will need a modem to connect your computer to a telephone line. Most modems also provide faxing capabilities. You can purchase either an internal or an external modem. There is no difference in performance between internal and external modems. An internal modem plugs into an expansion slot inside your computer; this means that an internal modem will not occupy any extra space on your desk. Internal modems are also less expensive, since they do not require an external case or a separate power supply. Disadvantages of internal modems are that they increase internal heat, do not show visible status lights, and can cause computer damage if the modem malfunctions or was not properly installed. One advantage of selecting an external modem is that you don't need to open the computer's case to install the modem, and it is portable. External modems also have lights that tell the user what the modem is doing, such as whether data is being sent or received. The external modem does not drain the system unit's power. It can also be transferred to new equipment when you upgrade the system.

The most important consideration in selecting a modem is its speed or *baud rate.* You should select a modem with a data transfer speed of at least 28,800 bits per second (bps). A high-speed modem is compatible with lower-speed modems. A 28,800 bps modem can communicate with a 14,400 bps or a 2,400 bps modem. Other considerations in selecting a modem are available software support, reliability (minimal errors), versatility, message buffering, call duration logging, error correction ability, and voice data switching.

An intelligent modem can perform many functions that are more complicated than receiving and transmitting characters over the telephone lines. It allows for dialing, answering, and hanging up the phone on command; redialing the last number called; and recalling a series of phone numbers. A "dumb" modem does not possess internal instructions for dialing or hanging up. It does not recognize whether it is originating the call or answering it. (A person usually has to set the modem switch manually to either "originate" or answer.") It has to be instructed as to the speed at which to operate.

Automatic features are available for different types of modems, including

- *Auto log on.* Log-on information is provided automatically.
- *Auto answer.* The modem is able to get calls and data without the computer operator's intervention.
- *Auto dial.* The modem can automatically place a call.
- *Auto redial.* This feature keeps calling a busy number until the call goes through.
- *Directory dialing.* This feature allows dialing from a directory of numbers that have been saved in a smart telecommunications software program.
- *Number chaining.* Allows it to respond to a busy signal by dialing other numbers.
- *Line test.* The modem tests the telephone line.
- *Answer-back strings.* The modem responds to an incoming call by giving identification codes or messages.
- *Self-test.* The modem verifies its own functionality.
- *Software disconnection.* This refers to the modem's ability to hang up the phone.
- *Dial tone connection.* The modem listens for a dial tone, dials 9 to get an outside line, and then waits for a second dial tone.
- *Line-sound monitoring.*

Types of Telecommunications

There are several different ways you can use telecommunications. Most people tend to engage in the following types of activities:

- *Electronic mail* (e-mail) is available on most systems, and it allows you to send and receive messages in your mailbox. Your e-mail messages may be private or public. You can send a private message to another user who has an electronic mailbox. You can also send a public message that can be read by everyone on the system.
- *Real-time conferencing* takes you one step beyond e-mail. As soon as you type your message, the recipient is able to get the message immediately and can then respond. Real-time conferencing (also called *chatting*) is similar to talking to someone on the telephone; however, instead of talking, you type your messages. Real-time conferencing offers at least two advantages over telephone conferencing. First, many users can communicate simultaneously. Second, a written record can be kept of all statements. Problem situations may be solved more quickly.
- *File transfer* is frequently used in telecommunications. You can either *download* or *upload* files. Downloading involves copying files from an online system to your own computer. Uploading is the reverse process; that is, you send a copy of files from your computer to the online system. Most commercial online services and BBSs have software that can be downloaded. Some services also allow you to upload software. Generally, the software that is downloadable is either public domain or *shareware*. You can try this software for free; however, if you continue to use shareware software, you are expected to pay a small registration fee. Note: a buffer is a temporary storage area holding information such as that downloaded from an online service.
- *Online research* is possible on almost any topic. There are specialized databases for stock market data, accounting and tax information, marketing data, management updates, production information, legal cases, computer information, and a wide variety of other topics. There are also databases that provide indexes and abstracts of business and financial articles from thousands of publications.
- Online transactions are now becoming the norm in many industries. It is possible to do banking and order merchandise online. It is easy to check the cash balance, find out what checks have cleared, or contact your bank's service online. Everything from financial specifics to economic data is online. Businesses can place orders with suppliers and receive orders from customers.

COMPUTER NETWORKS

The productivity of organizations has increased tremendously via the use of computers. Due to the major advances in computer technology, this period of history has come to be called the *information age.* Computer networks play a dominant role in transmitting information to users.

A computer network is simply a set of computers (or terminals) interconnected by transmission paths. These paths usually take the form of telephone lines; however, other media, such as wireless and infrared transmission, radio waves, and satellite communications, are possible. The network serves one purpose: the exchange of data between the computers and/or terminals.

The considerations in selecting a network medium are as follows:

- Technical reliability
- Type of business involved
- The number of managers who will need to access or update data simultaneously
- Physical layout of existing equipment
- The frequency of updating
- Number of microcomputers involved
- Compatibility
- Cost
- Geographic dispersion
- Type of network operating software available and support
- Availability of application software
- Expandability in adding additional workstations
- Restriction to PCs (or can cheaper terminals be used?)
- Ease of access in sharing equipment and data
- Need to access disparate equipment like other networks and mainframes
- Processing needs
- Speed
- Data storage ability
- Maintenance
- Noise
- Connectability mechanism
- Ability of the network to conduct tasks without corrupting data moving through it
- Appearance
- Fire safety

ADVANTAGES OF NETWORKS

Computer networks provide several advantages. Most organizations are geographically dispersed, with offices located all over the world. Computers at each site need to transfer and exchange data—frequently on a daily basis, and sometimes even in real time. A network provides the means to exchange data.

Even if the organization is not geographically dispersed and has only one office, networks can serve useful functions. Networks permit efficient sharing of resources. For example, if there is too much work at one site, the network allows the work to be transferred to another computer in the network. Such load sharing enhances productivity by allowing a more even utilization of an organization's resources.

Backup capability is an especially important feature of networks. For instance, if one computer fails, another computer in the network can take over the load. This might be critical in certain industries such as financial institutions.

Networks can be used to provide a very flexible work environment. An organization can allow its employees to connect to the network and work from home or *telecommute*. A network makes it easier for employees to travel to remote locations and still have access to critical data such as sales for last week or research data from a project.

DATA FLOW

Data flows among computers in a network using one of three methods. *Simplex* transmission operates in one direction only. An example of simplex transmission is radio or television transmission. Simplex transmission is rare in computer networks because one-way transmission is not particularly useful. *Half-duplex* transmission is found in many systems. In a half-duplex system, information can flow in both directions. However, it is not possible for the information to flow in both directions simultaneously. In other words, once a query is transmitted from one device, it must wait for a response to come back. A *full-duplex* system can transmit information in both directions simultaneously; it does not have the intervening stop-and-wait aspect of half-duplex systems. For high throughput and fast response time, full-duplex transmission is frequently used in computer applications.

Data switching equipment is used to route data through the network to its final destinations. For instance, data switching equipment is used to route data around failed or busy devices or channels.

In designing the network, one must consider three factors. First, the user should get the best response time and throughput. Minimizing response time entails shortening delays between transmission and receipt of data; this is especially important for interactive sessions between user applications. Throughput involves transmitting the maximum amount of data per unit of time.

Second, the data should be transmitted along the least-cost path within the network, as long as other factors such as reliability are not compromised. The least-cost path is generally the shortest channel between devices and involves the use of the fewest number of intermediate components. Furthermore, low-priority data can be transmitted over relatively inexpensive telephone lines, while high-priority data can be transmitted over expensive high-speed satellite channels.

Third, maximum reliability should be provided to ensure proper receipt of all data traffic. Network reliability includes not only the ability to deliver error-free data but also the ability to recover from errors or lost data in the network. The network's diagnostic system should be capable of locating problems with components and perhaps even isolating the component from the network.

NETWORK TOPOLOGIES

The network *configuration* or *topology* is the physical shape of the network in terms of the layout of linking stations. A *node* refers to a workstation. A bridge is a

connection between two similar networks. Network protocols are software imple-
mentations providing support for network data transmission. A server is a microcomputer or a peripheral device performing tasks such as data storage functions
within a local area network (LAN). Network servers are of several types. A dedicated
server is a central computer used only to manage network traffic. A computer that
is used simultaneously as a local workstation is called a *nondedicated* server. In
general, dedicated servers provide faster network performance, since they do not
take requests from both local users and network stations. In addition, these machines
are not susceptible to crashes caused by local users' errors. Dedicated servers are
expensive and cannot be disconnected from the network for use as stand-alone
computers. Nondedicated servers have a higher price-to-performance ratio for companies that need occasional use of the server as a local workstation.

The most common types of network topologies are described below.

HIERARCHICAL

The hierarchical topology (also called vertical or tree structure) is one of the most
common networks (Figure 8.1). The hierarchical topology is attractive for several
reasons. The software to control the network is simple and the topology provides a
concentration point for control and error resolution. However, it also presents potential bottleneck and reliability problems. It is possible that network capabilities may
be completely lost in the event of a failure at a higher level.

HORIZONTAL

The horizontal topology (or bus topology) is popular in local area networks (Figure
8.2). Its advantages include simple traffic flow between devices. This topology
permits all devices to receive every transmission; in other words, a single station

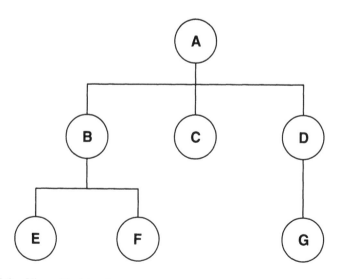

FIGURE 8.1   Hierarchical topology.

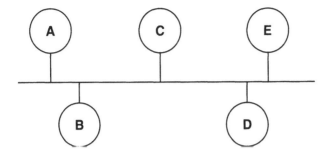

FIGURE 8.2   Horizontal topology.

broadcasts to multiple stations. The biggest disadvantage is that, since all computers share a single channel, a failure in the communication channel results in the loss of the network. One way to get around this problem is through the use of redundant channels. Another disadvantage with this topology is that the absence of concentration points makes problem resolution difficult. Therefore, it is more difficult to isolate faults to any particular component. A bus network usually needs a minimum distance between taps to reduce noise. Identifying a problem requires the checking of each system element. A bus topology is suggested for shared databases, but it is not good for single-message switching. It employs minimum topology to fill a geographic area, at the same time having complete connectivity.

STAR

The star topology (Figure 8.3) is a highly popular configuration, and it is widely used for data communication systems. The software for star topology is not complex,

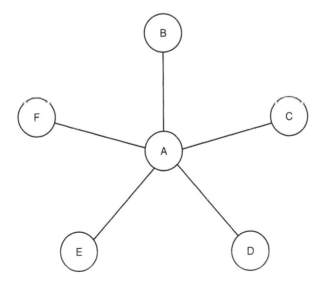

FIGURE 8.3   Star topology.

and controlling traffic is simple. All traffic emanates from the hub or the center of the star. In a way, the star configuration is similar to the hierarchical network; however, the star topology has more limited distributed processing capabilities. The hub is responsible for routing data traffic to other components. It is also responsible for isolating faults, which is a relatively simple matter in the star configuration.

The star network, like the hierarchical network, is subject to potential bottlenecks at the hub, which may cause serious reliability problems. One way to minimize this problem and enhance reliability is by establishing a redundant backup of the hub node. A star network is best when there is a need to enter and process data at many locations with day-end distribution to different remote users. Here, information for general use is sent to the host computer for subsequent processing. It is easy to identify errors in the system, since each communication must go through the central controller. While maintenance is easily conducted, if the central computer fails, the network stops. There is a high initial cost in setting up the system, because each node requires hookup to the host computer in addition to the mainframe's cost. Expansion is easy, because all that is needed is to run a wire from the terminal to the host computer.

RING

The ring topology (Figure 8.4) is another popular approach to structuring a network. The data in a ring network flows in a circular direction, usually in one direction only. The data flows from one station to the next station; each station receives the data and then transmits it to the next.

One main advantage of the ring network is that bottlenecks, such as those found in the hierarchical or star networks, are relatively uncommon. There is an organized structure. The primary disadvantage of the ring network is that a single channel ties

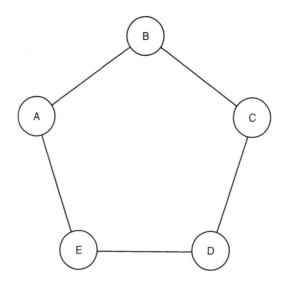

FIGURE 8.4   Ring topology.

all of the components in a network. The entire network can be lost if the channel between two nodes fails. Establishing a backup channel can usually alleviate this problem. Other ways to overcome this problem include using switches to automatically route the traffic around the failed node and installing redundant cables.

A ring network is more reliable and less expensive when there is a minimum level of communication between microcomputers. This type of network is best when there are several users at different locations who have to access updated data on a continual basis. Here, more than one data transmission can occur simultaneously. The system is kept current on an ongoing basis. The ring network permits managers within the firm to create and update shared databases. With a ring, there is greater likelihood of error incidence as compared to a star, because data are handled by numerous intervening parties. In light of this, the manager should recommend that data in a ring system make an entire circle before being removed from the network.

Mesh

The mesh topology (Figure 8.5) provides a very reliable, although complex, network. Its structure makes it relatively immune to bottlenecks and other failures. The multiplicity of paths makes it relatively easy to route traffic around failed components or busy nodes.

Wide Area Networks and Local Area Networks

Networks may be broadly classified as either wide area networks (WANs) or local area networks (LANs). The computers in a WAN may be anywhere from several miles to thousands of miles apart. In contrast, the computers in a LAN are usually closer together, such as in a building or a plant. Data switching equipment can be used in LANs, but not as frequently as it is in WANs.

The channels in WANs are usually provided by an interchange carrier, such as AT&T or MCI, for a monthly fee plus usage cost. These channels are usually slow and relatively error prone. In contrast, the channels in a LAN are usually fast and relatively error free; the user organization usually owns these channels.

The major differences in WANs and LANs dictate that their topologies usually take on different shapes. A WAN structure tends to be more irregular. Since an organization generally leases the lines at a considerable cost, an attempt is usually made to keep the lines fully utilized. To keep the lines fully utilized, data is often

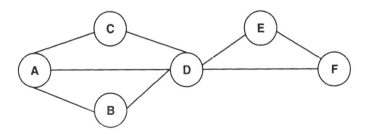

FIGURE 8.5 Mesh topology.

routed for a geographical area through one channel; hence, the irregular shape of the WAN network.

The LAN topology tends to be more structured. Since the channels in a LAN network are relatively inexpensive, the owners of a LAN are generally not concerned with the maximum utilization of channels. Furthermore, since LANs usually reside in a building or a plant, such networks tend to be inherently more structured and ordered. LANs are flexible, fast, and compatible, and they maximize equipment utilization, reduce processing cost, reduce errors, and provide ease of information flow. LANs use ordinary telephone lines, coaxial cables, fiber optics, and other devices like interfaces. Fiber optics result in good performance and reliability, but they are expensive. LAN performance depends on physical design, protocols supported, and transmission bandwidth. Bandwidth is the frequency range of a channel and reflects transmission speed along the network. Transmission speed is slowed down as more devices become part of the LAN.

Two or more LANs may be interconnected. Each node becomes a cluster of stations (subnetworks). The LANs communicate with each other.

ADVANTAGES OF INTERFACING NETWORKS

- Total network costs are lower.
- There is flexibility in having individual subnetworks meet particular needs.
- More reliable and higher-cost subnetworks can be used for critical activities, and vice versa.
- If one LAN fails, the other LAN still functions.

DISADVANTAGES OF INTERFACING NETWORKS

- Complexity is greater.
- Some network functions may not be able to go across network boundaries.

ELECTRONIC DATABASES

There has been a tremendous growth in the online database industry throughout the world in terms of the number and type of databases, producers, and vendors. Never before has management had real-time access to such a vast amount of informational resources. Online business databases improve decision making and analysis, allow management to add value by creating new products and services through information exchange and processing, and improve the bottom line. Online databases are a resource to be converted to useful information for decision-making purposes. The real measure of the industry, however, is its actual use as measured by the number of online searches. Estimates produced by the major word-oriented database vendors show that the number of online searches increased from fewer than 1 million in 1974 to almost 60 million in 1993. These figures do not include financial transaction databases, such as databases for stocks, electronic ordering, etc. If they did, the total searches would be many times higher.

One way to classify databases is according to the presentation methodology. The methodologies include text, number, image (video), audio, electronic services, and software. The earliest public databases were text-based, and they still are the predominant type of database. As of 1994, text-based databases represented over 70% of all databases and are continuing to grow in number. The user performs searches using text phrases to find specific information. Text-based databases include bibliographic, directory, dictionary, full text, and others.

Numeric databases are used primarily for transactions and for obtaining statistical information. They actually represent a declining proportion of all database types and in 1994 were less than 20% of all online databases.

Multimedia audio and graphical databases are in the process of development and are gaining popularity. As of 1994, they represented 5% of all databases, but their actual number increased more than fivefold. One application of a multimedia database is in the real estate industry, where clients can be taken on a "virtual visit" of a particular property without leaving the office. Bulletin board services (BBSs) are another form of online database that offers a wide variety of downloadable data.

Commercial online services, such as America Online, CompuServe, Prodigy, Microsoft Network, and GEnie have extensive access to various business database providers. Their primary function is to be a conduit for delivering databases developed by these providers.

The World Wide Web (Web) portion of the Internet has a rapidly increasing series of online business databases. These databases use multimedia graphical and audio features with hypertext links to other data and resources. Users need a web browser to read a graphical Web database. Web online business databases are a valuable resource, because they link to all other Internet resources, including text files, Telnet (standard Internet protocol for remote terminal connection service), Gophers (a distributed information service that makes available hierarchical collections of information across the Internet), Usenet newsgroups (a collection of thousands of topically named newsgroups and members associated with them on the Internet), and other portions of the Internet, as required.

Another form of a multimedia database is represented by the development of a vast number of CD-ROM business databases that interrelate audio, video, and text and allow the user search and download capabilities.

Faxback services are becoming popular and are a major source of timely business information. They are easy to use and provide a wide variety of information by just using a fax machine or a fax modem.

Finally, there are many online U.S. government databases. These high-quality databases contain extremely useful information and are often free of charge.

COMMERCIAL ONLINE SERVICES

These services are steadily increasing in popularity, are designed to be user friendly, and normally have graphical user interface (GUI) software with access to the Internet, including the Web. Pricing options vary widely, and each service should be consulted directly. A partial listing of the most popular services is given below.

- *America Online (AOL) (800-827-6364).* AOL is user friendly and utilizes an excellent GUI software and Web browser. It has a news and finance section, which includes stock quotes, business news, public discussion forums, and extensive business databases including Morningstar. America Online's information content is primarily news oriented. News services, such as Reuters, ABC, Time magazine, the New York Times, CNN, and UPI, are available on AOL. One can obtain financial news and stock quotes and make stock purchases on AOL. Stock portfolios can also be valued automatically with updated stock quotes. *Business Week, Worth,* and *Investor's Business Daily* are also available online. A wide assortment of business software is available for downloading. AOL has several forums on taxes, personal finance, and business strategy.
- *AT&T Business Network (800-838-3952).* Although a new online service provider, the AT&T Business Network provides a variety of online services and features full Internet access.
- *CompuServe (800-848-8199).* This service can be accessed using any standard communications software, and it also provides its own GUI, CompuServe Information Manager. CompuServe provides access to a wide variety of business databases, program packages, encyclopedia references, legal advice, stock quotes, news and e-mail services. Extensive news is provided by the Associated Press (AP), and the information is updated continuously. Over 700 forums on a wide variety of subjects are available online. The Easy Sabre's Bargain Finder can be used to search for the lowest available airfare. CompuServe's Fundwatch allows one to search for mutual funds most suitable to the investor's criteria from a database of 4,800 funds. CompuServe has a huge library of business and general interest software available for download.
- *Delphi (800-695-4005).* Delphi is a complete commercial online service with Internet access. However, Delphi's services are not competitive with those of other online providers. Accessing information on the Internet using Delphi can be difficult. Delphi's Internet is text-based. Delphi is expected to be replaced by a new online service in a joint venture with MCI Communications Corp.
- *Dialog (800-334-2564).* This service can be accessed using any standard communications software as well as its own DialogLink software. It is an online business information service that has searchable company information databases, bibliographic references, newsletters, and related publications. Dialog provides access to more than 450 databases, including TRW, Moody's Corporate Profiles, and D&B Donnelly.
- *Dow Jones News Retrieval (609-452-1511).* This service can be accessed using any standard communications software as well as its own Dow Jones Link GUI software. This service provides access to the *Wall Street Journal, Barrons,* the *Washington Post,* and Dow Jones News Service.
- *GEnie (800-638-9636).* A possible alternative to CompuServe, GEnie has extensive resources for business users. Many of the business services available on GEnie are also available on CompuServe, but with lower

fees. GEnie lacks a true graphical interface, so its text-based screens don't look as attractive. GEnie has a large library of business software that can be downloaded. It is fairly easy to navigate through GEnie and locate information.

- *Hoover (617-868-4442).* This service requires special software as well as Lotus Notes. It prompts the user in a database search form and provides the results to a Lotus Notes network database.
- *LEXIS/NEXIS (800-346-9759).* This service uses its own research software used for searching in specific industries, including public relations and law. It is the most popular database of legal information including case decisions and previous testimony of expert witnesses. Besides case records, files of state and federal codes and regulations are available on everything from banking to hazardous wastes. This includes law review and journal articles. It has a collection of U.S. patents and public records data including real estate transactions, and corporate reports filed with government agencies. Individual libraries exist on LEXIS such as a bankruptcy library. This approach ensures that the user is in the right place, pulling together relevant filings and cases from all jurisdictions, along with applicable codes and reference materials. There are also electronic editions of basic legal reference tools, such as the *Martindale-Hubbell Law Directory,* for locating practicing attorneys by state or by specialty or verifying the credentials of the opposing counsel. Also, LEXIS contains the *American Law Reports,* which is a useful legal research tool. LEXIS contains thousands of unpublished decisions that are not available in any library. The LEXIS online database includes the *Department of State Bulletin,* the *Federal Judiciary Almanac,* the *American Maritime Cases, Model Rules of Professional Conduct, Opinions of the American Bar Association Committee on Ethics and Professional Responsibility,* the *Environmental Law Reporter,* the *National Insurance Law Service,* the legislative history of securities acts, the *RIA Federal Tax Coordinator 2d,* and the Interstate Commerce Commission decisions, opinions, and orders. The LEXIS online service allows you to search geographically and narrow down the search by state or country. The LEXIS online service is organized into libraries and files facilitating information searches. Examples of important libraries (one selects a library as a means of narrowing down the files in which the searching will be done) include GENFED (files containing federal cases and other federal materials), MEGA (case law from a different jurisdiction), CODES (statutes of a particular jurisdiction), and STATES (files, cases, and other materials from a particular state). Once a library is selected, one or more files can be selected. LEXIS online is easy to use and can perform searches that would be time consuming, if not unimaginable, by conventional methods.
- *Microsoft Network (MSN).* MSN offers content similar to America Online and CompuServe.
- *Prodigy (800-776-3449).* This is an easy-to-use online service. It stresses investment/business news and financial services. Prodigy is rapidly

expanding its business services without sacrificing its traditional family focus. It includes tools for researching stocks and mutual funds, and for placing trading orders with discount brokers.

- *Total Online Tax and Accounting Library (TOTAL) (800-862-4272).* An online service available to the members of American Institute of Certified Public Accountants (AICPA). TOTAL allows access to a variety of online services including LEXIS (Legal Information Services), NEXIS (News Information Services), and NAARS (National Automated Accounting Research System).
- *West Law Tax.* It provides legal and tax information.

THE U.S. GOVERNMENT'S STAT-USA ONLINE SERVICES

The U.S. government has moved aggressively to provide extensive online database access. The Economics and Statistics Administration of the U.S. Department of Commerce has created STAT-USA for providing U.S. government online databases. It has several databases on the Internet at http://www.stat-usa.gov with an Internet mail address at stat-usa@doc.gov. STAT-USA received the National Performance Review's Hammer Award, which recognizes those Federal agencies leading the way in "Creating a Government that Works Better, and Costs Less."

STAT-USA publishes the most timely business and economic information that the federal government has to offer. It eliminates the need to call from agency to agency to find the report that you need. STAT-USA gathers the most crucial, timely business and economic information from more than 50 Federal agencies and distributes them from a central source, saving countless hours in research time.

STAT-USA/Internet provides more than 300,000 reports and statistical series (the equivalent of seven sets of encyclopedias) online, including press releases, trade leads, and reports that are released on a daily or weekly basis. Searching is done using *Inquery*, an award-winning natural-language search-and-retrieval program that greatly simplifies locating files.

Access to the Economic Bulletin Board/Lite Edition (EBB/LE) is included as part of a STAT-USA/Internet subscription. Quarterly, annual, and Class C subscription group rates are available. For more information on the EBB/LE, or to place an order, call (202) 482-1986 or send e-mail to stat-usa@doc.gov. Companies interested in obtaining access for multiple users should call 202-482-1986 for information on the available pricing options. STAT-USA/Internet databases include the following:

- *Budget of the United States.* STAT-USA offers budget files, free of charge, in ASCII and in Adobe's Portable Document Format, and it makes them searchable using Inquery. The *Budget* contains the budget message of the president, the president's budget proposals, analytical perspectives, and historical tables.
- *Bureau of Economic Analysis (BEA) Economic Information.* This is an authoritative online news release source for *Survey of Current Business* issues, and for detailed data files from BEA's national, regional, and international economic accounts.

- *Bureau of Economic Analysis, U.S. Department of Commerce.* This contains GDP press releases (complete) with corporate profits, economic indicators summary text file; leading, coincident, and lagging indexes release (text and tables in text format); and personal income and outlays.
- *Bureau of the Census, US. Department of Commerce.* This covers new construction, durable goods, shipments and orders, new home sales, housing starts, manufacturing and trade inventories and sales, advance retail sales, shipments, inventories and orders, and U.S. international trade in goods and services—formerly merchandise trade (complete release).
- *Bureau of Labor Statistics, U.S. Department of Labor.* Contains the Employment Situation (complete release), Consumer Price Index (full release), Producer Price Index (text/tables), and Productivity and Cost Preliminary (complete release).
- *Daily Economic Press Releases.* Provides state and local government bond rates, trade opportunities, 10:00 A.M. and 12:00 P.M. daily foreign exchange rates, the daily treasury statement, treasury rate quotations, and yield curve points.
- *Economic Bulletin Board/Lite Edition.* The Economic Bulletin Board/Lite Edition is a comprehensive Internet source for government-sponsored economic releases and business leads. The EBB/LE offers a small subset of the files available on STAT-USA's modem-based Economic Bulletin Board (EBB) system, thus its title "Lite Edition." Economic news and business leads are available the minute they are released on the EBB/LE, and it gives in-depth analyses of markets, products, and economic trends. The EBB/LE provides searchable databases containing export promotion information; the Trade Opportunity Program (TOPS) and market research reports with daily updates and three months of archives; and the U.S. Department of Agriculture's Agricultural Trade Leads.
- *Federal Reserve Board (FRB).* Offers a summary of commentary on current economic conditions by Federal Reserve District, industrial production and capacity utilization, FRB bank credit, FRB consumer credit report, FRB foreign exchange rates, FRB selected interest rates, FRB money stock data, and FRB aggregate reserves.
- *The Global Business Opportunities Service (GLOBUS).* GLOBUS is an international marketplace for U.S. businesses, providing billions of dollars in procurement opportunities from all over the world. Currently, GLOBUS contains the Commerce Business Daily, and Small Purchase Opportunities from the Defense Logistics Agency.
- *The Census Bureau's Merchandise Trade Export and Import Statistics.* These are available on a commodity level as well as a country level.
- *The Economic Bulletin Board (EBB).* This is the world's leading source of government-sponsored business data. Begun in 1985, it helped launch the era of electronic reporting and today is still the most used bulletin board of its kind. On the EBB, late-breaking business developments are reported within 30 minutes after they are received from contributing federal agencies. In-depth analyses of markets, products, and economic

trends are also provided. The EBB has a vast collection of files. The list of available files alone is 471 pages. The EBB collects, collates, and publishes data from more than 35 federal agencies.

ONLINE BUSINESS DATABASES

There are many online business databases. There has been about a 5% annual increase in total business databases since 1988. They cover an enormous number of subjects, including census, bibliographic, education, aerospace, and newspaper data, to name just a few.

The following online business databases are a selected listing of the numerous databases available. For complete online business database listings, the reader is urged to consult the Gale Directory of Databases (Detroit: Gale Research, Inc.).

- *ABA Banking Journal.* This is a database of the complete text of the *ABA Banking Journal*, covering the commercial banking industry. It is updated monthly, and it is available through LEXIS/NEXIS. It is produced by the Simmons-Boardman Publishing Corporation, New York, NY 10014 (212-620-7200).
- *ABEL.* This is a bibliographic database containing more than 15,000 citations to items listed in the Official Journal of the European Communities, covering legislation enacted by the Commission of the European Communities. It is available online from the Commission of the European Communities (CEC), and is updated daily. It is produced by the Commission of the European Communities, Office for Official Publications, Luxembourg (Phone 0352-499282563).
- *ABI/INFORM.* This is a service having more than 675,000 citations, with abstracts, to articles appearing in more than 1,200 international periodicals. It is available on a wide number of commercial services and is updated weekly or monthly depending on the service. IT is produced by UMI/Data Courier, Louisville, KY 40202-2475 (502-583-4111).
- *ACBAS.* ACBAS is a directory of more than 1,400 publicly available French, German, and English-language online business databases. It is updated monthly. Produced by Yves Balbure, Malmaison, France (Phone 01-47518431).
- *Access Business Online.* This is your all-in-one business center. It offers business executives headline news, press releases, classifieds, links to financial markets, company profiles, upcoming trade shows and seminars, search capability of vendors in various industries, and much more. Exec-U-Net is an excellent tool for business executives to communicate with other business executives and senior professionals. Some examples of topics included on the information matrix are Market News and Business Connections, Independent Business, Wall Street and World Wide Finance, GeoPolitical Strategist, and Import/Export Exchange.
- *Advertising and Marketing Intelligence (AMI).* AMI is a bibliographic database abstracting articles from 75 advertising, marketing, and media

publications. It includes information on products and services. It is updated daily and is available on LEXIS/NEXIS, and it is produced by the New York Times Company, Parsipanny, NJ 07054 (201-267-2268).

- *FinanceNET...FASAB.* The Federal Accounting Standards Advisory Board provides up-to-date information on issues in public financial management and accounting matters. In addition to available newsgroups and mailing lists to which one may subscribe, FASAB offers much more. Publications, legislation, exposure drafts, and newsletters are among many of the available topics to sift through at this web site. For those involved with the FASAB, there is a calendar of events listed as well as the latest meeting minutes and highlights.
- *Internal Auditing World Wide Web.* This is a comprehensive web site for internal auditors.
- *Kaplan's Audit Net Resource List.* This is a monthly updated directory of accounting and auditing resources.
- *Moody's Investors Service, Inc.* Moody's is a corporate and municipal bond financial service. It is available online through Dialog (212-553-0546).
- *NAARS (National Automated Accounting Research System).* NAARS contains the full text, including footnotes and auditor's report, of the financial statements of more than 4,200 company annual reports for each year on file. NAARS also includes the complete text of a wide variety of authoritative accounting literature such as Statement of Accounting Standards (SAS), Accounting Research Bulletins (ARB), and Accounting Standards Executive Committee (ASEC) position papers and issue papers.
- *Netsurfer Focus: Computer and Network Security.* This one contains guidance on computer security.
- *New York State Society of CPAs' Luca Online.* This is a database of accounting, auditing, and tax information.
- *Rutgers Accounting Web.* This is one of the most comprehensive accounting indices available. There is a link to nearly every accounting-related site on the Internet. The Rutgers web server serves as a web site for the American Institute of CPAs (AICPA), Institute of Management Accountants (IMA), Institute of Internal Auditors (IIA), Financial Accounting Standards Board (FASB), and the American Accounting Association (AAA), just to mention a few. You can access numerous publications and documents from the AICPA site. There is also a database on "Improving Business Reporting "that can be accessed through the AICPA web site. Another feature of the AICPA web site is the "AICPA Documents on Call via Fax." The code numbers for each of the documents are given. The Institute of Management Accountants offers case studies in management accounting practices and techniques such as implementing activity-based costing. Its research publications are listed in an annotated bibliography in chronological order. The Institute of Management Accountants displays upcoming events. The FASB site contains a listing of everything having to do with the FASB. All of its statements and interpretations are listed.

Hundreds of accounting firms, including the "Big 6," can be accessed at this web site.

INTERNET SERVICES AND THE WORLD WIDE WEB

A rapidly growing number of databases are available through the Internet. These databases use four types of internet services. They are Telnet, anonymous file transfer protocol (FTP), Gopher, and the World Wide Web.

Gophers use a series of menus to easily access any type of textual information available on the Internet. While there are some stand-alone Gopher services, the wide majority interconnect with other Gopher services, allowing simple information access. The Gopher's ease of use results from a simple standard menu interface.

Gopher is a menu-driven system for reaching Internet sites and retrieving information found at that site. The result of a Gopher search may be a document that can be read and saved, or a database that is searched according to a user-supplied keyword. For example, a good Gopher site for an accountant to visit might be gopher://riceinfo.rice.edu/11/Subject/Economics, where all kinds of government data can be found like the current U.S. budget, journal publications, law-related Gopher sites, Library of Congress links, management accounting research, economic development, statistics, trade journals, U.S. Small Business Administration, and so on. There are at least 50 or more sites listed on this page that will link the accountant to all kinds of useful information. And that is just one example. Some of the various sites listed will link the accountant to other sites with many other useful links or information.

Another communication link that the Internet offers is the Usenet. The Usenet is a bulletin board that contains thousands of topics. Users discuss these topics through the bulletin board. Each bulletin board contains a separate topic. The user chooses a desired subject to view and goes to that group. Under that group, a list of topics for discussion will come up. The user can then choose the discussions to read and can even respond to the discussions. Many topics on the Usenet pertain to accountants. One example of a topic that accountants would be interested in is taxes under the group misc.taxes. Kent Information Services, Inc., and TAPNet provide one bulletin board available for managerial accountants and accounting professionals. The accountants discuss problems and different procedures for doing things on this line. It is very useful because it is another source of knowledge. TAPNet provides tax practice issues, information on tax and accounting software, and management accounting issues. The magazine *Management Accounting* adds to this bulletin board every night.

Telnet permits users to access and log in to a remote Internet computer site and then run the computer software at that site. For example, a user who telnets over to locis.loc.gov will access the Library of Congress information system. From there, it is possible to search for documents contained in the Library of Congress.

Telnet is the Internet standard protocol for remote terminal connection service. It uses a series of commands to communicate with other computers. On the Internet, Telnet acts as the intermediary between your computer, the local computer, and the other computer, referred to as the *remote* computer. To reach a particular computer, a user would have to enter a Telnet address and then "Telnet" to the remote computer.

FTP, or File Transfer Protocol, enables Internet users to copy computer files from a remote server to the user's computer. FTP sites contain thousands of documents, publications, programs, graphics, and online books that can be useful for the accountant.

Anonymous FTP allows a user to retrieve documents, files, programs, and other archived data from anywhere on the Internet. By using the special user identification (user ID) of "anonymous" the network user will bypass local security checks and will have access to publicly accessible files on the remote system without having to establish a user ID and password. Anonymous FTP is an important and widely used Internet service.

The fastest growing and probably the most creative online business databases are appearing on the "Web." The Web accesses all portions of the Internet and allows information to be presented in highly creative multimedia formats using video, color graphics, animation, sound (including voice and music), and hypertext links between other text and databases with data downloading capabilities.

Management is finding that the Web is an excellent "market-space" not only for gathering information using "search engines," but also as a simple and inexpensive marketing format where home pages can be established with links to a database catalog of products and online documentation. For example, a hypertext link on a customer's computer in New York City can point to a picture on a supplier's computer in L.A. to place an order. Each computer within the Web is called a Web *site*. A host computer provides access to the site.

Web browser software is necessary to use the Web. Browsers can even be downloaded. Public World Wide Web browsers are available on certain Telnet hosts. However, browser software installed on the user's terminal will give the most effective utilization of the Web. They have full multimedia capabilities and the ability to connect to any Web site. In addition, Web search tools are also necessary to do online word searches. A growing number of these *Web crawlers* are currently available, and most are free. Their names include Yahoo, Lycos, and WebCrawler. The WWW is becoming the choice Internet location for online business databases.

Online databases are constantly being added and, for that matter, removed or relisted at a different address. Making a database available online requires a large financial and managerial investment. Site addresses are changed for financial as well as technical reasons. Databases must be continually updated and maintained. Therefore, the reader is cautioned that addresses do change, and the following is only a selected list of online business databases on the Internet. After each of the following database listings, an Internet address is given that was current at the time this material was compiled.

- *Academe This Week.* Provides access to the contents of the *Chronicle of Higher Education.* It contains summaries of the articles and provides a searchable index of more than 1,600 current job announcements (http://www.chronicle.merit.edu:70/11).

- *Advertising Law Internet Site.* This site provides a guide to FTC regulations on advertising, guidelines on choosing a business name, guides to state business opportunity laws, and privacy concerns about customer mailing lists (http://www.webcom.com/~lewrose/home.html).
- *Asia Pacific Business and Marketing Resources.* Contains information on business and management in Asia. Other resources include market reports for specific countries and access to SEC filings and patent data for 1994 (gopher.hoshi.cic.sfu.ca:70/11/ dlam/business).
- *Basic Legal Citation.* Provides an introduction to legal citation for the beginner (http://www.law.cornell.edu/citation/citation.table.html).
- *Building Industry Exchange (BIX).* Provides educational, communication, and informational services to the building industry; including a global directory, a virtual industrial park, and an employment center (http://www.building.org).
- *Bureau of Economic Analysis (BEA).* This is the Bureau of Economic Analysis home page sponsored by the US. Department of Commerce. It provides access to recent Survey of Current Business issues as well as a link to STAT-USA for downloading statistical information (http://www.stat-usa.gov/BEN/Services/beahome.html).
- *Canadian Business Infoworld.* A Canadian business directory including business resources, stock market information, and job information (http://csclub.uwaterloo.ca/u/nckwan).
- *Canadian Consulate General (travel/immigration).* Contains information on immigration and temporary visits to Canada. It also includes details on the application process, fee schedule, and list of Canadian visa offices in the United States (gopher://cwis syr.edu/70/1/admin/ois/canada).
- *Commerce Information Locator Service (CLIS).* Assists the user in finding relevant business, economic, scientific, social, and technical information (http://www.fedworld.gov).
- *Commercial Sites Index.* A directory of commercial services, products, and information on the Internet (http://www.directory.net).
- *Construction and Engineering Industries.* This is the Environmental Dynamics Design, Inc. construction network, which offers Internet access and a bulletin board service for members of the architecture, engineering, and construction industries (http://www.aecnet.com).
- *Dun & Bradstreet Information Services.* Dun & Bradstreet's home page contains information on marketing a business globally, tactical marketing, predicting slow payers, managing vendors, and researching effectively. Dun & Bradstreet offers users Business Background Reports on more than 10 million U.S. companies. The Business Background Reports contain company history, business background of its management, special events, recent newsworthy events, and an operations overview. In addition, through its web site, Dun & Bradstreet offers Customer Service and Solutions and Services. Customer Service provides telephone numbers and addresses of Dun & Bradstreet offices. "Solutions and Services" contains informative tips on effective business techniques for many com-

mon areas of business such as purchasing, planning, and credit/risk assessment (http://www.dbisna.com).

- *EGOPHER.* This is the "entrepreneur's gopher," presented by St. Louis University on the Internet. It contains loads of information for small businesses and/or entrepreneurs, including "how to's" and financial opportunities (gopher://avb.slu.edu/11gopher$root%3a%5bdata21._general._entrepreneurship%5d).
- *Engineering Information Inc. (EI Inc.).* Engineering Information Inc. (known as EI) was created for a community of engineers wanting to share their own research results and learn about what others were doing. EI has been instrumental in identifying, organizing, and facilitating easy access to the published engineering literature of the world. EI brings engineers information globally, either directly or through information specialists (http://www.ei.org/).
- *EXPO Guide Home Page.* This is an index of trade shows, searchable by date, location, or keyword (http://www.expoguide.com).
- *Federal Government Agency Directory.* Contains a list of federal agencies on the Internet (http://www. lib.lsu.edu/gov/fedgov.html).
- *Federal Reserve Bank of Philadelphia.* This site contains information about the Federal Reserve Bank and its activities. It contains, among other things, publications and working papers, an index of articles published by the Federal Reserve, and the text of the *Business Review* (gopher://simon.wharton.upenn.edu:70/11/fed).
- *Federal Reserve Board.* Contains a variety of information, including flow of funds tables, industrial production and capacity utilization, reserves of depository institutions, weekly series on assets and liabilities of large commercial banks, selected interest rates, money stock measure and components, and other Federal Reserve data tables. The URL for this site is gopher://town.hall.org:70/11/other/fed.
- *The Federal Web Locator.* A central location for locating all U.S. federal government World Wide Web site information. This web site is sponsored by the Villanova Center for Information, Law and Policy (http://www.law.vill.edu/fed-agency/fedwebloc. html).
- *Fedworld Information Network.* Contains a collection of tax forms and instructions from the IRS, including instructions and publications. You can also browse lists of IRS forms. It provides a list of web servers, ftp, gopher, and Telnet sites, organized by the National Technical Information Service (NTIS) subject categories. It has scientific, technical, and business-related titles, including reports, databases, and software (http://www.fcdworld.gov).
- *FinanceNet.* Provides accountants, auditors, and financial managers with an opportunity to share information to improve financial management in government. FinanceNet reaches across the world to provide listings of government asset sales for the general public while providing electronic document libraries, mailing lists, discussion forums, major related resources, and best of the "'Net" to link and inform public and private

sector financial management professionals in government, federal, state, and local (http://www.financenet.gov).

- *Franchise Source.* Those seeking a franchise opportunity should start with this directory of businesses. It is searchable by initial investment category or type of business (http://www.axxs.com/source.html).
- *Help for Small Business.* U.S. Internal Revenue Service (IRS) small business advice including lists of the forms businesspeople should be using, and information on how to contact the IRS. You can log onto this site at http://www.ustreas.gov/treasury/bureaus/irs/irssba.html.
- *Holt's Stock and Option Market Reports.* Contains the Holt reports. Among other services, it provides daily updates on AMEX, NASDAQ, NYSE Indices, and foreign markets. This Gopher site is accessible at gopher://wuecon.wustl.edu:671/11/holt.
- *Insurance and Financial Planning.* A complete online glossary of insurance and financial planning terms where terms are arranged alphabetically (http://www.bus.orst.edu/faculty/nielson/glossary/glos_idx.htm).
- *Insurance Industry.* This is for the insurance Industry Information News Page, which compiles international stories and reports pertaining to property and casualty, life, and health insurance available for a registration fee (http://www.newspage.com).
- *International Trade Law Project.* Provides information for legal research on international trade law (http://ananse.irv.uit.no/trade_law/nav/trade.html).
- *Internet Bankruptcy Library.* This site offers frequently asked questions (FAQs) on bankruptcy filings, news updates, a directory of international bankruptcy and insolvency professionals, and pointers related to bankruptcy issues (http://bankrupt.com).
- *Internet Business Center.* This is an extensive site providing detailed information on every aspect of electronic business, especially marketing (http://www.tig.com).
- *Internet Business Opportunity Showcase (IBOS).* This is an advertising space intended to match entrepreneurs with potential investors (http://www.clark.net/pub/ibos).
- *Internet Law Library, Code of Federal Regulations (CFR).* Gives partial access to, and search capabilities for, the Code of Federal Regulations (http://www.pls.com:8001/his/ctr.html).
- *Internet Marketing Archives.* An award winning site! Here are the fully indexed, searchable entries of the Internet Marketing List (http://www.popco.com/hyper/internet-marketing).
- *Internet Shopkeeper.* This is a WWW-based shopping mall. It is a place to set up shop on the Internet. It provides shop/store rates and ordering information, and keyword searching on all current shops registered (http://www.ip.net/shops.html).
- *InterNIC Directory of Directories (dirofdirs).* The Directory of Directories (dirofdirs) enables users to obtain references to information resources, products, and services associated with the Internet. It includes pointers to such resources as computing centers, network providers, information serv-

ers, white and yellow pages directories, library catalogs, data and software archives, training services and related services. This site is accessed at gopher://ds2.internic.net/11/dirofdirs.

- *IOMA Business Page.* The Institute of Management and Administration provides a massive number of links on this page. One has access to any sort of business newsletter including business news, stock prices, sales improvement information, and even a self-help page for small business owners. Whether managing a law or accounting office, a defined contribution investment plan, or a computer network, professionals from virtually every industry can find invaluable, career-enhancing information in this site (http://ioma.com/ioma).
- *IRS Tax Form Database.* Contains more than 400 IRS forms, schedules, and electronic services as well as extensive tax information and help (http://www.irs.ustreas.gov/).
- *Legal Information Institute.* This site is a comprehensive Internet guide to legal sources, including current Supreme Court decisions. It is maintained by Cornell Law School's Legal Information Institute (http://www.law.cornell.edu).
- *McNeil's Tax Sites.* Contains a comprehensive list of tax resources including federal and state tax forms and domestic and foreign tax laws (http://www.best.com/~ftmexpat/html/taxsites.html).
- *NAFTA Watch.* A forum for NAFTA-inspired business opportunities in Mexico. It provides a fax or e-mail subscription service and is located at http://www.aescon.com/naftam/index.htm.
- *NAFTAnet Home Page.* This is a vast site with an exorbitant amount of NAFTA/GA1T export information with links. It is sponsored by the magazine Mexico Business (http://www.nafta.net).
- *National Bureau of Economic Research Home Page.* This site contains information on the bureau with links to online data, major programs and projects, and publications. It includes an index to National Bureau of Economic Research publications and working papers. The database has links to other sites with economic data (http://nber.harvard.edu/).
- *National Business Incubation Association (NBIA).* This Internet service provides assistance for start-up or fledgling firms. The database includes a directory of NBIA servers, member information, electronic network service (Bater-link), and convention and meeting information (http://www.nbia.org/).
- *National Locator & Data.* This provides access to 950 million names and phone numbers. It provides database reports on a wide range of subjects, including commercial credit reports, corporate records, workman's compensation claims, and public record databases, motor vehicle reports, social security number tracing, marriage/divorce records searches, and many more (http://www.iu.net/hodges).
- *Networth.* This database on more than 5,000 no-load mutual funds includes fund profiles, performance reports, prospectuses, and financial newsletters (http://networth.galt.com).

- *Online Career Center (OCC).* The OCC works with the Internet, Prodigy, GEnie, CompuServe, America Online, and other national online networks to develop the most economical, effective network for employment advertising, outplacement services, and communications. The OCC advertises state, regional, national, or international employment positions in all fields for human resource management. It has a database of resumes and allows keyword searches. It also has a database of company information and profiles and provides outplacement assistance for employees through employers nationwide and has online communications with job candidates from their homes or offices (http://www.occ.com/occ/index.html).

- *Overseas Business Reports (OBR).* Provides information on the economic environment of various countries. The database contains information on trade agreements, economic outlook, government attitude towards trade, economic policy, fees, customs, recent trends, and list of organizations and contacts (gopher://lumslvma.umsl.edu:70/1 1/library/govdocs/obr).

- *Population and Housing.* Demographic information provided by the U.S. Census Bureau, including numbers and descriptive narrative; ethnicity data; and data map, which provides information by state and county (http://www.census.gov/pop.html).

- *Providers of Commercial Internet Access (POCIA).* Provides commercial Internet access including domain names and Web sites. The address is http://www.teleport.com.

- *Public Domain Financial Data.* Contains daily stock prices for U.S. and Canadian stocks. This ftp site contains a list of mutual fund company telephone numbers and provides daily stock market summaries (ftp://dg-rtp.dg.com/pub/misc.invest).

- *Quote Server.* Provides 15-minute delayed quotes for stocks traded on the NYSE, AMEX, NASDAQ, and OTC exchanges. The site also provides information on bonds traded on the NYSE and AMEX. The database contains information on mutual funds and money market funds (http://www.secapl.com/cgi-bin/qs).

- *QuoteCom.* Provides quotes for stocks of 45,000 companies, foreign stocks, and commodity market information. It also contains Hoover company profiles, Standard and Poor's (S&P's) Stock Guide, and S&P s MarketScope Alerts and charts (http://www. quote.com).

- *Small Business Administration (SBA) Online.* The U.S. Small Business Administration home page. Information about starting a small business is presented including financial aspects. The SBA site has frequently updated "hot-links" for new and exciting business-related news on the Web (http://www.sbaonline.sba.gov).

- *SEC EDGAR.* This searchable S.E.C. online database provides access to financial information on all publicly-traded companies. This site offers Daily SEC News and Digest, press releases, SEC enforcement actions, and rule-making proposals and final rules. SEC forms are here as well (http://www.sec.gov/edgarhp.html).

- *Security APL Quote Server.* Provides information on stocks such as the exchange, full name, last trading place with date and time, currency, amount and percentage of change, volume, number of trades, bid, ask, day high and low, 52-week high and low, and a list of WWW hyperlinks to other sites if available (http://www.secapl.com).
- *State Tax Index.* Maxwell Labs, Inc., provides a partial list of tax forms for several states (http://www.scubed.com/tax/state/state_index.html).
- *Stockmaster.* This page provides recent stock market information, including previous day's closing prices and one-year graphs of historical prices. It is updated automatically, usually between 7:00 PM and 9:00 PM EDT, from an e-mail source in California, to reflect the current day's closing information. It consists of general market news and quotes for selected stocks. Not all stocks are included. It also includes stock charts of price and volume movement, and mutual fund charts of price movement (http://www.ai.mit.edu/stocks.html).
- *STO's Internet Patent Search System.* Provides search forms for determining patent class using the *Manual of Classification* or the *Index to Classification,* retrieve patent titles using class/subclass code, and/or retrieve patent abstracts using a patent number. The address of this Web site is http://sunsite.unc.edu/patents/intropat.html.
- *Taxing Times.* Contains federal and state tax forms and information that can be downloaded (http://www.scubed.com:8001/tax/tax.html).
- *The Construction Site.* Provides the construction industry with information on advertising, legal matters, and trade secrets (http://www.constr.com).
- *The Federal Reserve Bank of Chicago.* The database contains information on the financial markets, monetary policy, and Federal Reserve publications (http://www.frbchi.org/).
- *The Internet Companion.* This site contains the full text of the book, *The Internet Companion.* It provides general information about the Internet, discusses using other online resources, and furnishes information on getting started using the Internet (anonymous ftp: ftp.world.std.com; Path: /OBS/Tracy. LaQuey File name:The.Internet.Companion.no-controls).
- *THOMAS: Legislative Information on the Internet.* Provides access to recently proposed and/or passed U.S. Government legislation including an e-mail directory of Congress, CSPAN online, and other forms of legislative information (http://thomas.loc.gov).
- *Thomas Register Supplier Finder.* Free online version of the Thomas Register. Search on a product or service and retrieve information on the companies that offer it (http://www.thomasregister.com).
- *US. Bureau of Labor Statistics (BLS).* Second to the U.S. Census Bureau in terms of statistical output. It has extensive data on employment, unemployment, forecasts, etc. (http://stats.bls.gov).
- *U.S. Census Bureau.* Contains tables and narrative interpretations for census summaries of manufacturers, retail, service, and wholesale industries (http://www.census.gov).

- *U.S. Central intelligence agency (CIA)*. This is a very useful site where the CIA publishes *The World Factbook, Factbook on Intelligence, CIA Maps and Publications Released to the Public, Chiefs of State and Cabinet Members of Foreign Governments, Intelligence Literature: Suggested Reading List*, and *Handbook of International Economic Statistics* (http://www.odci.gov/cia/publications/pubs.html).

- *U.S. Chamber of Commerce*. The Chamber Mall presents everything one would expect from their local chamber on a national scale: training, information, and assistance to small businesses. This site is located at http://www.uschamber.org/chamber.

- *U.S. Copyright Law*. This is presented by the Legal Information Institute at Cornell Law School. It contains the U.S. Copyright Act, U.S. Copyright Regulations, copyright decisions of the U.S. Supreme Court (since May, 1990), Berne Convention, Convention for the Protection of Producers of Phonograms, International Convention for the Protection of Performers, and Producers of Phonograms and Broadcasting Organizations (http://www.law.cornell.edu:80/topics/copyright.html).

- *U.S. Department of State Press Briefings*. Contains transcripts of daily briefings since 1991 (gopher://dosfan.lib.uil.edu/ID1%3a2784%3aDOS%20Press%20Briefs/confs).

- *U.S. Department of the Treasury, Internal Revenue Service (IRS)*. Contains a hypertext guide to all federal tax forms, other information, and the Internal Revenue Services' daily tax publication, *The Digital Daily* (http://www.irs.ustreas.gov/basic/cover.html).

- *U.S. Patent Law*. Provides Title 35 of the U.S. Code, patent decisions of the U.S. Supreme Court (since May, 1990), Patent Cooperation Treaty, Paris Convention for the Protection of Industrial Property, and the Patent Office Reform Panel Final Report (1992) provided by Cornell University (http://www.law.cornell.edu:80/topics/patent.html).

- *United States Patent and Trademark Office*. Provides keyword searching of index of trademark goods and services as well as trademark and patent application advice. The USPTO has transcripts of hearings including software patents, information security, and biotechnology as well as posting patent laws, and Federal Register notices (http://www.uspto.gov).

- *University of Michigan Statistics*. Provides access to U.S. Department of Commerce statistical files of information on employment, export, GNP, and everything in between (gopher://una.hh.lib.umich.edu:70/1 1/ebb).

- *World Bank Documents*. This site contains various World Bank documents (http://ftp.worldbank.org/html/extpb/Publications.html).

- *World Telephone Code Information*. A detailed country telephone code listing (gopher://gopher.austin.unimelb.edu.au/11/phones/other-phone).

- *Yahoo Search*. This is perhaps the most notorious Internet search engine. Yahoo is recommended as a good beginning point for subject-specific searching (http://www.yahoo.com/search.html).

CD-ROM BUSINESS DATABASES

There are a wide variety of CD-ROM business databases. Their quality varies, but almost all have multimedia features. A partial listing follows:

- *Research Institute of America (RIA) Tax Service.* A comprehensive database of tax information including IRS regulations and rules, and case law.
- *24HR Virtual Assistant by Microforum.* An online help line for popular software; provides shortcuts, advice, and instruction on how to utilize features of various software including word processing, spreadsheets, and databases.
- *Microsoft Quick Shelf.* An excellent multimedia reference library containing the *American Heritage Dictionary,* the original *Roget's Thesaurus,* the *Columbia Dictionary of Quotations,* the *Concise Columbia Encyclopedia, Hammond Intermediate World Atlas,* the *People's Chronology,* the *World Almanac* and *Book of Facts.*
- *The National Economic Social and Environmental Data Bank (NESE-DB).* Developed by STAT-USA of the U.S. Department of Commerce. The NESE-DB is the definitive source of information on socio-economic programs and trends in the United States. It provides in-depth coverage of economic trends, education, health issues, criminal justice, and the environment. It contains complete contents of the NESE-DB, including more than 100 books, magazines, reports, and tables too numerous to list individually. However, the following topics give an idea of the breadth of information available: budget of the United States, business statistics, capital and equipment, consumer expenditures information, economic conversion, employment and retraining program information, education in the U.S. historical trends, projections and indicators, employment statistics, energy information, financial statistics, government policy statements and analysis, health statistics of U.S. citizens, highway and airline transportation statistics, pollution data and toxic chemical release statistics, regional housing information, regional population projections to 2040, regional economic, demographic, and environmental information, small business information sources and indicators, U.S. and overseas industrial production statistics, U.S. economic conditions, U.S. fisheries statistics, U.S. government securities quotations, U.S. industry statistics by commodity, U.S. national economic accounts, and weather averages for cities and metropolitan areas. CD-ROM disks are produced quarterly in the months of November, February, May, and August. The cost of a single quarterly disk is $95, and an annual subscription of four disks is $360.
- *The National Trade Data Bank/CD-ROM (NTDB).* A subscription service of the Department of Commerce's STAT-USA. It has a trade library of more than 190,000 documents (three encyclopedias' worth) of information. It provides small and medium-sized companies immediate access to information that, until now, only Fortune 500 companies could afford. Topics on the NTDB include export opportunities by industry, country,

and product; foreign companies or importers looking for specific products; how-to market guides; demographic, political, and socio-economic conditions in hundreds of countries; and much more. The NTDB offers trade information from more than 20 federal sources. The NTDB has more than 200,000 documents (over one gigabyte). The CD-ROM version of the NTDB is updated monthly. The NTDB/CD-ROM provides information on agricultural commodity production and trade, basic export information, capital markets and export financing, country reports on economic and social policies and trade practices, energy production, supply and inventories, exchange rates, export licensing information, guides to doing business in foreign countries, international trade terms directory, how-to guides, international finance assistance, international trade regulations/agreements, employment and productivity, maritime and shipping information, market research reports, overseas contacts, overseas and domestic industry information, price indexes, small business information, state exports, state trade contacts, trade opportunities, U.S. export regulations, U.S. import and export statistics by country and commodity, U.S. international transactions, world fact book, and world minerals production. The NTDB is available for use free of charge at most Commerce district offices and at nearly 1,000 federal depository libraries. In the United States, Mexico, and Canada it is $40 for a single monthly issue (two disks) and $360 for an annual subscription (12 monthly two-disk issues). Export counseling is provided by the Commerce Department at 1-800-USA-TRADE.

- *Select Phone by Prophone.* A complete phone book having listings from every white pages phone book in the USA. It also provides reverse search capabilities to search by name, area code, zip code, phone number, city, state, business category, or SIC code. It allows unlimited downloading of more than 84 million residential and business listings for mail merge and telemarketing.

- *Standards* (two-disk set) by InfoMagic. An inclusive collection of domestic and international communication standards with documentation. It includes networking, telecommunications, and data communications standards including ISDN and modems.

- *Statistical Abstract of the United States.* Produced by the U.S. Department of Commerce and the Economics and Statistics Administration, it provides the complete *Statistical Abstract of the United States.* The CD-ROM, like the book, is a statistical reference and guide to more than 250 statistical publications and sources from government and private organizations. It has 1,400 tables and charts from more than 250 sources. Text and tables can be viewed or searched with the accompanying software. Some of the areas covered include vital statistics, education, elections, finances, and population data. The tables can be printed as they exist, or the user can download the Lotus 1-2-3 file and use it directly in a spreadsheet. For any businessperson needing comprehensive government data, the CD-ROM version of the *Statistical Abstract* is an absolute necessity. The CD-ROM can be ordered from the Bureau of the Census, Data User Services Division, Washington, DC 20233 or telephone 301-457-4100; fax 301-457-4714.

- *Toolworks Reference Library* by Software Toolworks. A winner of the "Best CD Program" award, the *Toolworks Reference Library* is an essential business reference source. It has the *New York Public Library Desk Reference, Webster's New World Thesaurus, Webster's New World Guide to Concise Writing, Webster's New World Dictionary Third College Edition, J. K. Lasser's Legal and Corporation Forms for the Smaller Business, Webster's New World Dictionary of Quotable Definitions,* and the *National Directory of Addresses and Telephone Numbers.*

- *U.S. Global Trade Outlook.* Produced by the U.S. Department of Commerce, this is the CD-ROM version of the 224-page *U.S. Global Trade Outlook, 1995-2000* and features all 140 color graphics and tables of the print version. Its electronic page images duplicate the printed copy in color including all graphics and tables, and can be viewed, printed, and searched as well as having all necessary software to run on Macintosh and Windows platforms. The pages are formatted in Adobe Acrobat portable document format (.pdf), and the CD-ROM comes with a licensed copy of the Acrobat Reader software, giving both Windows and Macintosh computers full access to the electronic document for viewing, printing, and searching. The CD-ROM also contains the complete ASCII text of the *U.S. Global Trade Outlook* in chapter-by-chapter text files, which you can print or view with your own word processing software. In addition, the CD-ROM features 119 Industry Trends tables created with the input of the U.S. International Trade Administration's industry analysts. These 119 spreadsheet files contain updated statistics for many of the industries and groupings formerly covered in the *U.S. Industrial Outlook* (they contain historical information and estimates through 1994, but do not include forecasts.). This is a valuable tool for business researchers tracking industry shipments, employment, capital investment, imports, and exports.

- *World Factbook* by Quanta Press. This is the *CIA World Factbook,* which contains data on 249 countries and territories worldwide. The major areas covered on the disk are geography, disputes, environment, population and vital statistics, government economy, industry, communications, and infrastructure.

FAXBACK SERVICES

Most faxback services offer an index of documents. The user should choose the index first to select relevant documents. Except for the Export Hotline, all of the following faxback services are government sponsored and are free, notwithstanding the long distance phone call that may be required.

- *AMERI-FAX (202-482-1495).* This is an automated fax-on-demand service sponsored by the U.S. Commerce Department. It provides documents

on the North American Free Trade Agreement (NAFTA), the Summit of
the Americas, and conducting business in Canada and Mexico. It also
includes a Latin America section providing economic reports on Latin
American and Caribbean countries. This faxback service is extremely
useful for those interested in Mexican and Latin American markets and
receiving instructions on completing the NAFTA certificate of origin
customs documentation. The Canadian section also provides useful trade
information.

- *BISNIS Fax Retrieval System (202-501-3144).* An automated fax-on-
demand service sponsored by the U.S. Department of Commerce and the
International Trade Administration. It provides a fax retrieval service for
the Russian Federation including business contacts, import and export
documents, periodicals, e-mail services, electronic databases, trade over-
views, banking, tariff schedules, trade shows, and related items.

- *Canada Business Service Centre Faxback System.* An automated fax-on-
demand service sponsored by Industry Canada. It provides numerous
documents in several areas including agriculture, business startup and
management, communications, environment, marketing and strategic alli-
ances, research and development, science and technology, taxation, trade,
and tourism. The Canada Business Service Centre Faxback System provides summary information on a wide variety of Canadian business issues
and government programs. Canada Business Service Centre Faxback
phones are as follows: 604-775-5515 (Vancouver), 306-956-2310 (Saska-
toon),204-984-5527 (Winnipeg), 416-954-8555 (Toronto), 514-496-4010
(Montreal), 506-444-6169 (Frederic/on), 902-426-3201 (Halifax), 902-
368-0776 (Charlotte/own), and 709-772-6030 (St. John's).

- *Eastern Europe Flashfax (202-482-5745).* An automated fax-on-demand
service sponsored by the U.S. Department of Commerce. It provides
information on Eastern Europe including current trade and business opportunities, sources of financing, multilateral development banks, venture
capital, pending trade events, country information, and newsletters.

- *Export Hotline (617-248-9393).* An automated fax-on-demand service
sponsored by AT&T, Business Week, Delta Air Lines, the *Journal of
Commerce,* the National Association of Manufacturers, United States
Council for International Business, and the U.S. Department of Commerce. It provides more than 4,500 reports on 78 countries and more than
50 industries. It has an extensive electronic yellow pages of more than
10,000 companies as well as more than 5,000 Japanese importers. It has
a market research export hotline menu including general documents on
how to export, government programs, trade shows, how to import, etc.
Additionally, the Export Hotline provides research on more than 78 countries as well as the European Union (EC) and NAFTA, including industry
analyses and marketing strategies. Company profiles are listed by four-
digit harmonized codes.

- *Faxlink Information Service.* An automated fax-on-demand service sponsored by the Canadian Department of Foreign Affairs and International

Trade in Ottawa. Two services are provided. The Faxlink Information Service provides information relating to Canadian business contacts, government programs, industry sector profiles, press releases, and newsletters. This service is an export service directed at the Canadian businessperson providing "how to" information as well as giving primary business contacts. The Faxlink International Information Service is targeted at the foreign businessperson and ISO investor. It provides business contacts as well as giving information on Canada's infrastructure and business investing environment. The phone number for the Faxlink Information Service is 613-944-4500, whereas the phone number for the Faxlink International Information Service is 613-944-6500.

- *GATT/Uruguay Round Fax Retrieval System (202-501-3144).* An automated fax-on-demand service sponsored by the U.S. Department of Commerce. It provides an overview of the Uruguay Round trade agreement including how to get membership in the World Trade Organization and GATT. It also includes trade opportunities for American states as well as providing 30 separate industry specific reports. The service provides 21 topical and special reports on a wide range of issues including the textile agreement, antidumping, intellectual property rights, etc.

- *Japan Export Promotion Hotline (202-482-4565).* An automated fax-on-demand service sponsored by the Japan Export Information Center at the U.S. Department of Commerce. It provides information on doing business in Japan including how to build business relationships, the Japanese distribution system, business negotiations, direct marketing, the Japanese beer market, trademark registration, customs clearance and regulations, interpretation/translation firms, Japanese banking, fact sheets, and construction and reconstruction opportunities

- *NAFTA FACTS (202-482-4464).* To help companies learn more about NAFTA and other aspects of doing business in Mexico, the U.S. Department of Commerce's Office of Mexico has set up NAFTA FACTS, a free automated fax delivery system. NAFTA FACTS includes documents on numerous topics, including specific NAFTA provisions, NAFTA rules of origin and customs information, tariff schedules, and doing business in Mexico. Specific documents of interest include "Dates and Locations for NAFTA Customs Rules for Exporters Seminars" (document #4001);"Making the NAFTA Rule of Origin Determination" (document #5001); Copy of the NAFTA Certificate of Origin (document #5002); "Completing the NAFTA Certificate of Origin" (document #5003); "Documents Needed for Exporting Your Product to Mexico" (document #8401); and "Mexican Government Standards and Labeling Regulations" (document #8404).

- *STAT-USA/FAX (202-482-0005).* An automated fax-on-demand service sponsored by the U.S. Commerce Department's STAT-USA. It is a valuable source for current business, economic, and international trade information produced by the U.S. federal government. The service is accessible 24 hours/day, seven days/week. STAT-USA/Fax is a subscriber-based service, but anyone may access the system as a guest user. Follow the voice prompts and enter "2" for guest access. Guest users may request product brochures, release schedules general and technical information, sample files, and a subscription order form. Each user is limited to two downloads per call, and a subscriber may download up to six files per day. Any user may receive an unlimited number of guest files per day. When prompted for a document code, enter "800" for a list of available information titles and codes, and enter "801" for a schedule of information release dates and times.

- *The USTR Fax Service (202-395-4809).* This automated fax-on-demand service is sponsored by the Office of the United States Trade Representative. It provides recent trade press releases, reports, treaties, and announcements from that office. Essentially, it gives the latest U.S. executive trade policies regarding various nations and regions of the world. It is an effective tool for understanding difficulties in certain regions and assessing new trade opportunities resulting from changes in international trade policies. It also explains the implications of trade treaties such as the General Agreement on Trade and Tariffs (GATT) and gives tariff announcements.

- *Trade Information Center Hotline (202-501-3144).* This is an automated fax-on-demand service sponsored by the U. S. Department of Commerce and the International Trade Administration. This fax service provides general export information, information on specific U.S. government export programs, alternative trade finance options, electronic information services including trade leads, information on the National Trade Data Bank (NTDB), national trade data bank locations in the U.S., a U.S. national export directory by state and industry, and desk officers.

9 The Intranet

Intranet utilization in corporate America is rapidly growing. Because intranets use Internet technology, there is ready access to external data. In effect, intranets are internal web sites. An intranet is an important tool to use in business and is developed and used by the company itself. An intranet is easy to install and flexible (what is developed for one platform may be used for others).

Corporate managers must have a knowledge of intranet structure and organization, because it relates to accounting, tax, audit, control, and security issues. Managers, customers, employees, stockholders, potential investors, creditors, loan officers, government agent representatives (SEC, IRS), and other interested parties can access the database or information in a company through web browsers (interfaces) such as Netscape Navigator and Microsoft's Internet Explorer. Management may set up an intranet to improve operating efficiencies and productivity and to reduce operating costs (e.g., distribution expenses), time, and errors. Of course, keeping information on the intranet current takes time and resources. Proper controls must be established to guard against unauthorized access of the company's data through the Internet. One security device is the use of firewalls (barriers) to protect the company's intranet by unauthorized access and to prevent misuse of the intranet by outsiders who might otherwise be able to alter accounting and financial information, steal property, obtain confidential data, or commit other inappropriate or fraudulent acts. Furthermore, add-on security tools are available to restrict users by preventing them from performing certain acts or from viewing certain "restricted" information.

In an intranet, one protocol connects all users to the web server, which is run on standard protocols supported by any computer.

INTRANET EXPLOSION

Information system (IS) and functional department managers quickly saw the power of this new communications medium as a resource to be leveraged on the corporate network as well. Forrester Research did a study finding that two-thirds of large companies already had or are contemplating some use of intranet business applications. Surveyed companies identified the intranet as a powerful tool to make information more readily available within and outside the company.

With businesses under significant pressure to empower employees and to better leverage internal information resources, intranets furnish a very effective communications platform—one that is both timely and extensive. A basic intranet can be set up in days and can eventually act as an "information hub" for the whole company, its remote offices, partners, suppliers, customers, investors, creditors, consultants, regulatory agencies, and other interested parties.

Intranets provide the following features:

- Easy navigation (internal home page provides links to information)
- Ability to integrate a distributed computing strategy (localized web servers residing near the content author)
- Rapid prototyping (can be measured in days, or even hours in some cases)
- Accessible via most computing platforms
- Scaleable (start small, build as requirements dictate)
- Extensible to many media types (video, audio, interactive applications)
- Can be tied to "legacy" information sources (databases, existing word processing documents, groupware databases)

The benefits to these features are many, including the following:

- An intranet is inexpensive to start, requires minimal investment in dollars or infrastructure.
- Open platform architecture means large (and increasing) numbers of add-on applications.
- A distributed computing strategy uses computing resources more effectively.
- An intranet is much more timely and less expensive than traditional information (paper) delivery.

CALENDAR-DRIVEN VS. EVENT-DRIVEN STRATEGY

One of the key drivers in the intranet adoption curve is how they allow businesses to evolve from a "calendar" or "schedule" based publishing strategy to one of an "event-driven" or "needs-based" publishing strategy. In the past, businesses published an employee handbook once a year, regardless of whether policies changed to coincide with that publication date. Traditionally, even though these handbooks may have been outdated as soon as they arrived on the users' desks (and were promptly misplaced), they would not be updated until the next year.

With an intranet publishing strategy, information can be updated instantly. If the company adds a new mutual fund to the 401K program, the content on the benefits page can be immediately updated to incorporate that change, and the company internal home page can have a brief announcement about the change. Then, when employees refer to the 401K program, they have the new information at their fingertips. Content can be changed or updated to reflect new rules at any time.

INTRANETS REDUCE COST, TIME TO MARKET

Intranets dramatically reduce the costs (and time) of content development, duplication, distribution, and usage. The traditional publication model includes a multistep process including creation of content, migration of content to the desktop publishing environment, production of the first draft, revision, final draft production, duplication, and distribution.

The intranet publishing model includes a much shorter process, skipping many of the steps involved in the traditional publication model. In the intranet model, revision becomes part of the updating process while the original content is available to end users, thus dramatically reducing the time it takes for the information to become available to the user. As the information is centrally stored and always presumed to be current, the company will not have to retrieve "old" information from employees, thus saving updating expenses.

This new publishing model significantly reduces both costs and the time frame. Assuming that the corporate local area network (LAN) environment can support intranet activities (and most can), the information technology (IT) infrastructure is already in place. Furthermore, most popular intranet web servers can run on platforms widely found in most companies (Intel Pentium class computers, Apple Macintosh, Novell NetWare, etc.), so that little if any additional infrastructure is required.

Organizations estimate that the traditional model may entail physical duplication and distribution costs of as high as $15 per employee—costs separate from the content development or testing phases. An organization with 10,000 employees may find potential cost savings of moving to an intranet policy for a single application alone—the employee policies and benefits manual—of $150,000. This cost savings does not even consider the additional value in an intranet solution, which makes information more easily available to staff, thus improving their productivity and morale.

PRACTICAL APPLICATIONS

The uses of intranets (internal webs) by companies are unlimited, including:

- Furnishing outside CPAs with accounting, audit, and tax information
- Providing marketing and sales information to current and prospective customers or clients
- Providing information to salespersons in the field and managers at different branches (e.g., sales and profit reports, product tracking, transaction analysis)
- Furnishing resource needs and reports to suppliers
- Communicating corporate information to employees, such as company policies and forms, operating instructions, job descriptions, time sheets, human resource data and documents, business plans, newsletters, marketing manuals, phone directories, schedules, and performance reports
- Assisting in employee training, development, and technical support
- Transferring information to government agencies (e.g., Department of Commerce, SEC, IRS)
- Furnishing current and prospective investors with profitability, growth, and market value statistics

- Providing lenders and creditors with useful liquidity and solvency data
- Providing project, proposal, and scheduling data to participating companies in joint ventures
- Providing press releases and product/service announcements
- Giving legal information to outside attorneys involved in litigation matters
- Providing trade associations with input for their surveys
- Accessing and searching databases and rearranging information
- Furnishing information to outside consultants (e.g., investment management advisors, pension planners)
- Providing insurance companies with information to draft or modify insurance coverage
- Allowing for collaborative workgroups such as letting users access various drafts of a specific project document interactively and add annotations and comments (e.g., Ford's intranet links design engineers in the U.S., Europe, and Asia)
- Furnishing economic statistics about the company to economic advisors
- Facilitating database queries and document requests
- Providing spreadsheets, database reports, tables, checklists, and graphs to interested parties
- Displaying e-mail

Site maps (e.g., tables of contents) should be included so users may easily navigate from each node (element) and should be visible through frames or panels.

An intranet requires web application development for its internal network such as appropriate web servers. For quick response time, there should be a direct connection to the server. Web browsers may be used to achieve cross-platform viewing and applications for a wide variety of desktops used within the company. The use of web technology (e.g., web servers) allows each desktop having a web browser to access corporate information over the existing network. Therefore, employees in different divisions of the company located in different geographic areas (e.g., buildings) can access and use centralized and/or scattered information (cross section).

There are many client/server applications within and among companies, such as cross-platform applications. The major element in an intranet is the web server software, which runs on a central computer and serves as a clearinghouse for all information. Web servers for an intranet are available from many vendors, including the following:

- IBM (800-426-2255): Internet Connection Server for MVS
- Microsoft (800-426-9400): Internet Information Server (comes with Microsoft's NT Server)
- Netscape (415-528-2555): Fast Track and Commerce Server for Windows NT
- Lotus (800-828-7086): InterNotes Web Publisher
- CompuServe (800-848-8199): Spry Web Server for Windows NT
- Quarterdeck (800-683-6696): Web Server and Web Star for Windows 95/NT

The author believes that the advantages of Microsoft's Windows NT Server are higher security and easier upgradeability to more powerful hardware at a later date as application needs increase.

In addition, there are many intranet tool vendors, such as Illustra Information Technologies (http://www.illustra.com, 510-652-8000) and Spider Technologies (http://www.w3spider.com, 415-969-7149). Frontier Technologies' Intranet Genie, as an intranet tool, includes a fairly secure Web server, HTML authoring instructions and guidelines (discussed below), a Web browser, and e-mail functions. Regardless of the operating system used (e.g., Windows, UNIX, Mac OS), many intranet tools are available.

HYPERTEXT MARKUP LANGUAGE

The author recommends the use of hypertext markup language (HTML) in developing intranets, because it provides an easier graphical user interface (GUI) to program than Windows environments such as Motif or Microsoft Windows. HTML is a good integration tool for database applications and information systems. It facilitates the use of hyperlinks and search engines, enabling the easy sharing of identical information among different responsibility segments of the company. Intranet data usually goes from back-end sources (e.g., mainframe host) to the web server to users (e.g., customers) in HTML format.

COMMON GATEWAY INTERFACE

Most web applications run through a mechanism in the web server referred to as the *common gateway interface (CGI)*. CGI is used to connect users to databases. Most CGI programs are written in TCL or Perl (a scripting language). However, because these languages involve printing source code from the web server, there is an unsecured situation from a control and security standpoint. Other deficiencies are relative slowness in applications, nonexistant or inadequate debuggers, and maintenance problems. Consider other languages for the CGI such as C or C++.

The following approach is recommended for CGI business applications:

1. In developing web applications for intranets, code management tools are needed to enable different participants in a corporate project or activity to communicate and work together. You must also use tools for database design, modeling, and debugging. In this connection, the following web sites, among others, provide helpful information to corporate managers:
   - Basic HTTP
     (http://www.w3. org/hypertext/www/protocols/http/http2.html)
   - HTML browser list
     (http://www.w3.org/hypertext/www/clients.html)
   - Web server comparison chart
     (http://www.proper.com/www/seners-chart.html)
   - HTML specifications from the WWW Consortium
     (http://www.w3.org/hypertext/www/markup/markup.html)

- Introduction to CGI
  (http://hoo.hoo.ncsa.uiuc.edu/docs/cgi:/overview.html)

2. Because new technological developments require flexibility on your part, you should not commit to a particular server or browser. You should set up your system so that it may accommodate many servers and browsers.

3. Make sure your HTML user interface is separate from the database and application logic.

SETTING UP AN INTRANET

Intranet applications are scaleable, i.e., they can start small and grow. This feature allows many businesses to "try out" an intranet pilot—to publish a limited amount of content on a single platform and evaluate the results. If the pilot looks promising, additional content can be migrated to the intranet server.

PROPOSED CONTENT

Companies must ascertain whether data should be made available via a web server, via e-mail or by some other means. If the data is of general importance, such as company travel guidelines or mileage reimbursement, it can be posted on a web server so that when employees and travel agents, among others, require this information, they can click on "Travel Guidelines" from the human resources page and obtain the most current information.

Many businesses find building web interfaces to "legacy information" as a key application. With tools such as Purveyor's Data Wizard, HTML Transit, and Web-DBC, end users can build simple point-and-click access to this legacy information without any programming, making it available to nontechnical users through their web browser. Key database applications include customer records, product information, inventory, technical problem tracking, call reports, etc. In addition, individuals can quickly set up seminar or training registration forms for short-term use, loading the registrants' information into an easily manipulated database.

Conversely, interoffice e-mail may be more appropriate for "interrupt-driven" time-sensitive information, especially for a focused group of recipients. "Our most important customer is coming in March 2, so please attend the briefing at 9 A.M." In this case, the web server can be used as an extended information resource. "Before the meeting, check the internal web server link for current customers for updated information concerning this account."

ENHANCEMENTS

Intranets can provide efficient access to other external information resources, including group access to mailing lists, threaded discussion groups, and stock/bond quotes. In this way, the oft-accessed information can be aggregated at the firewall and efficiently dispersed within the company, thus reducing external bandwidth and connectivity requirements.

Multithreaded discussion group software, or conferencing applications, can run on the same platform as the intranet application, providing further chances to discuss company issues and the content that resides on the server.

INTRANETS COMPARED TO GROUPWARE

Intranets and *groupware* are not mutually exclusive. Many companies find that groupware (work flow, collaborative computing, etc.) is appropriate for certain focused applications, while intranets are suitable for migrating existing content to online delivery. Others find a powerful combination in groupware and a web server (e.g., Lotus InterNotes engine for publishing Notes databases on the web).

Ultimately, each application strategy has its merits. Beyond this, intranet applications and web servers make an excellent foundation for web-based groupware, allowing businesses to employ a web-centric intranet system strategy and leverage the nearly ubiquitous web browser and the powerful navigational aids provided by HTML.

SUMMARY

The application of Internet technologies in an intranet environment can dramatically increase the flow and value of organizational information. The corporate manager can gain quick and timely access to a much wider variety of existing information residing in a variety of original forms and sources, including word processing files, databases, spreadsheets, Lotus Notes, and other resources. In addition, traditional paper-based information distribution can be replaced by intranet applications, lowering costs and increasing the timeliness of information flow.

Intranet applications can start as small "pilots" and scale upward over time, gradually providing or facilitating access to an increasing breadth of information, thus improving both employee productivity and satisfaction, and eventually bolstering the company's competitive position.

An *extranet* is an extended intranet that creates virtual private networks between companies, business partners, and clients.

10 Information Systems Development and End-User Computing

Information systems development can be a complex task and may involve many employees working collaboratively. In this process, many existing small information systems may be combined into a large one so that all business functions can be integrated through information systems, or a new information system may be created from the ground up. Developing information systems within a planned framework often creates a better system and helps organizations to avoid the necessity of patching together a collection of incompatible information systems. Therefore, the development of a successful information system is not a trivial task. It requires a thorough understanding of existing business processes, discipline, organizational policies, expertise in this field, a vision of the future, and good communication skills. The rationale behind triggering the development of an information system could be to catch an opportunity or to solve a problem.

- *Catching an opportunity.* An *opportunity* is defined as a potential improvement in business such as an increase in sales, more efficient operations, or a gain in competitive advantages. Catching an opportunity is considered to be a *proactive* activity in business, whereas solving a problem is considered to be *reactive*.
- *Solving a problem.* A *problem* is defined as an undesired situation or unforeseen circumstances. For example, a business realizes that the cost of operations is not competitive anymore, or the customer service does not meet the requirement level. A good information system can provide a solution that leads to the solution of a current problem.

THE SYSTEMS DEVELOPMENT LIFE CYCLE

The systems development life cycle (SDLC) consists of several distinct phases and subphases, known by different names. The SDLC approach assumes that the life of an information system starts with a need and follows with an assessment of the functions that the system will fulfill. It ends when the benefits of the system no longer outweigh its maintenance cost. A new system is then constructed for another life cycle. The SDLC includes five major phases (see Figure 10.1).

System Analysis

The purpose of system analysis is to establish in detail what the proposed system will do. This includes establishing the objectives of the new system and conducting an analysis of its costs and the benefits to be derived. Two steps are involved in this process: feasibility analysis and requirements analysis.

Feasibility Study

A feasibility analysis consists of three steps: the technical feasibility study, the economic feasibility study, and the operational feasibility study. The *technical feasibility study* investigates whether the proposed system is technically feasible and whether the technology is sophisticated enough to accomplish the task. The *economic feasibility study* involves the financial status and the cost-benefit analysis of the proposed system. The potential benefits, including savings and extra revenue, must be greater than the potential cost, including maintenance. It does not make sense to build a system whose cost exceeds its income. The *operational feasibility study* investigates whether the system is operational and if the technology is available. Technology availability does not guarantee that the system will be operational. For example, running a system for 24 hours a day is possible *technologically* but *infeasible due to budget constraints or government regulations.* In general, a feasibility

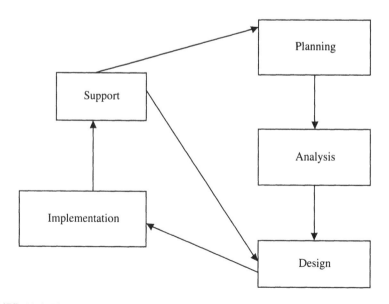

FIGURE 10.1 Five steps of the system analysis phase.

study consumes 5 to 10% of a project's resources. The question is, how much time will be spent on the development process?

Requirements Analysis

The principal objective of requirements analysis is to produce the requirements specifications for the system, which specify what the system will do if implemented. The requirements can be used to establish understanding among future users, developers, and management, and they can serve as a contract among all parties.

A typical requirement analysis includes the following:

- What kind of output will the system produce? What input will be needed to generate this output?
- What volume of data will be handled? How many users can be served?
- What type of user interface will be provided?
- What kinds of obligations, in terms of usage and maintenance of the system, are required for users and developers?

System Analysis Alternatives

To perform a good system analysis, information collection is an important step. There are different ways to collect information for the purpose of system analysis.

Collecting information from users. Collecting information from users is usually done by means of an interview. The interview process should be planned in advance to make sure that managers from different levels can be questioned. Two types of questions are to be asked.

- *Open-ended questions* such as, "How can this process be improved?" These give the interviewee the opportunity to find potential problems and create new solutions. The answer may be unorganized but could be very helpful in terms of finding possible opportunities.
- *Closed-ended questions* such as, "Do you maintain an audit trail for this type of transaction?" These generally provide the interviewer with a short answer such as yes, no, or a brief response.

Collecting information from existing systems. If the proposed system will replace the existing system, or if it is similar to the existing system, the requirements for the proposed system may be derived from the existing one.

Collecting information from analyzing business functionality. Decision analysis call help establish the information needs of an individual manager. This method consists of the following steps:

- Identify the key decision a manager makes.
- Identify the steps for the decision-making process.
- Identify the information needed for decision making.
- Identify the input (usually the raw data) and output (usually the information) of the information systems.

SYSTEM DESIGN

Logical Design

The *logical design* is a translation of the user requirements into detailed functions of the system. The steps involved in logical design are as follows:

- The output of the proposed system and the input used to produce this output are identified.
- The components of the hardware and software are identified.
- The user interface is designed.
- The database management system is designed.
- The program that will constitute the system is designed.
- The procedures to be employed in the operating system are specified.
- The controls that will be incorporated in the system are specified.

Physical Design

The objective of *physical design* is to produce a complete specification of all system modules and their interfaces. The system's design must conform to the purpose, scale, and general concept of the system that management approved during the requirements analysis phase.

SYSTEM OUTPUT

When designing user output, consider the following six important factors:

Content. This refers to the actual pieces of data included among the outputs provided to users. For example, the content of a weekly report to a sales manager might consist of salesperson's name, sales calls made during the week, and the amount of each product sold to each major client category.

Form. This specifies how the content is presented to users. Content can be presented in various forms: quantitative, nonquantitative, text, graphics, audio, and video.

Output volume. *Volume* is commonly used in technology to measure the amount of activity taking place at a given time. The amount of data output required at any one time is known as *output volume.*

Timeliness. This refers to when users need outputs. Some outputs are required on a regular, periodic basis—perhaps daily, weekly, monthly, quarterly, or annually.

Media. The input/output *medium* is the physical substance or device used for input, storage, or output. The two most widely used media are paper and display. Paper involves printer or plotter hardware, whereas display involves a monitor or display terminal.

Format. Format refers to the manner in which data are physically arranged. This arrangement is called *output format* when referring to data output on a printed report or on a display screen.

System Input

User inputs should be designed next, after the outputs are designed. The input issues to consider are content, timeliness, media, format, and volume.

Content. The analyst should consider the types of data that need to be gathered to generate user outputs. Sometimes the data needed for a new system is not available within the organization—but a close substitute might be. For example, cost data sometimes can be cleverly manipulated into useful substitute information.

Timeliness. When inputs must enter the system is critical, because outputs cannot be produced until certain inputs are available. Hence, a plan must be established regarding when different types of' inputs will enter the system.

Media. The input media are the devices used to enter the data, such as display workstations, magnetic tapes, magnetic disks, keyboards, optical character recognition (OCR), pen-based computers, and voice, to name a few.

Format. After the data content and the media requirements are determined, input formats are considered. When specifying record formats, for instance, the type and length of each data field, as well as any other special characteristics, must be defined.

Input volume. Input volume relates to the amount of data that must be entered in the computer system at any one time. In some decision-support systems and many real-time transaction-processing systems, input volume is light. In batch-oriented transaction-processing systems, input volume can be heavy.

Determining Processing Requirements

This determination helps the project team to decide which types of application software products are needed and, consequently, the degree of processing the system needs to handle. This leads the system developers to decisions regarding the systems software and computer hardware that will most effectively get outputs to users.

User Interface

User interface design is the specification of a conversation between the system user and the computer. This conversation generally results in either input or output, and possibly both. There are several types of user interface styles. Traditionally, these styles were viewed as alternatives. However, with recent movements toward designing systems with graphical user interfaces, a blending of all styles can be found.

Menu selection. The more traditional user interaction dialogue strategy is menu selection. This strategy presents a list of alternatives or options for the user. The system user selects the desired alternative or option by keying in the number or letter that is associated with that option.

Menu bars. Menu bars are used to display horizontally across the top of the screen or window a series of choices from which the user can select.

Pull-down menus. Pull-down menus provide a vertical list of choices to the user. A pull-down menu is made available once the user selects a choice from a menu bar. The choices are typically organized from top to bottom according to the frequency in which they are chosen.

Cascading menus. This type of menu must be requested by the user from another higher-level menu.

Iconic menus. An iconic menu uses graphic representations for menu options. Iconic menus offer the advantage of easy recognition. The use of graphic images helps the user to memorize and recognize the functions available within an application. Instead of menus, some traditional applications were designed using a dialogue around an instruction set (also called a *command language interface*). Because the user must learn the syntax of the instructions set, this is suitable only for dedicated users.

Question-answer dialogue. Question-answer dialogue strategy is a style that was primarily used to supplement either menu-driven or syntax-driven dialogues. The simplest questions involve *yes* and *no* answers. Question-answer dialogue is difficult, because you must try to consider everything that the system user might do wrong!

Direct manipulation. The newest and most popular of the user interface styles allows direct manipulation of graphical objects appearing on a screen. Essentially, this user interface style focuses on using icons, or small graphic images, to suggest functions to the user. A trash can icon, for instance, might symbolize a delete command.

ACQUISITION

At the end of the design phase, the firm has a reasonably good idea of the types of hardware, software, and services it needs for the system being developed. These physical items are identified after the logical design of the system model is finished.

THE VENDOR MARKETPLACE

Today, thousands of technology-related vendors exist, and a single organization might buy from hundreds of companies before meeting its full set of processing needs. The technology industry can be broken down into three primary market segments: hardware, software, and services.

- *Hardware.* The hardware segment of the computer industry consists of firms that make computer units (that is, system units), peripheral devices, and/or communications devices. Some firms primarily produce mainframes, others minicomputers, and still others microcomputers. Some firms have products in all three markets, and many make peripherals as well as computer units. Several of these firms produce software as well.

It is possible to lease computer hardware (enter into a contract with a vendor to possess and use a computer system over a specified time period, for a specified payment) or to buy it.

- *Software*. Unlike hardware, software is usually licensed rather than leased or purchased. Its use may be licensed on a single-payment basis (the standard practice for microcomputer software) or on a monthly basis (common for mainframe software). Such licensing agreements give the organization the right to use the software.

- *Services*. Many firms in the computer industry supply services, including software and hardware maintenance, creation and maintenance of banks of financial data that other companies can access, provision of communications networking capability, remote access to computing facilities, data processing and system integration (system development), advice, programs or applications development, education, and so on. The availability of such services has given many companies the option of outsourcing their information-processing activities; that is, contracting with another firm to provide the information-processing services that were previously provided in house.

THE REQUEST FOR PROPOSAL

Firms may approach vendors to acquire hardware, software, or services in various ways. One method is to send vendors a document called a *request for proposal (RFP)*. This document outlines the firm's system needs and requests that interested vendors submit a formal proposal detailing how they will satisfy those needs.

EVALUATING VENDOR PROPOSALS

The proposals or bids are evaluated, and a selection is made. Two useful procedures to aid in this process are the *vendor rating system* and the *benchmark test*. In a vendor rating system, vendors are quantitatively scored with respect to how well their systems stack up against a specific set of criteria.

In a benchmark test, one or more programs (or sets of data) are prepared by the potential buyer and then processed under the hardware or software of the vendors being considered. The collection of programs and data submitted by the potential buyer is called a *benchmark*. The benchmark should reflect the type of work that the vendor's hardware and software will actually perform, thereby providing a realistic indication of how well that hardware will do when used for real applications.

CONTRACTING WITH VENDORS

After a vendor is chosen, a *contract* is signed. A contract is a document, enforceable in a court of law, that defines such items as the basic agreement; the parties to the agreement; the goods, services, and monies exchanged; and the continuing expectations; plus the course of action if either party fails to live up to expectations.

CONSTRUCTION

Once the software development tools are chosen, the construction of the system begins. System construction is predominantly programming by translating input, output, and processes into programs. After the program module is completed, it is tested by means of *walk-through* and simulation. In a walk-through, system analysts follow the logic of the program and compare it with what they know the result should be. In *simulation,* the team runs the program with the data. After the modules of the application are completed and tested, the modules are integrated into one coherent program.

SYSTEM TESTING

It is critical to test the entire integrated system. System testing consists of test runs for the purpose of finding errors. The system is checked against the system requirements originally defined in the analysis phase by running typical data through the system. The quality of the output is examined, and processing times are measured to ensure that the original requirements are met. This is a crucial step in the development effort, since many unforeseen impediments can be detected and fixed before the system is introduced for daily use.

IMPLEMENTATION

Implementation, also called *delivery,* consists of two steps: training and conversion.

   Training. Staff members must he trained in one of several ways, such as *class training,* which takes advantage of the economical use of instructors, or *on-the-job training,* in which people learn by doing. Training can be achieved by using multimedia technology and other training software in which employees can train themselves and learn the system at their own pace.

   Conversion. Conversion takes place when an operation switches from the old system to the new system. There are the broad ranges of activities that prepare the intended users for work with the new system and for "owning" it. The operators need time to get used to new systems, and a lot of effort is required to test the system. In this stage, services to other departments and to customers may be delayed, and data may be lost.

EXPLORING THE PROTOTYPING ALTERNATIVE

A *prototype* is an original information system that serves as a model for the production of other information systems with similar goals and functionality. In the manufacturing industry, a prototype refers to an actual physical product that is later mass-produced for marketing. IS prototyping is different from manufacturing prototyping in how it is produced. IS prototyping tends to use a more interactive approach than a systematic approach. The users and developers are consistently interacting, revising, and testing the prototype system until it evolves into an acceptable application. This approach is totally different from the traditional step-by-step analysis and development process.

The purpose of prototyping is to develop a system from a working model as quickly as possible. This working model is then revised and tweaked, as developers and users work together. A typical development process consists of the following steps:

- Quick development of a working model
- Test by users, with feedback and suggestions
- Modification of the system based on feedback and suggestions

Studies have shown that prototyping has become a popular approach to system development, since it requires fewer staff members than the traditional approach. This implies that prototyping costs less than the traditional approach. Prototyping also significantly shortens the time required to complete the system development process. However, the risk is that, since the analysis phase is reduced to a minimum level to save time and cost, incompatibilities and other unforeseen mishaps may occur. For example, the documentation process can be complicated when the system is complete.

KNOWING WHEN TO PROTOTYPE

Prototyping is an efficient approach to development in two situations. The first is when the system is small in scale, because the risk involved in the lack of thorough analysis is minimal. If the development takes longer than planned, the overall cost is still likely to be smaller than if a full SDLC were performed. The second is when the system deals with unstructured problems; it leads to de facto prototyping. The developer interviews the experts and builds a crude system; then the experts try to improve it. If users cannot specify all the requirements at the start of the project, the developers have no choice but prototype, and the users can communicate their requirements as the development proceeds.

KNOWING WHEN NOT TO PROTOTYPE

Prototype is not recommended if a system is large or complex, because it requires a significant investment of resources. A system failure could entail great financial loss. Prototyping should be avoided when the system is designed to interface with other systems. The requirements and integration must be analyzed carefully to reduce the risk of damage to the existing system. For example, a payroll system or a large order-entry system is rarely prototyped.

OUTSOURCING OPTIONS

A company no longer has to develop its own information system, because many companies specializing in IS services provide expertise and economies of scale that no single company can achieve. However, with regard to whether to develop a system in house or to outsource its development, top managers should ask basic questions: What are the core business competencies? What are the specialties that the company should continue to do by itself? What does the company do outside of its specialty that could be done better by an organization that specializes in that area?

Many companies realize that IT is not among their core competencies and should not be a focus of their efforts. With this change in business operations, outsourcing has come to mean two different things:

1. A short-term contractual relationship with a service firm to develop a specific application for the organization
2. A long-term contractual relationship with a service firm to take over all or some of the IS functions

The advantages of outsourcing are as follows:

- *Improved cost clarity.* The client knows exactly what the cost of the IS functions will be over the period of the contract.
- *Reduced license and maintenance fees.*
- *User concentration on core business.* Outside experts manage IT, freeing executives from managing an IS business so that they can concentrate on the company's main business.

INTEGRATING END-USER COMPUTING

THE END-USER ENVIRONMENT

End users are persons who need the outputs produced by application software to perform their jobs. *End-user computing (EUC)* is the involvement of end users, such as employees, managers, or executives, in the development and use of the information system. As the field of end-user computing evolves, more end users are becoming directly involved in satisfying their own data and information needs.

FACTORS ENCOURAGING END-USER COMPUTING

A complete list of the applications that motivate end-users to employ computing resources or to acquire their own computing resources would be extensive. Many end users' applications fall into one or more of the following eight areas:

Data entry. Data entry refers to entering data into the computer system. Many data-entry operations are part of transaction-processing operations. In this case, the entry application was probably developed by computer professionals and not by end users.

Document processing. Document processing includes such activities as the preparation of memos, letters, and other types of correspondence, as well as such tasks as electronic document management and routing. Document routing is often performed by electronic mail and the image processing system.

Data management. Data management refers to the set of computing and development activities involved with maintaining large computerized banks of data. It refers to the types of activities that constitute data management, as well as the file and database management software used to implement these activities.

Extract reports. Extract reports are business reports that use data extracted from files or databases. A user can create a report that consists only of selected records from a file. A user can also do arithmetic on report records and sort records in various ways.

Display retrieval. Preparing extract reports normally involves permanent hard-copy output, formatting information into a report style, and completeness attributed to the report. Display retrieval, on the other hand, involves temporarily summoning only a few pieces of output to the display screen.

Schedules and lists. Schedules and lists consist of outputs as budgets, profit-and-loss statements, and annuities.

Analysis. Analysis involves drawing conclusions from a set of data. Analysis can be performed by end users in numerous ways, such as sensitivity analysis or statistical analysis.

Presentation. Many end users need to put information into a highly presentable form. For instance, presentations made at a meeting often require that information be shown in an easily understood or graphical format.

MANAGING END-USER COMPUTING

According to Thomas Gerrity arid John Rockart, three principal approaches to management of end-user computing (EUC) exist.

Monopolist Approach

End-user development is often perceived as a threat to the power of an IS department. As end users acquire their own systems, they depend less on the resources of the IS department to meet their needs. The IS department has thwarted the onrush of end-user computing by convincing management that computer professionals should control all information processing. The monopolist approach is the strategy for an IS department attempting to retain its power.

Laissez-Faire Approach

The laissez-faire approach is in direct contrast to the monopolist approach. In this approach, end-user computing should be left completely to the discretion of the end users themselves. Unfortunately, this approach can easily lead to chaos. End-user computing costs, which may already be substantial, can zoom out of control. As each user group does what it wants, the proliferation of technologies can make systems integration a nightmare.

Information Center Approach

The newest, and often the most sensible, approach to the management of EUC is the information center. This approach enables users to retain the authority to care for their own need (most end users operate under normal budgetary constraints and are motivated to spend funds wisely) and, if properly managed, provides some control over the unbridled proliferation of end-user systems.

ADVANTAGES AND PROBLEMS

Increased Individual Performance

Perhaps the single most important benefit of EUC is increased individual performance froth the viewpoints of both effectiveness and efficiency. Most people agree that decision support system (DSS) tools in the hands of informed managers usually make those managers much more effective.

Easier and More Direct Implementation

With end-user development, it is more likely that the final system will be exactly what the end user wants and expects.

Technological Literacy

As users become more sophisticated with end-user tools, it is likely that benefits will accrue that management never expected.

Competitive Advantage

Numerous examples exist in which companies employed end-user technologies to establish a competitive advantage. In these instances, benefits to the organization may include shifting inventory carrying costs to the supplier, greater control over suppliers, increased ordering efficiency, enhanced quality of incoming supplies, and easier shopping for the best price.

Reducing the Applications Backlog

As end users become capable of meeting their own computing needs, both the visible and invisible applications backlogs may lessen.

CHALLENGES AND PROBLEMS

From a management perspective, three of the most critical challenges associated with end-user computing and development are cost control, product control, and data control.

Problems Arising from EUC

1. The cost of EUC often cannot be measured effectively.
2. Many end-user-related costs are not formally justified in any way.
3. Some end-user computing costs are not optimized at the enterprise level.
4. End users often buy products that are incompatible with those bought by other end users, with whom someday they might have to integrate applications.
5. End users often solve the wrong problems or apply the wrong tools and models.
6. The information center staff often does not follow up properly after initial end-user needs appear to be satisfied.
7. End users typically do not apply rigorous data integrity or accuracy controls, making the results they get from their systems less reliable than those obtained from formal systems.
8. End users typically have little security or backup on their systems.
9. Some end users get carried away with their computer systems, using them inefficiently or ineffectively, to the detriment of their main job functions.
10. End users are typically deficient at documentation and setting up audit trails.
11. End users often fail to upgrade their systems.

TOOLS FOR SYSTEMS DEVELOPMENT

COMPUTER-AIDED SYSTEMS ENGINEERING TECHNOLOGY

Computer-aided system engineering (CASE) is the application of computer technology to systems development activities, techniques, and methodologies. CASE tools are programs (software) that automate or support one or more phases of a system development life cycle. The technology is intended to accelerate the process of developing systems and to improve the quality of the resulting systems.

THE HISTORY AND EVOLUTION OF CASE TECHNOLOGY

The history of CASE dates back to the early to mid-1970s. The ISDOS project, under the direction of Dr. Daniel Teichrowe at the University of Michigan, developed a language called *Problem Statement Language (PSL)* for describing user problem and solution requirements for an information system into a computerized dictionary. A companion product, called *Problem Statement Analyzer (PSA),* was created to analyze the problem and requirement statement for completeness and consistency. The real breakthrough came with the advent of the IBM personal computer. Not long thereafter, in 1984, an upstart company called Index Technology (now known as INTERSOLV) created a PC software tool called Excelerator. Its success established the CASE acronym and industry. Today, hundreds of CASE products are available to various systems developers. It is important to realize that modern CASE technology is still very young, but the technology is improving at a staggering rate. New tools are emerging monthly. The best existing products are improving annually.

THE FRAMEWORK OF THE CASE TOOL

CASE framework is based on the following popular terminology:

- The term *upper-CASE* describes tools that automate or support the "upper," or front-end, phases of the systems development life cycle: systems planning, system analysis, and general systems.
- The term *lower-CASE* describes tools that automate or support the "lower," or back-end, phases of the life cycle: detailed systems design, systems implementation, and systems support.
- The term *cross life cycle CASE* refers to tools that support activities across the entire life cycle. These include activities such as project management and estimation.

CASE Tools for Systems Planning (Upper-CASE)

Upper-CASE tools for systems planning are intended to help analysts and consultants capture, store, organize, and analyze models of the business. These models and their evaluation help the information systems planners define and prioritize the following:

- Business strategies that are being (or will be) implemented; complementary information systems and information technology strategies to be implemented
- Databases that need to be developed
- Networks that need to be developed
- Applications that need to be developed around the databases and networks

CASE Tools for System Analysis and Design (Upper-CASE)

Upper-CASE tools for system analysis and design are intended to help system analysts better express users' requirements, propose design solutions, and analyze the information for consistency, completeness, and integrity. This information helps analysts to accomplish the following:

- Define project scope and system boundaries
- Model and describe the current information system (if required in the methodology)
- Model and describe the users' business requirements for a new information system
- Prototype requirements for the purpose of discovery or verification
- Design a computer-based information system that will fulfill users' business requirements
- Prototype specific design components (such as screens and reports) for the purpose of verification and ease of use

CASE Tools for Systems Design and Implementation (Lower-CASE)

Lower-CASE tools for detailed design and systems implementation are intended to help designers and programmers more quickly generate applications software. This includes the following:

- Helping programmers more quickly test and debug their program code
- Helping programmers or analysts to automatically generate a program code from analysis and design specifications
- Helping designers and programmers to design and automatically generate special or detailed system design components like screens and databases
- Automatically generating complete application code from analysis and design specifications

CASE Tools for Systems Support (More Lower-CASE)

Lower-CASE tools support the maintenance activities for production information systems. For systems support, these tools are intended to help analysts, designers, and programmers react to inevitable, ever-changing business and technical environments, including the following:

- Helping programmers restructure existing or old program code to be more maintainable
- Helping programmers and analysts react to changing user requirements
- Helping analysts and programmers re-engineer programs to accommodate newer technology (such as changing the "preferred" database management system)
- Helping analysts and programmers determine when the costs of maintaining a system exceed the benefits of maintaining the system (in other words, "Is it time to start over?")
- Helping analysts recover any reusable information from obsolete programs as a prelude to taking that information back to upper-CASE tools and redeveloping a major, new information system

CASE Tools that Support Cross Life Cycle Activities

A wide variety of CASE tools support activities across the entire system development life cycle.

Project management is one cross life cycle activity common to most projects. A wide variety of project management software packages exist, because numerous professions use them. Project management tools help managers plan, schedule, report on, and manage their projects and resources. But some project management tools have crossed into CASE by virtue of their interfaces to other CASE tools.

One growing category of cross life cycle CASE technology is that of *process managers*. Process management software provides the necessary online guidance and expertise. The best process managers, such as Rapid System Development's

Hyper Analyst, are actually capable of invoking (starting) CASE tools at appropriate times in the methodology.

Another category of cross life cycle CASE is *estimation*. Attempting to accurately assess the size of a project (or system) and then to estimate the time and cost to complete the project is very difficult. But now how do you estimate size and cost? *Function points* is a formal, mathematically based technique.

Yet another cross life cycle activity is *documentation*. The deployment of CASE technology creates a wealth of documentation. Tools like KnowledgeWare's ADW/DOC allow you to design a custom work product or deliverable, and then automatically retrieves the appropriate diagrams, specifications, or information. It can even incorporate word processing and spreadsheet files.

THE ARCHITECTURE OF THE CASE TOOL

The center of CASE tool architecture is a database called a *repository*, which is a developer's database. Here the developers can store diagrams, descriptions, specifications, applications programs, and any other working by-products of systems development. Synonyms include design database, dictionary, and encyclopedia. Most first-generation CASE tools had stand-alone, proprietary repositories. A CASE tool could read and write only from its own repository. Second-generation CASE tools were frequently built around a shared repository. These tools not only share a repository; they make the workbenches highly dependent on one another.

FACILITIES AND FUNCTIONS

To use a repository, we obviously need input and output facilities as follows:

- *Graphic facilities* are used to diagram or model information systems using various techniques.
- *Description facilities* are used to record, delete, edit, and output non-graphical information and specifications.
- *Prototyping facilities* are used to analyze or design components such as inputs, outputs, screens, or forms.
- *Inquiry and reporting facilities* are used to extract information and specifications out of the repository. They can support simple inquiries such as, "Tell me about the input called ORDER," or more complex inquiries such as, "Provide me a listing of every input or file that contains any field that includes a two-character date field."
- *Quality assurance facilities* analyze graphs, descriptions, and/or prototypes for consistency, completeness, and conformance to generally accepted "rules" of systems development.
- *Decision support facilities* analyze information in the repository to provide support for decisions.
- *Documentation facilities* are used to assemble graphs, repository descriptions, prototypes, and quality assurance reports into formal documents or deliverables that can be reviewed by project participants.

- *Transform facilities* automate or assist the transformation of something into another form.
- *Generators* automatically translate user requirements and/or technical designs into working applications and programs.
- *Data-sharing facilities* provide export and import repository information between different local repositories of the same CASE tool.
- *Security and version control facilities* maintain the integrity of repository information.
- *Housekeeping facilities* establish user accounts, project directories, user privileges, tool defaults and preferences, backup and recovery, and so forth.

THE BENEFITS OF THE CASE TOOL

- *Increased productivity.* CASE automates many of the most tedious clerical activities of developers. It reduces the time needed to complete many tasks, especially those involving diagramming and associated specifications.
- *Improved quality.* CASE can eliminate or substantially reduce omissions and defects that would prove very costly to correct during system implementation or support.
- *Better documentation.* An early benefit of CASE is higher-quality documentation. CASE tools also make it easier to maintain documentation.
- *Reduced lifetime maintenance.* The net benefit of higher-quality systems and better documentation should be reduced costs and effort required for maintaining systems. This, in turn, creates more time and resources for new systems development.

11 Accounting Information Systems and Packages

This chapter discusses several software applications of particular interest to accountants. The discussion includes the major players in the area and some important features to look for when considering a particular type of software.

Many factors must be weighed when selecting a computer software package. Besides determining the software features currently needed and required in the future, the buyer must have a thorough understanding of the firm's existing system and whether proposed software will integrate with all areas of that system and the business.

Some of the basic considerations include features and capabilities, compatibility and integration, ease of customization, ease of use, written documentation and technical support, price, and vendor's reputation and stability.

In the DOS world, vendors tried to top each other by constantly enhancing features. With the advent of Windows, they compete by concentrating on improving integration and customization. With Windows interfaces, data can more easily be linked and exchanged with all types of applications, such as spreadsheets, databases, and even e-mail. Thus, compatibility with existing systems and data is an extremely important consideration when selecting new software. Likewise, customization of input screens and reports to conform to a firm's needs can more easily be done, and capabilities vary between packages.

Although the price of a system is an important consideration, it should never be the deciding factor. Often, the cost of software is relatively insignificant when compared to the costs of implementation, training, ongoing maintenance, and support. Training costs can be reduced if the program has good context-sensitive online help. Installation will be much simpler if the program has a checklist or "wizard" that actually walks the user through the installation procedure.

Before buying any package, try calling the customer support department of the vendor. Customer support can give you detailed information about the features of a package. Vendors typically offer a demo or a free or low-cost trial of their computer software product. You might also get information about specials or discounts available to professionals such as practicing accountants.

BENEFITS OF WINDOWS INTERFACE

Accountants have been slow to migrate to the Windows interface. However, that movement has been accelerating, and a growing number of vendors offer software with a Windows interface. In fact, most new software packages are Windows-based and provide a graphical representation of documents such as the check, purchase order, invoice, and reports in a WYSIWYG (what you see is what you get) format.

The Windows environment makes it easy to format reports exactly as the user wants them to look. An important advantage of the Windows interface is the ability to perform "event-driven" input. In a typical DOS system, one must navigate through an inflexible menu system and, before entering into another operation, one must back out of the old operation. In Windows, you can freely and much more efficiently move among activities as needed, thus input is "event-driven."

With Windows, one can have several applications, as well as documents, open on the desktop and active at the same time. Thus, you can transport or move data among them much more readily. As indicated, the ability to easily transfer data between applications has increased the need to make sure that a software purchase is compatible with, and can integrate with, your current programs and applications.

Essentially a standard feature in a Windows-based product is the ability to *drill down* to the detail level of on-screen reports. Using a mouse, you can click on an item or amount in a report. This opens up (called *drilling down*) the underlying source document for this report. For even more detail, you can further drill down on this report. This process can be continued until you reach the bottom level transaction. For example, in an accounts receivable aging schedule, you can click or drill down to get a list of customers whose accounts are more than 90 days old. You can then further click on a specific customer and find other information, such as the customer's credit limit and information about other outstanding invoices and transactions.

ACCOUNTING SOFTWARE

The fundamental task of accounting software is to automate the routine chore of entering and posting accounting transactions. This information is organized in an electronic format so as to produce financial statements and can be accessed immediately to assist in the management of the firm.

An accounting software package consists of a series of highly integrated modules. Each module corresponds to a specific accounting function (e.g., payroll, accounts receivable, and accounts payable). In an integrated system, after the details of the transaction are entered in one of the modules, the chart of accounts from the general ledger is "read." The transaction is then automatically posted to the accounts in the general ledger. For example, when a sale on account is entered in the accounts receivable module, a debit is automatically made to the accounts receivable account in the general ledger and an offsetting credit made to the general ledger sales account.

Synex Systems' F9 software does financial reporting including variance and ratio analysis. Activity Financial's Activity package also prepares financial statements.

In Peachtree Accounting, the user also has the ability to enter data or perform tasks within a module by use of navigation aids. These aids, which are a graphical representation of the task flow of a module, can appear on the bottom of each screen. For example, in the navigation aid for payables, the user can directly enter purchases or record payments, print checks, and maintain vendor information and the general ledger.

MODULE DESCRIPTIONS

The basic features typically required by a firm, and often integrated in an accounting software package, include general ledger, accounts receivable and invoicing accounts payable and purchase order processing, inventory, payroll, job costing, and fixed assets.

General Ledger

The general ledger is the heart of the accounting system. It contains the chart of accounts of the business. A general ledger module should contain a sample chart of accounts that can be customized to a particular business. In addition, it should contain predefined reports that support budget data and prior year comparisons that can be tailored to a firm's specific needs. Other essential features include the capability to generate automatic reversing and recurring journal entries, having at least 13 periods open at one time, and the ability to make prior period adjustments or post entries to another year without closing the current year.

Accounts Receivable and Invoicing

The accounts receivable and invoicing functions are often combined in the same module. This module allows you to enter sales data and permits extensive sales analysis. It provides customer receivables management by tracking customers' balances and generates invoices and/or monthly statements, as well as aging reports. It should allow for setting up credit limits for each customer, provide for flexible billing options, and offer the ability to apply partial payments to specific invoices or to the oldest balance. For faster processing, online inquiry should show the complete customer record at a glance, including balances and unpaid invoices, and it should allow you to make changes *on the fly*.

Accounts Payable and Purchase Order Processing

Accounts payable and purchase order processing can also be combined in a single module. The module tracks obligations to vendors and determines a best payments schedule, prints checks, and provides for the distribution to accounts. It should allow for enhanced management of order processing by tracking orders from the start to the receipt of goods. It should be able to detect supply problems and thus permit early planning for alternate sources. To analyze vendor performance, it must track the complete purchase and delivery history of vendors and allow for easy access to this information.

Inventory

This module automatically tracks inventory as purchases or sales are made and maintains cost and price data for each inventory item. In an integrated system, the inventory main file, which stores the product's number, is checked when a sales invoice is created in the accounts receivable module. If sufficient inventory is on hand, the amount of the sale is reduced from the balance. Likewise, when inventory is purchased, the inventory quantity is automatically increased. The module should help improve inventory management by alerting the user when it is time to reorder, identifying slow moving items and analyzing performance by item and category.

Payroll

The payroll module maintains default information for each employee (e.g., rate of pay and income tax withholding information). The module calculates the wages to be paid, prints checks, and keeps track of deductions, sick and vacation days, and other such information. It maintains information for government reporting (e.g., 941, W-2, unemployment, and state tax forms). For cost control, it should be able to provide for expense distribution or integrate with a costing module.

Job Costing

A job costing module allows you to track and report on the costs, income, and profitability of individual jobs or projects. This is done by assigning a job ID number to purchases, sales, and employee hours. A job cost module should provide for an accurate audit trail, detailed income, expenses and committed costs, as well as the tracking of other user-defined categories. For example, Maxwell Business Systems' JAMIS is a job costing accounting package that tracks costs by project, contract, or organization over multiple years.

Fixed Assets

Fixed assets usually represent a significant investment by a firm, so it is essential to keep track of them—but extremely tedious to do so. Tracking fixed assets and the repetitive calculation of depreciation is well suited for he computer. Most accounting software packages include a fixed asset module or capabilities to control fixed assets. It is also possible to purchase dedicated stand-alone fixed asset packages.

Fixed asset software can handle large amounts of data and a variety of depreciation methods for financial accounting and tax purposes. It should be able to maintain detailed information about each asset, including a description of the asset, its location, date placed in service, and estimated useful life. It should also be able to track additions and disposal as well as basis adjustments. An example of a fixed asset package is Decision Support Technology's BASSETS Fixed Asset System.

Before purchasing an accounting package, check if it has a fixed asset module, or capabilities sufficient for your needs. If not, ask if the vendor produces a stand-alone version, or would recommend a third party vendor. Before purchasing a stand-alone fixed asset software package, make sure that it allows for easy sharing of information with your general ledger, tax packages, and other data repositories.

MARKET LEADERS

There are a number of accounting software products. They can conveniently be categorized as (a) low-end, (b) mid-level, and (c) high-end packages.

In a May 1996 article in the *Journal of Accountancy*, the best low-end packages were reviewed. Not too long ago, if an accounting package cost less than a few thousand dollars, it would have very few features and would not be recommended to a client. However, the market has changed significantly. Figure 11.1 shows seven low-end products reviewed in the May 1996 article. They all cost about $250 or less, are all Windows-based, and have significant features and power.

Each year CIS, Inc. evaluates accounting software packages that have proven to be popular, versatile, in widespread use, and possessing solid vendor support. Listed in the figure are the systems that were reviewed in the fall 1995 edition. They can be considered mid-level packages.

The February 1996 issue of CFO magazine contains a discussion of high-end accounting software. This category is extremely young, and the marketplace is very chaotic. Thus, only the top three products are listed in the figure. R/3 from SAP A.G. of Walldorf, Germany is the most dominant player in the marketplace. The next two players are far behind. The price range for each of these products is over $1 million.

WRITE-UP SOFTWARE

With the development of easy-to-use and inexpensive accounting software, many companies who previously relied on CPAs to keep their books are doing it themselves. CPA firms can counter this trend with dedicated write-up software that is easy-to-use and provides more features so as to add value to their write-up services.

Write-up software should allow you to do more than just record transactions. One of the biggest features to look for is the ability to easily create an array of printouts and reports that a client might need. This includes being able to link and transfer data from other software packages and applications.

Another important feature is the ability to customize the input screen so that it is consistent with the layout of the client's source documents, thereby reducing unneeded keystrokes. Easy setup is another means to reduce the cost of write-up service. The package should contain sample company data and should provide the ability to copy common information and make changes to default information included in the setup *on the fly*.

MAJOR PLAYERS

There are many products in the write-up area. Recently, 8 write-up products were reviewed by *Accounting Today* and 16 by *Accounting Technology*. Figure 11.2 lists

Low-End

DacEasy Accounting &
  Payroll
DacEasy
800-322-3279

**Mind Your Own Business
  Accounting**
BEST!WARE
800-322-6962

One-Write Plus
NEBS Software
800-388-8000

Simply Accounting
4 Home Productions
800-733-5445

Mid-Level

ABS
American Business Systems
800-356-4034

AccountMate Premiere
SourceMate
800-877-8896

**Peachtree Accounting for
  Windows**
Peachtree Software
800-228-0068

Profit
Great Plains
800-926-8962

QuickBooks for Windows
Intuit
800-624-8742

Accounting Visdion/32
Intellisoft
800-933-4889

ACCPAC 2000
Computer Associates
408-432-1764

ACCPAC Plus
Computer Associates
408-432-1764

Avista
Avista Software
404-564-8000

BusinessWorks for Windows
State of the Art
800-854-3415

**CYMA Professional
  Accounting Series**
CYMA Software
800-292-2962

Great Plains Accounting
Great Plains Software
800-456-0025

Great Plains Dynamics
Great Plains Software
800-456-0025

LIBRA Accounting
Libra Software
800-453-3827

Maeola
Maeola Software
800-468-0834

MAS 90
State of the Art
800-854-9415

Open Systems
Open Systems Software
800-328-2276

Platinum
Platinum Software
800-999-1809

RealWorld
RealWorld Software
800-678-6336

SBT Professional
SBT
800-944-1000

Solomon III Btrieve
Solomon Software
800-476-5666

Solomon IV
Solomon Software
800-476-5666

SouthWare
SouthWare Software
800-547-4179

High-End

R/3 System
SAP America
610-725-4500

Oracle Applications
Oracle
800-ORACLE1

PeopleSoft
PeopleSoft
800-947-7743

FIGURE 11.1 Accounting software.

five products included in both reviews. Most products in this area are DOS based.
It can be argued that a DOS system is better than a Windows system for write-up—a
very intensive data entry application. Due to all the features of a Windows product,
repetitive data entry can be slower as compared to a DOS product. However, there's
no telling what will happen in the future, and most development money is being
spent in the Windows environment.

Datawrite Client Accounting	PDS Client Accounting	Write-Up Solutions II
SCS/Compute	Professional Design Systems,	Creative Solutions
800-326-1040	Inc.	800-968-8900
	800-628-9802	
Peachtree Client Write-Up	**Write-Up Plus**	
Peachtree Software	UniLink	
800-228-0068	800-456-8321	

FIGURE 11.2 Write-up software.

TAX PREPARATION SOFTWARE

Computer technology has had a significant impact on the way tax returns are prepared. Computerized tax return preparation lets the user prepare a return quickly and accurately, and it allows the user to quickly analyze different tax planning strategies. Some software packages have built-in tools for tax research and allow for the electronic filing of tax returns. This software also lets the user easily do "what-if" planning and then quickly makes all the necessary changes. Furthermore, data can be imported directly from accounting packages or electronic spreadsheets into tax preparation software.

While tax preparation software can help with tax planning, one should consider a dedicated tax research package for serious tax research. Most CD-based tax services can effectively replace the printed version of tax services. A major advantage of using CD-based tax services is having the ability to do electronic keyword searches. This can greatly facilitate the tax research process and make it much more efficient. In addition, it is easier to maintain and store all this information on a CD, thereby saving a good deal of library storage space.

The industry is going through rapid and significant changes in terms of features and key players in the marketplace. As with other software, improvements are continuous. One of the major improvements in the last few years has been the introduction of Windows versions of products. The switch to Windows seems to have been resisted and has been slow in starting. However, as more people upgrade their hardware, the switch to Windows will accelerate further, and it will inevitably become the platform of choice.

The tax software industry is fiercely competitive and continues to go through consolidations and shakeouts. Thus, it makes sense to deal with the larger, better known vendors whose products are more likely to be supported in the future.

MARKET LEADERS

The leading tax software packages can be categorized into the following segments:

Lower-cost alternatives. The price for this category is generally under $1,000. In spite of their low price, their features compare favorably with the higher-priced products. The five products included in this category are listed in Figure 11.3.

Lower-Cost Alternatives	Digitax	TaxWorks
	Cold River Software Inc.	Laser Systems
	800-432-1065	801-552-8800
ProSeries		
Intuit	**Lacerte Software**	**Nax Machine**
800-934-1040	**Corporation**	SCS/Compute Inc.
	800-765-7777	
Tax/Pack Professional		**Ultra Tax**
Alpine Data Inc.	**LMS/Tax**	Creative Solutions Inc.
800-525-1040	SCS/Compute Inc.	800-968-8900
	800-488-0779	
Tax Relief		**High-End**
Micro Vision Software	**Package EX**	
800-829-7354	ExacTax Inc.	
	800-352-3638	**A-Plus-Tax**
TAX$IMPLE		Arthur Andersen
TAX$IMPLE	**Pencil Pushers Tax Software**	800-872-1040
800-323-2662	Damirus Corp.	
	800-370-2500	**Go System & EasyGo**
Veritax		CLR/Fast-Tax
Cold River Software	**Professional Tax System**	800-327-8829
800-837-4829	Tax and Accounting Software	
	Corp. (TAASC)	**Prosystem fx**
Mainstream	918-493-6500	CCH Inc.
		800-457-7639
	RAM	
CPASoftware	RAM Software Inc.	
CPA Software	800-888-6217	
904-434-2685		

FIGURE 11.3 Tax software.

Mainstream. These packages are suitable for mainstream tax practices. They are generally easy to use and learn but are not intended to handle every situation that may arise. The packages in this category are generally more powerful than those in the lower-cost category.

High-end. This group is marketed for use by multistate regional and national firms. These packages are able to handle the most complex returns and track their progress through large offices.

AUDIT SOFTWARE

Audit software is used by accountants to perform audits efficiently and effectively. Software audit tools include automated workpapers, data extraction software, and trial balance software.

Products such as APG (Audit Program Generator) by the American Institute of Certified Public Accountants (AICPA) and the optional add-on modules allow you to prepare customized audit programs. It eliminates the photocopying, cutting, and pasting usually required when creating the audit program and guides users through the engagement.

Data extraction software, such as IDEA (Interactive Data Extraction and Analysis), also by the AICPA, allows auditors to access clients' files for audit testing. The auditor can either access the client's live data or obtain a copy of the company's data files on tape or disk. Data extraction software allows the auditor to audit *through the computer.* The auditor can, for example, select a sample of accounts receivables for confirmations or perform analytical reviews and do ratio analysis. Transactions may be compared to predetermined criteria. Linton Shafer's Audit Sampling Software packages select random numbers and dates. It handles multiple ranges and evaluates results, and it performs compliance and substantive testing.

Trial Balance software, such as the AICPA's ATB (Accountant's Trial Balance), helps the auditor organize client's general ledger balances into a working trial balance. The auditor can then perform adjustments and update account balances. The calculation of financial ratios is extremely simple with trial balance software. This type of software aids in the preparation of financial statements. While trial balance software is designed primarily for audits, it can be used instead of write-up software for compilation and review services.

Price Waterhouse Researcher is an accounting, auditing, and reporting research system on a single CD-ROM. Equivalent to a 100,000 page library, PW Researcher includes generally accepted accounting principles (GAAP), generally accepted auditing standards (GAAS), Securities and Exchange Commission (SEC) regulations, and U.S. Cost Accounting Standards. The information on the CD includes American Institute of CPAs (AICPA), Financial Accounting Standards Board (FASB), SEC, and Emerging Issues Task Force (EITF) publications, along with Price Waterhouse guidance, analysis, and interpretations. The CD is updated quarterly and also includes international accounting and auditing standards. The easy-to-use database may be searched using a key word or phrase. Users may make personal notes and markers. The author highly recommends this excellent product.

Price Waterhouse TeamMate is an electronic working paper system that helps automate the working paper preparation, review, reporting, and storage process. It includes standard and free-form schedule templates, an automatic tick mark system, and a powerful cross-referencing capability. PW TeamMate also integrates popular spreadsheet, word processing, and imaging software. There are hypertext links between documents and applications, enabling the auditor to jump backward through related numbers in reports or spreadsheets to the original data. The search, cross-referencing, and retrieval capabilities allow the auditor to automatically correct errors in all affected documents. The working paper review features include automatic exception reporting, a working paper navigation system, and text and voice annotation. For example, the auditor can obtain a directory of all review notes pertaining to a document. The reporting features include key audit point summarization, report drafting, audit status reports, and time summaries. Financial data is quickly accessed by the sorting and filtering tools. A standard index provides a branch and node system for all papers. There is a simultaneous multi-user feature so auditors/reviewers can work with the same document set, even if they are working in various locations. PW TeamMate improves the quality, productivity, and effectiveness of the auditors' work.

Price Waterhouse Controls facilitates the documentation, evaluation, and testing of internal controls. The software expedites the collection and summarization of controls in place, appraises their effectiveness, and identifies areas of risk exposure. PW Controls can be used by auditors to document particular business processes. Control weaknesses are identified with resultant recommendations for improvement. The auditor can view control effectiveness at different levels within the company (e.g., by activity, by business unit). A comparison and analysis may be made of the relative control performance of different operating units.

Price Waterhouse Chekhov is a software package that automates the completion of checklists.

Figure 11.4 contains a number of audit software packages. Each contains one or more features previously discussed.

SPREADSHEETS

More than any other product, the electronic spreadsheet has made the capabilities of microcomputers evident to the business community. An electronic spreadsheet allows the user to work with data in a huge number of rows and columns. The user works with this data in a columnar spreadsheet, a format familiar to accountants. A big advantage of the spreadsheet is that it eliminates the need to perform manual calculations and can perform powerful computer-aided operations.

The spreadsheet has become a valuable tool in business planning, since it permits the user to perform "what-if" scenarios. Inputs can be continuously changed, and the results will automatically be recalculated throughout the spreadsheet. Thus, the effect of alternative decisions is easily determined and planning greatly facilitated. The use of templates is another important feature of spreadsheets. Templates provide the format and contain the formulas that are used to repeatedly solve various business applications. Since one doesn't have to be a programmer to construct a template, all firms can now more easily use the vast power of the computer to help make better decisions in the management of a firm.

ACE for Windows	ATB	IDEA
CLR Professional Software	AICPA	AICPA
800-241-3306	800-862-4272	800-862-4272
ACL	AuditVision	Perfect Balance
ACL Software	Peer Software	PPC
604-669-4225	800-613-2331	800-323-8724
APG	CA-PanAudit Plus/PC	Workpapers Plus
AICPA	Computer Associates	Cogent Technologies
800-862-4272	800-225-5224	717-283-2257
	GuideWare	
	PPC	
	800-323-8724	

FIGURE 11.4 Audit software.

MAJOR PLAYERS AND SELECTION CONSIDERATIONS

The chief players in the spreadsheet field have been reduced to three:

- Lotus 1-2-3, from IBM Corp.
- Microsoft Excel, from Microsoft Corp.
- Quattro Pro, from Corel

In actuality, all the players have the same basic features. Although a particular feature may currently be lacking in a specific spreadsheet, that feature may very well be included in the next upgrade of that product. Therefore, the decision of which product to buy should not be based primarily on features. More importantly, be certain the planned spreadsheet supports, and is compatible with, the major applications of your business. Thus, make sure that the spreadsheet can directly access your databases and that any macros or templates that have already been developed are compatible with the proposed acquisition.

MANAGING RISK USING FUZZY ANALYSIS

A unique spreadsheet, FuziCalc, takes the computational complexity out of fuzzy arithmetic. This spreadsheet allows us to easily incorporate ranges or intervals in our analysis and assign different weights to the ranges. Implicit in any type of decision analysis is the assumption that judgmental inputs can be accurately repre-sented by a single precise number. However, it generally is not possible to quantify judgment with such precision. Most of the traditional tools for decision analysis are *crisp*. By *crisp* we mean that the tools require precise inputs. In contrast, most of the problems facing managers are *fuzzy*, vague, or imprecise. Traditionally, managers have incorporated imprecision in their analysis through probability theory. An alter-nate framework, based on the fuzzy set theory, allows imprecision in data analysis It allows the decision maker to benefit from the structure of quantitative decision analysis without forcing the user to provide very precise numerical inputs

From a practical perspective, fuzzy analysis is easy to do using the FuziCalc spreadsheet. There are no new techniques to learn. Anyone familiar with a conven-tional spreadsheet can quickly adapt to the FuziCalc spreadsheet. All fuzzy data can be represented by "belief graphs." Belief graphs are the heart of the FuziCalc spreadsheet. Fuzzy data inputs are made using belief graphs. The simplest way to represent a fuzzy number is to use a triangular shape. A minimum of three points are required to represent any fuzzy number. A triangular fuzzy number has many practical applications. To construct a triangular fuzzy number of sales price, we need to determine the highest, the most likely, and the lowest sales price. Let's assume our estimates for the highest, the most likely, and the lowest sales price are $35, $25, and $20, respectively. A belief graph of this fuzzy triangular number can then be constructed as shown in Figure 11.5.

Let's contrast the fuzzy number in Figure 11.5 with the crisp number 25 in Figure 11.6. A crisp number does not have a range of values; its belief graph is a straight line.

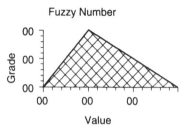

FIGURE 11.5 Belief graph of fuzzy triangular number.

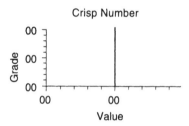

FIGURE 11.6 Belief graph of crisp number.

FuziCalc provides five common shapes to represent fuzzy data. The five shapes from FuziCalc's Gallery are shown in Figure 11.7.

The triangular shape was discussed earlier; its use is appropriate when the user has a single best estimate of the most likely value and can specify the endpoints of the range. Sometimes it is not possible for the user to give one best estimate of the most likely value. A trapezoidal fuzzy number would be most appropriate when only a range of most likely values can be given. The user may select the multipeaked shape to represent fuzzy numbers where the low and high values are more likely than the middle values. The tent shape is most appropriate where all of the values in the range have a high possibility of occurring. The rocket shape might be used when the user believes a wide range exists, but a narrow range within it has a much better possibility. The five shapes will be sufficient for the needs of most users. However, FuziCalc allows users to easily alter the shape to represent any fuzzy number.

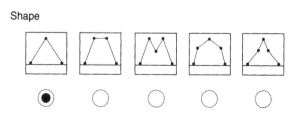

FIGURE 11.7 Common shapes of fuzzy data.

It is possible to add, subtract, multiply, and divide fuzzy numbers just like regular *crisp* numbers. The advantage of using the FuziCalc spreadsheet is that users don't need to concern themselves with the complex underlying computations.

FuziCalc's primary strength is in modeling under uncertainty. Beyond that, FuziCalc offers little to spreadsheet users. As a spreadsheet, FuziCalc offers only the very basic features. Users of conventional spreadsheets might even find working in FuziCalc a little frustrating. Many of the features that one is accustomed to in conventional spreadsheets are missing in FuziCalc. Thus, it would be used to supplement, rather than to replace, a conventional spreadsheet. FuziCalc is sold by FuziWare, Inc., 800-472-6183.

ACTIVITY-BASED COSTING SOFTWARE

An activity-based costing (ABC) system accumulates costs on the basis of production or service activities at a firm. Basically, it assigns costs by activity and links them to specific products. It is argued that the resulting cost data is much more realistic and precise as compared to the data obtained from a traditional costing system. Aided by computer software designed for ABC, the management accountant can more easily and accurately accumulate cost information and perform "what-if" testing. With this data, management is in a better position to evaluate and make decisions regarding its operations and products. There is a good deal of software that the management accountant can use to aid in accumulating cost data. Some software packages are actually spreadsheet applications; others are modules of mainframe packages. The winter 1994 issue of the *Journal of Cost Management* reviewed nine cost management software packages. All these packages are for use on a personal computer, and most were designed for activity-based costing or activity-based management. Figure 11.8 separates these packages into two categories: those developed by independent vendors and those supported or developed by a big-six CPA firm. It should be noted that some products include consulting support as part of the overall package.

Price Waterhouse's ACTIVA is a comprehensive activity-based costing (ABC), profitability, and performance management software tool. Its features and capabilities include budgeting and planning, product costing and pricing, cost management and

Independent Vendors	QUOTE-A-PROFIT	ACTIVA
	Manufacturing Management	Price Waterhouse
	Systems, Inc.	314-425-0500
NetProphet	216-428-4068	
Sapling Software		**The Profit Manager Series**
416-678-1661	**Big-Six CPA Firms**	KPMG Peat Marwick
		313-983-0321
CMS-PC		
ICMS	**TR/ACM**	**ABCost Manager**
817-633-2873	Deloitte & Touche	Coopers & Lybrand
	617-261-8615	312-701-5783

FIGURE 11.8 ABC software.

analysis, decision support, process improvement, activity-based management, and variance determination and evaluation. Developed using state-of-the art client/server technology, its additional features include capital investment analysis, production sourcing, distribution logistics, and foreign currency appraisal. ACTIVA aids in measuring the profitability by customer, product, service, market, process, and distribution channel. ACTIVA can support many users conducting diverse applications in multiple locations worldwide. The software contain sophisticated security features.

Lead Software's Activity Analyzer assigns activities to cost objects and calculates by activity costs and profitability. Profitability may be determined by product, service, customer, and territory. Armstrong Laing's Hyper ABC is a multidimensional, multiperiod activity-based management system. Sapling Software's Net Prophet combines activity-based costing and management, process view analysis, budgeting, capacity planning, and constraint checking.

ABC helps in determining what a product or process should cost, areas of possible cost reduction, and value-added vs. nonvalue-added aspects. Activity-based costing is beneficial in appraising value-chain functions. Furthermore, costs are a function of their consumption factors such as number of employees, units produced, labor hours, and so on.

12 Financial Management Information Systems and Packages

Finance has been an important functional area for virtually all types of organizations. The finance area monitors cash flow and profitability. Well conceived financial information systems are capable of providing financial managers with timely information, which is vital to success in today's competitive global economy. History has witnessed the results of poor financial decisions. Banks and savings institutions have gone into bankruptcy because of bad decisions and unfavorable economic conditions. Companies with too much debt and leverage have also gone bankrupt. On the contrary, good financial decisions have resulted in growing and prosperous organizations.

A financial management information system provides financial information to all financial managers within an organization. Specifically, the financial MIS assists the financial manager in performing required responsibilities, which include the following:

- Financial analysis and planning—analyzing historical and current financial activity and determining the proper amount of funds to employ in the firm; that is, designating the size of the firm and its rate of growth.
- Investment decisions—allocating funds to specific assets (things owned). The financial manager makes decisions regarding the mix and type of assets acquired as well as modification or replacement of assets.
- Financing and capital structure decisions—projecting future financial needs and raising funds on favorable terms; that is, determining the nature of the company's liabilities (obligations). For instance, should funds be obtained from short-term or long-term sources?
- Management of financial resources—monitoring and controlling the use of funds over time and managing cash, receivables, and inventory to accomplish higher returns without undue risk.

Figure 12.1 shows the inputs, function-specific subsystems, and outputs of a financial MIS.

Inputs	Subsystems	Outputs
Strategic goals	Financial forecasting	Financial forecasts
Transaction processing system	Financial data from departments (profit/loss and costing)	Funds management
Internal accounting		Financial budget planning and control
External sources	Financial intelligence	

FIGURE 12.1 Overview of a financial MIS.

INPUTS TO THE FINANCIAL MANAGEMENT INFORMATION SYSTEM

Decisions supported by the financial MIS require diverse information needs. The sources, both internal and external, are briefly discussed below.

CORPORATE STRATEGIC GOALS AND POLICIES

The strategic plan covers major financial goals and targets. Earnings growth, and loan ratios, and expected returns are some of the measures that can be incorporated in the strategic plan. The plan often projects financial needs three to five years down the road. More specific information needs, such as expected financing needs, the return on investment (ROI) for various projects, and desired debt-to-equity ratios, evolve directly from the strategic plan.

THE TRANSACTION PROCESSING SYSTEM

Important financial information is captured by a number of internal accounting systems. One is the *order entry system,* which enters the orders into the accounting system. Another is the *billing system,* which sends bills or invoices to customers. A third is the *account receivable system,* which collects the funds. Other key financial information is also collected from almost every transaction processing application—payroll, inventory control, accounts payable, and general ledger. Many financial reports are based on payroll costs, the investment in inventory, total sales over time, the amount of money paid to suppliers, the total amount owed to the company from customers, and detailed accounting data.

EXTERNAL SOURCES

Information from and about the competition can be critical to financial decision making. Annual reports and financial statements from competitors and general news items and reports can be incorporated into MIS reports to provide units of measure or as a basis of comparison. Government agencies also provide important economic and financial information. Inflation, consumer price indexes, new housing starts, and leading economic indicators can help a company plan for future economic conditions. In addition, important tax laws and financial reporting requirements can also be reflected in the financial MIS.

FINANCIAL MIS SUBSYSTEMS AND OUTPUTS

Financial decisions are typically based on information generated from the accounting system. Depending on the organization and its needs, the financial MIS can include both internal and external systems that assist in acquiring, using, and controlling cash, funds, and other financial resources. The financial subsystems, discussed below, include financial forecasting, profit/loss and costing, and financial intelligence systems. Each subsystem interacts with the transaction processing system in a specialized, functionally oriented way and has informational outputs that assist financial managers in making better decisions. The outputs are financial forecasts, management of funds reports, financial budgets and performance reports such as variance analysis used for control purposes.

FINANCIAL FORECASTING

Financial forecasting, the process of making predictions on the future growth of products or the organization as a whole, is based on projected business activity. For example, expected sales of goods and services can be converted into expected revenues and costs. The sales price per unit and production cost factors can be multiplied by the number of units expected to be sold to arrive at a forecast value for revenues and costs. Fixed costs such as insurance, rent, and office overhead are estimated and used to determine expected net profits on a monthly, quarterly, or yearly basis. These estimates are then incorporated into the financial MIS. The financial forecasting subsystem relies on input from another functional subsystem (namely, the marketing forecasting system) to determine projected revenues.

Having an estimate of future cash flows can be one of the first steps for sound financial management. Financial managers and executives use this valuable information to project future cash needs. For instance, an organization's managers will know in advance that, in some months, additional cash might be required, while in other months excess cash will have to be invested. Improperly managed cash flow is one of the major causes of business failure and bankruptcy. Financial forecasting can help financial executives avoid cash-flow problems by predicting cash-flow needs.

PROFIT/LOSS AND COST SYSTEMS

Two specialized financial functional systems are profit/loss and cost systems. Revenue and expense data for various departments are captured by the transaction processing system (TPS) and become a primary internal source of financial information. Many departments within an organization are *profit centers,* which means that they track total expenses, revenues, and net profits. An investment division of a large insurance or credit card company is an example of a profit center. Other departments may be *revenue centers,* which are divisions within the company that primarily track sales or revenues, such as a marketing or sales department. Still other departments may be *cost centers,* which are divisions within a company that do not directly generate revenue, such as manufacturing or research and development. These units incur costs with little or no revenues. Data on profit, revenue, and cost centers are gathered (mostly through the TPS but sometimes through other channels as well), summarized, and reported by the financial MIS.

FINANCIAL INTELLIGENCE

Financial intelligence is responsible for gathering data and information from stockholders, the financial community, and the government. Since the financial function controls the money flow through the firm, information is needed to expedite this flow. The day-to-day flow of money from customers and to vendors is controlled by the internal accounting subsystem. The financial intelligence subsystem is concerned with flows other than those involved in daily operations. This system seeks to identify the best sources of additional capital and the best investments of surplus funds.

Most of the information flows from the firm to the stockholders in the form of annual and quarterly reports. Stockholders have an opportunity to communicate information (complaints, suggestions, ideas, etc.) to the firm through the stockholder relations department. Also, once a year, an annual stockholders meeting is held in which stockholders can learn first hand what the firm is doing. Very often, stockholders use these meetings as an opportunity to communicate directly with top management. Information gathered informally from stockholders is seldom entered into the computerized system, but it is disseminated by verbal communication and written memo to key executives in the firm.

The relationship between the firm and the financial community also receives attention from financial management. There should be a balanced flow of money through the firm, but this equilibrium is not always achieved. At times, additional funds are needed, or investments of surplus funds are desired. It is the responsibility of the financial intelligence subsystem to compile information on sources of funds and investment opportunities. An important indirect environmental effect influences this money flow through the firm. The federal government controls the money market of the country through the Federal Reserve System. There are various means of releasing the controls to expedite the money flow and of tightening the controls to reduce the flow.

The firm therefore must gather information from both financial institutions and the Federal Reserve System. This information permits the firm to remain current on national monetary policies and trends and possibly to anticipate future changes. A variety of publications can be used for this purpose. They are prepared by both the financial institutions and the government. Two examples are the *Monthly Economic Letter* prepared by the City Bank of New York and the *Federal Reserve Bulletin* prepared by the Federal Reserve System.

In addition to the need to acquire funds, the firm frequently must invest surplus funds on either a short- or long-term basis. These funds can be invested in a number of different ways—in United States Treasury securities, commercial paper, or certificates of deposit (CDs). Since the terms and rates of return for some of these vary over time, it is necessary to monitor these investment opportunities continually so that the optimum ones can be used when needed.

Gathering information from the financial environment is the responsibility of the financial intelligence subsystem. As with the other two functional intelligence subsystems, the information is usually handled outside the computer system. This subsystem is one area where computer use could improve.

Two major financial dailies are worth mentioning as a great source of financial intelligence. the *Wall Street Journal (WSJ)* and *Investor's Business Daily (IBD)*. The *WSJ* contains news of happenings throughout the business community. It provides especially informative descriptions of the economic environment in which businesses operate. Simply by reading a periodical such as the *WSJ,* you can keep up with many of the important environmental influences that shape a manager's decision strategy.

Each day, the front page contains a "What's News" section in columns 2 and 3. The "Business and Finance" column offers a distillation of the day's major corporate, industrial, and economic news. The "World-Wide" column captures the day's domestic and international news developments. "Special Reports" appears in column 5 each day. On Monday, "The Outlook" provides an economic overview, analyzing the economy from every conceivable angle. On Tuesday, the "Labor Letter" addresses work news of all kinds—government policy, management, unions, labor relations, and personnel. Wednesday brings the "Tax Report," which alerts readers to new tax trends. The "Business Bulletin" appears each Thursday and tries to spot emerging trends. The idea is to make information available while managers can still act on it. Finally, every Friday brings the "Washington Wire," providing an interpretation of government policy and its possible impacts on business.

Published by William O'Neil & Co., Inc., *Investor's Business Daily* reports daily coverage of (1) "The Top Story," the most important news event of the day, (2) "The Economy," sophisticated analysis of current economic topics and government economic reports, (3) "National Issue/Business," a major national and business issue of our time, (4) "Leaders & Success," profiles of successful people and companies, (5) "Investor's Corner," coverage of a wide variety of personal finance topics including investment ideas, and (6) "Today's News Digest," 35 to 40 brief but important news items of the day.

FUNDS MANAGEMENT

Funds management is another critical function of the financial MIS. Companies that do not manage and use funds effectively produce lower profits or face possible bankruptcy. Outputs from the funds management subsystem, when combined with other aspects of the financial MIS, can locate serious cash flow problems and help the company increase returns. Internal uses of funds include additional inventory, new plants and equipment, the acquisition of other companies, new computer systems, marketing and advertising, raw materials, and investments in new products. External uses of funds are typically investment related. On occasion, a company might have excess cash from sales that is placed into an external investment. Current profitability is only one important factor in predicting corporate success; current and future cash flows are also essential. In fact, it is possible for a profitable company to have a cash crisis; for example, a company with significant credit sales but a very long collection period may show a profit without actually having the cash from those sales.

Financial managers are responsible for planning how and when cash will be used and obtained. When planned expenditures require more cash than planned activities are likely to produce, financial managers must decide what to do. They may decide to obtain debt or equity funds or to dispose of some fixed assets or a whole business segment. Alternatively, they may decide to cut back on planned activities by modifying operational plans, such as ending a special advertising campaign or delaying new acquisitions, or to revise planned payments to financing sources, such as bondholders or stockholders. Whatever is decided, the financial manager's goal is to balance the cash available and the needs for cash over both the short and the long term.

Evaluating the statement of cash flows is essential if you are to appraise accurately an entity's cash flows from operating, investing, and financing activities and its liquidity and solvency positions. Inadequacy in cash flow has possible serious implications, including declining profitability, greater financial risk and even possible bankruptcy.

Financial management also involves decisions relating to source of financing for, and use of, financial resources within an organization. Virtually all activities and decisions within an organization are reflected in financial information. One useful application of a real-time system to financial information involves inquiry processing. An online financial information system enables immediate response to inquiries concerning comparisons of current expenditure with budgeted expenditure, up-to-date calculations of profit center contribution, or information required for audit investigation.

The fund management subsystem can prepare a report showing cash flow for the next 12-month period. The report can be printed by a mathematical model that uses the sales forecast plus expense projections as the basis for the calculation.

Another application of real-time systems to financial management that has great potential is the area of computer models for financial planning, which is discussed later.

FINANCIAL BUDGETING, PLANNING, AND CONTROL

More and more companies are developing computer-based models for financial planning and budgeting, using powerful, yet easy-to-use, financial modeling languages such as Up Your Cash Flow and Comshare's Interactive Financial Planning System (IFPS). The models not only help build a budget for profit planning, they answer a variety of "what-if" scenarios. The calculations provide a basis for choice among alternatives under conditions of uncertainty. Furthermore, budget modeling can also be accomplished using spreadsheet programs such as Microsoft Excel.

In this section, we will illustrate the use of spreadsheet software such as Excel and stand-alone packages such as Up Your Cash Flow to develop a financial model. For illustrative purposes, we will present the following:

1. Three examples of projecting an income statement
2. Forecasting financial distress with Z score
3. Forecasting external financing needs—the percent-of-sales method

EXAMPLE 1

Given:

Sales for 1st month = $60,000
Cost of sales = 42% of sales, all variable
Operating expenses = $10,000 fixed plus 5% of sales
Taxes = 30% of net income
Sales increase by 5% each month

1. Based on this information, Figure 12.2 presents a spreadsheet for the contribution income statement for the next 12 months and in total.
2. Figure 12.3 shows the same as in (1), assuming that sales increase by 10% and operating expenses = $10,000 plus 10% of sales. This is an example of "what-if" scenarios.

EXAMPLE 2

Delta Gamma Company wishes to prepare a three-year projection of net income using the following information:

1. 2000 base year amounts are as follows:

Sales revenues	$4,500,000
Cost of sales	2,900,000
Selling and administrative expenses	800,000
Net income before taxes	800,000

2. Use the following assumptions:
   Sales revenues increase by 6% in 2001, 7% in 2002, and 8% in 2003.
   Cost of sales increase by 5% each year.
   Selling and administrative expenses increase only 1% in 2001 and will remain at the 2001 level thereafter.
   The income tax rate = 46%

Figure 12.4 presents a spreadsheet for the income statement for the next three years.

EXAMPLE 3

Based on specific assumptions (see Figure 12.5), develop a budget using Up Your Cash Flow (Figure 12.6).

A budget is a tool for both planning and control. At the beginning of the period, the budget is a plan or standard; at the end of the period, it serves as a control device

	1	2	3	4	5	6	7	8	9	10	11	12	Total	Percent
Sales	$60,000	$63,000	$66,150	$69,458	$72,930	$76,577	$80,406	$84,426	$88,647	$93,080	$97,734	$102,620	$955,028	100%
Less: VC														
Cost of sales	$25,200	$26,460	$27,783	$29,172	$30,631	$32,162	$33,770	$35,459	$37,232	$39,093	$41,048	$43,101	$401,112	42%
Operating ex.	$3,000	$3,150	$3,308	$3,473	$3,647	$3,829	$4,020	$4,221	$4,432	$4,654	$4,887	$5,131	$47,751	5%
CM	$31,800	$33,390	$35,060	$36,812	$38,653	$40,586	$42,615	$44,746	$46,983	$49,332	$51,799	$54,389	$506,165	53%
Less: FC														
Op. expenses	$10,000	$10,000	$10,000	$10,000	$10,000	$10,000	$10,000	$10,000	$10,000	$10,000	$10,000	$10,000	$120,000	13%
Net income	$21,800	$23,390	$25,060	$26,812	$28,653	$30,586	$32,615	$34,746	$36,983	$39,332	$41,799	$44,389	$386,165	40%
Less: Tax	$6,540	$7,017	$7,518	$8,044	$8,596	$9,176	$9,785	$10,424	$11,095	$11,800	$12,540	$13,317	$115,849	12%
NI after tax	$15,260	$16,373	$17,542	$18,769	$20,057	$21,410	$22,831	$24,322	$25,888	$27,533	$29,259	$31,072	$270,315	28%

FIGURE 12.2 Projected income statement.

	1	2	3	4	5	6	7	8	9	10	11	12	Total	Percent
Sales	$60,000	$66,000	$72,600	$79,860	$87,846	$96,631	$106,294	$116,923	$128,615	$141,477	$155,625	$171,187	$1,283,057	134%
Less: VC														
Cost of sales	$25,200	$27,720	$30,492	$33,541	$36,895	$40,585	$44,643	$49,108	$54,018	$59,420	$65,362	$71,899	$538,884	56%
Operating ex.	$6,000	$6,600	$7,260	$7,986	$8,785	$9,663	$10,629	$11,692	$12,862	$14,148	$15,562	$17,119	$64,153	7%
CM	$28,800	$31,680	$34,848	$38,333	$42,166	$46,383	$51,021	$56,123	$61,735	$67,909	$74,700	$82,170	$615,867	64%
Less: FC														
Op. expenses	$10,000	$10,000	$10,000	$10,000	$10,000	$10,000	$10,000	$10,000	$10,000	$10,000	$10,000	$10,000	$120,000	13%
Net income	$18,800	$21,680	$24,848	$28,333	$32,166	$36,383	$41,021	$46,123	$51,735	$57,909	$64,700	$72,170	$495,867	52%
Less: Tax	$5,640	$6,504	$7,454	$8,500	$9,650	$10,915	$12,306	$13,837	$15,521	$17,373	$19,410	$21,651	$148,760	16%
NI after tax	$13,160	$15,176	$17,394	$19,833	$22,516	$25,468	$28,715	$32,286	$36,215	$40,536	$45,290	$50,519	$347,107	36%

FIGURE 12.3 Projecting income statement.

	2000	2001	2002	2003
Sales	$4,500,000	$4,770,000	$5,103,900	$5,512,212
Cost of sales	$2,900,000	$3,045,000	$3,197,250	$3,357,113
	$1,600,000	$1,725,000	$1,906,650	$2,155,100
Selling & adm. exp.	$800,000	$808,000	$808,000	$808,000
Earnings before tax	$800,000	$917,000	$1,098,650	$1,347,100
Tax	$368,000	$421,820	$505,379	$619,666
Earnings after tax	$432,000	$495,180	$593,271	$727,434

FIGURE 12.4 Delta Gamma Company, Three-Year Income Projections (2000–2003).

Category	Assumptions

Sales: *alternative 1 from book Up Your Cash Flow*

Cost of goods sold: *Use 45% of sales*

Advertising: *59% of sales*

Automobile: *company has 4 autos at 1500 each. 4 x 1500 = 6000   12 = 1500/mo.*

Bad debts: *maintain at 29% of sales—1 hope*

Business promotion: *Prior year was $65000. 10% increase = $71500   12*

Collection costs: *Use 1000 per month*

Continuing education: *$10,000 for year =   12*

Depreciation: *$84,000 for year—use 2000 per month*

Donations: *$10,000 for year =   12*

Insurance—general: *agent said $24,000. use 2000 per month*

Insurance—group: *15 employees at 1,500 ea. = 37,500   12 = month #*

Insurance—life: *600 per month*

Interest: *expect to borrow 250 m at 15% = 37,500   12 = 3125 per month + other borrowings*

Office supplies: *2% of sales—and keep it there please!*

Rent: *4000 per month*

Repairs and maintenance: *use 400 per month*

Salaries: *Schedule the payroll per month*

Taxes and license: *Prior year was 1.5% of sales. use same this year.*

Taxes, payroll: *20% of monthly payroll*

Telephone–utilities: *$29,000 last year. Use 3300   12*

Travel – use $1000 per month.

FIGURE 12.5 Budget assumptions.

	Jan.	Feb.	Mar.	Apr.	May	Jun.	Jul.	Aug.	Sep.	Oct.	Nov.	Dec.	Total
Sales	$129,030	$129,030	$129,030	$129,030	$192,610	$192,610	$162,690	$129,030	$192,610	$129,030	$162,690	$192,610	$1,870,000
Cost of sales @ 45%	58,063	58,063	58,063	58,063	86,675	86,675	73,211	58,063	86,675	58,063	73,211	86,675	841,500
Gross profit	70,967	70,967	70,967	70,967	105,935	105,935	89,479	70,967	105,935	70,967	89,479	105,935	1,028,500
Advertising @ 5%	6,450	6,450	6,450	6,450	9,600	9,600	8,100	6,450	9,600	6,450	8,100	10,050	93,750
Automobile	500	500	500	500	500	500	500	500	500	500	500	500	6,000
Bad debts @ 2%	2,580	2,580	2,580	2,580	3,840	3,840	3,240	2,580	3,840	2,580	3,240	3,920	37,400
Business promotions	5,958	5,958	5,958	5,958	5,958	5,958	5,958	5,958	5,958	5,958	5,958	5,962	71,500
Collection costs	1,000	1,000	1,000	1,000	1,000	1,000	1,000	1,000	1,000	1,000	1,000	1,000	12,000
Continuing education	1,000	1,000	1,000	1,000	1,000	1,000	1,000	1,000	1,000	1,000	1,000	1,000	12,000
Depreciation	7,000	7,000	7,000	7,000	7,000	7,000	7,000	7,000	7,000	7,000	7,000	7,000	84,000
Donations	833	833	833	833	833	833	833	833	833	833	833	833	10,000
Dues & subscriptions	833	833	833	833	833	833	833	833	833	833	833	833	10,000
Insurance—general	2,000	2,000	2,000	2,000	2,000	2,000	2,000	2,000	2,000	2,000	2,000	2,000	24,000
Insurance—group	1,875	1,875	1,875	1,875	1,875	1,875	1,875	1,875	1,875	1,875	1,875	1,875	22,500
Insurance—life	600	600	600	600	600	600	600	600	600	600	600	600	7,200
Interest	3,125	3,125	3,125	3,125	4,375	4,375	4,375	4,450	4,450	4,450	4,450	4,450	47,875
Legal and accounting	1,000	1,000	1,000	1,000	1,000	1,000	1,000	1,000	1,000	1,000	1,000	1,000	12,000
Office supplies @ 2%	2,580	2,580	2,580	2,580	3,840	3,840	3,240	2,580	3,840	2,580	3,240	3,920	37,400
Rent	4,000	4,000	4,000	4,000	4,000	4,000	4,000	4,000	4,000	4,000	4,000	4,000	48,000
Repairs	400	400	400	400	400	400	400	400	400	400	400	400	4,800
Salaries	21,000	21,000	21,000	21,000	21,000	21,000	24,833	24,833	24,833	24,833	24,833	24,835	275,000
Taxes & license @ 1.5%	1,935	1,935	1,935	1,935	2,880	2,880	2,430	1,935	2,880	1,935	2,430	2,890	28,000
Taxes, payroll	4,200	4,200	4,200	4,200	4,200	4,200	4,966	4,966	4,966	4,966	4,966	4,970	55,000
Telephone—utilities	2,750	2,750	2,750	2,750	2,750	2,750	2,750	2,750	2,750	2,750	2,750	2,750	33,000
Travel	1,000	1,000	1,000	1,000	1,000	1,000	1,000	1,000	1,000	1,000	1,000	1,000	12,000
Profit	$(1,652)	$(1,652)	$(1,652)	$(1,652)	$24,451	$24,451	$7,546	$(7,546)	$20,777	$(7,576)	$7,471	$20,139	$85,075

FIGURE 12.6 Budget.

to help management measure its performance against the plan so that future performance may be improved. Each month, each manager with budget responsibilities receives a report showing actual expenditures compared with the budget and figures and appropriate variances so that unusual variances need to be addressed and properly rewarded or penalized.

In addition to the budget, the financial control system generates a number of performance measures or ratios that enable managers on all levels to compare their performance with benchmarks such as standards or targets. There are quite a few financial or operational ratios. A couple of ratios are given as an example. One popular ratio is the *current ratio,* which measures a firm's ability to pay short-term bills.

$$\text{Current ratio} = \frac{\text{Current assets}}{\text{Current liabilities}}$$

Another popular ratio is the *debt ratio,* which reveals the amount of money a company owes to its creditors. Excessive debt means greater risk to the company. The debt ratio is:

$$\text{Debt ratio} = \frac{\text{Total liabilities}}{\text{Total assets}}$$

FORECASTING FINANCIAL DISTRESS WITH Z SCORE

There recently have been an increasing number of bankruptcies. Will your company go bankrupt? Will your major customers or suppliers go bankrupt? What warning signs exist, and what can be done to avoid corporate failure?

Prediction models can help in a number of ways. In merger analysis, a prediction model can help to identify potential problems with a merger candidate. Bankers and other business concerns can use it to determine whether to give a new loan (credit) or extend the old one. Investors can use it to screen out stocks of companies that are potentially risky. Internal auditors can use such a model to assess the financial health of the company. Those investing in or extending credit to a company may sue for losses incurred. The model can help as evidence in a lawsuit.

Financial managers, investment bankers, financial analysts, security analysts, and auditors have been using early warning systems to detect the likelihood of bankruptcy. But their system is primarily based on financial ratios of one type or the other as an indication of financial strength of a company. Each ratio (or set of ratios) is examined independent of others. Plus, it is up to the professional judgment of a financial analyst to decide what the ratios are really telling us.

To overcome the shortcomings of financial ratio analysis, it is necessary to combine mutually exclusive ratios into a group to develop a meaningful predictive model. Regression analysis and multiple discriminant analysis (MDA) are two statistical techniques that have been used thus far.

Z-SCORE MODEL

This section describes the Z-score predictive model, which uses a combination of several financial ratios to predict the likelihood of future bankruptcy. Altman developed a bankruptcy prediction model that produces a Z score as follows:

$$Z = 1.2 \times X1 + 1.4 \times X2 + 3.3 \times X3 + 0.6 \times X4 + 0.999 \times X5$$

where X1 = working capital/total assets
       X2 = retained earnings/total assets
       X3 = earnings before interest and taxes (EBIT)/total assets
       X4 = market value of equity/book value of debt (net worth for privately held firms)
       X5 = sales/total assets

Altman established the following guideline for classifying firms:

Z score	Probability of Failure
1.8 or less	Very high
3.0 or higher	Unlikely
1.81 to 2.99	Not sure

The Z score is known to be about 90 percent accurate in forecasting business failure one year into the future and about 80 percent accurate in forecasting it two years into the future. There are more updated versions of Altman's model.

EXAMPLE 4

Navistar International (formerly International Harvester) continues to struggle in the heavy and medium truck industry and is selected for illustrative purposes. Figure 12.7 shows the 20-year financial history and the Z scores of Navistar. Figure 12.8 presents the corresponding graph.

The graph shows that Navistar International performed at the edge of the ignorance zone ("unsure area") for the year 1979. In 1980, though, the company started signaling a sign of failure. However, by selling stock and assets, the firm managed to survive. Since 1983, the company showed an improvement in its Z scores, although the firm continually scored on the danger zone. Note that the 1994 Z-score of 1.19 is in the high probability range of <1.81. The 1995 to 1998 Z-scores appear to be on the rise. This indicates that Navistar is improving its financial position and becoming a more viable business.

MORE APPLICATIONS OF THE Z SCORE

Various groups of business people can take advantage of this tool for their own purposes. For example,

	Balance Sheet					Income Statement			Stock Data	Calculations						Misc. Graph Data		
Year	Current Assets (CA)	Total Assets (TA)	Current Liability (CL)	Total Liability (TL)	Retained Earnings (RE)	Working Capital (WC)	Sales	EBIT	Market Value or Net Worth (MKT-NW)	WC/TA (X1)	RE/TA (X2)	EBIT/TA (X3)	MKT-NW/TL (X4)	Sales/TA (X5)	Z Score	Top Gray	Bottom Gray	Year
1979	3,266	5,247	1,873	3,048	1,505	1,393	8,426	719	1,122	0.2655	0.2868	0.1370	0.3681	1.6059	3.00	3	2	1979
1980	3,427	5,843	2,433	3,947	1,024	994	6,000	-402	1,147	0.1701	0.1753	-0.0688	0.2906	1.0269	1.42	3	2	1980
1981	2,672	5,346	1,808	3,864	600	864	7,018	-16	376	0.1616	0.1122	-0.0030	0.0973	1.3128	1.71	3	2	1981
1982	1,656	3,699	1,135	3,665	-1,078	521	4,322	-1274	151	0.1408	-0.2914	-0.3444	0.0412	1.1684	-0.18	3	2	1982
1983	1,388	3,362	1,367	3,119	-1,487	21	3,600	-231	835	0.0062	-0.4423	-0.0687	0.2677	1.0703	0.39	3	2	1983
1984	1,412	3,249	1,257	2,947	-1,537	155	4,861	120	575	0.0477	-0.4731	0.0369	0.1951	1.4962	1.13	3	2	1984
1985	1,101	2,406	988	2,364	-1,894	113	3,508	247	570	0.0470	-0.7872	0.1027	0.2411	1.4580	0.89	3	2	1985
1986	698	1,925	797	1809	-1889	-99	3357	163	441	-0.0514	-0.9813	0.0847	0.2438	1.7439	0.73	3	2	1986
1987	785	1,902	836	1259	-1743	-51	3530	219	1011	-0.0268	-0.9164	0.1151	0.8030	1.8559	1.40	3	2	1987
1988	1,280	4,037	1,126	1,580	150	154	4,082	451	1,016	0.0381	0.0372	0.1117	0.6430	1.0111	1.86	3	2	1988
1989	986	3,609	761	1,257	175	225	4,241	303	1,269	0.0623	0.0485	0.0840	1.0095	1.1751	2.20	3	2	1989
1990	2,663	3,795	1,579	2,980	81	1084	3,854	111	563	0.2856	0.0213	0.0292	0.1889	1.0155	1.60	3	2	1990
1991	2,286	3,443	1,145	2,866	332	1141	3,259	232	667	0.3314	0.0964	0.0674	0.2326	0.9465	1.84	3	2	1991
1992	2,472	3,627	1,152	3,289	93	1320	3,875	-145	572	0.3639	0.0256	-0.0400	0.1738	1.0684	1.51	3	2	1992
1993	2,672	5,060	1,338	4,285	-1,588	1334	4,696	-441	1765	0.2636	-0.3138	-0.0872	0.4119	0.9281	0.76	3	2	1993
1994	2,870	5,056	1,810	4,239	-1,538	1060	5,337	158	1469	0.2097	-0.3042	0.0313	0.3466	1.0555	1.19	3	2	1994
1995	3,310	5,566	1,111	4,696	-1,478	2199	6,342	262	966	0.3951	-0.2655	0.0471	0.2057	1.1394	1.52	3	2	1995
1996	2,999	5,326	820	4,410	-1,431	2179	5,754	105	738	0.4091	-0.2687	0.0197	0.1673	1.0804	1.36	3	2	1996
1997	3,203	5,516	2,416	4,496	-1,301	787	6,371	242	1374	0.1427	-0.2359	0.0439	0.3055	1.5553	1.32	3	2	1997
1998	3,715	6,178	3,395	5,409	-1,160	320	7,885	410	1995	0.0518	-0.1878	0.0664	0.3688	1.2763	1.51	3	2	1998

Notes: (1) To calculate Z score for private firms, enter net worth in the MKT-NW column. (For publicly held companies, enter market value of equity.)
(2) EBIT = earnings before interest and taxes.

FIGURE 12.7 Navistar International—NAV (NYSE) Z score—prediction of financial distress.

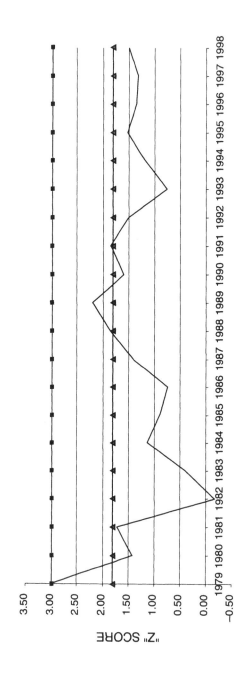

FIGURE 12.8 Z score graph (Navistar International).

1. *Merger analysis.* The Z score can help identify potential problems with a merger candidate.
2. *Loan credit analysis.* Bankers and lenders can use it to determine if they should extend a loan. Other creditors such as vendors have used it to determine whether to extend credit.
3. *Investment analysis.* The Z score model can help an investor in selecting stocks of potentially troubled companies.
4. *Auditing analysis.* Internal auditors are able to use this technique to assess whether the company will continue as a going concern.
5. *Legal analysis.* Those investing or giving credit to your company may sue for losses incurred. The Z score can help in your company's defense.

WORDS OF CAUTION

The Z score offers an excellent measure for predicting a firm's insolvency. But, like any other tool, one must use it with care and skill. The Z score of a firm should be looked upon not for just one or two years but for a number of years. Also, it should not be used as a sole basis of evaluation.

The Z score can also be used to compare the economic health of different firms. Here again, extreme care should be exercised. Firms to be compared must belong to the same market. Also, Z scores of the same periods are to be compared.

FORECASTING EXTERNAL FINANCING NEEDS—THE PERCENTAGE-OF-SALES METHOD

Percentage of sales is the most widely used method for projecting the company's financing needs. Financial officers need to determine the next year's fund requirements and the portion of it that has to be raised externally. This way, they can have a head start for arranging a least-cost financing plan.

This method involves estimating the various expenses, assets, and liabilities for a future period as a percentage of the sales forecast and then using these percentages, along with the projected sales, to construct pro forma balance sheets.

Basically, forecasts of future sales and their related expenses provide the firm with the information needed to project its future needs for financing.

The basic steps in projecting financing needs are as follows:

1. Project the firm's sales. The sales forecast is the initial most important step. Most other forecasts (budgets) follow the sales forecast.
2. Project additional variables such as expenses.
3. Estimate the level of investment in current and fixed assets that are required to support the projected sales.
4. Calculate the firm's financing needs.

The following example illustrates how to develop a pro forma balance sheet and determine the amount of external financing needed.

EXAMPLE 5

Assume that sales for 20X0 = $20, projected sales for 20X1 = $24, net income = 5% of sales, and the dividend payout ratio = 40%.

The steps for the computations are outlined as follows:

Step 1. Express those balance sheet items that vary directly with sales as a percentage of sales. Any item such as long-term debt that does not vary directly with sales is designated "n.a.," or "not applicable."

Step 2. Multiply these percentages by the 20X1 projected sales = $2.40 to obtain the projected amounts as shown in the last column.

Step 3. Simply insert figures for long-term debt, common stock, and paid-in-capital from the 20X0 balance sheet.

Step 4. Compute 20X1 retained earnings as shown in (b).

Step 5. Sum the asset accounts, obtaining a total projected assets of $7.20, and also add the projected liabilities and equity to obtain $7.12, the total financing provided. Since liabilities and equity must total $7.20, but only $7.12 is projected, we have a shortfall of $0.08 "external financing needed."

Figure 12.9 presents the projected balance sheet.

The major advantage of the percent-of-sales method of financial forecasting is that it is simple and inexpensive to use. To obtain a more precise projection of the firm's future financing needs, however, the preparation of a cash budget is required. One important assumption behind the use of the method is that the firm is operating at full capacity. This means that the company has no sufficient productive capacity to absorb a projected increase in sales and thus requires additional investment in assets.

FINANCIAL MODELING LANGUAGES

Remember that financial models are essentially used to generate pro forma financial statements and financial ratios. These are the basic tools for budgeting and profit planning. Also, the financial model is a technique for risk analysis and "what-if" experiments. The financial model is also needed for day-to-day operational and tactical decisions for immediate planning problems. For these purposes, computers are essential. In recent years, spreadsheet software and computer-based financial modeling software have been developed and utilized for budgeting and planning in an effort to speed up the budgeting process and allow CFOs to investigate the effects of changes in budget assumptions and scenarios.

These languages do not require any knowledge of computer programming on the part of financial officers. They are all English-like languages. Among the well known system packages are IFPS, SIMPLAN, EXPRESS, Encore! Plus, Venture, Cashe, and MicroFCS.

FINANCIAL ANALYSIS WITH SPREADSHEETS

Companies, large or small, profit-oriented or nonprofit, employing 100 or 10,000, etc., live or die by the extent of their powers in financial planning. There are other

	Present (20X0)	% of Sales (20X0 sales = $20)	Projected (20X1 sales = $24)	
Assets				
Current assets	2	10	2.4	
Fixed assets	4	20	4.8	
Total assets	6		7.2	
Liabilities and stockholders' equity				
Current liabilities	2	10	2.4	
Long-term debt	2.5	n.a.	2.5	
Total liabilities	4.5		4.9	
Common stock	0.1	n.a.	0.1	
Paid-in-capital	0.2	n.a.	0.2	
Retained earnings	1.2		1.92	(a)
Total equity	1.5		2.22	
Total liabilities and stockholders' equity	6		7.12	Total financing provided
			0.08	External financing needed (b)
			7.2	Total

a. 20X1 retained earnings = 20X0XI retained earnings + projected net income – cash dividends paid = $1.2 + 5%($24) – 40%[5%($24)] = $1.2 + $1.2 – $0.48 = $2.4 – $0.48 = $1.92

b. External financing needed = projected total assets – (projected total liabilities + projected equity) = $7.2 – ($4.9 + $2.22) = $7.2 – $7.12 = $0.08

FIGURE 12.9 Projected balance sheet in millions of dollars.

important contributing factors to success in business, but nothing can send a company into the abyss of Chapter 11 bankruptcy faster than a few major ill-fated financial decisions. Financial analysis is employed in an effort to be a bit more scientific about coming to a good financial decision. Questions must be asked about the company—and accurate answers found—to gain insight that will assist in determining the most prudent use of precious resources for some period in the future. The questions stem from numerous aspects of the business. Some are straightforward and easily answered: are profits greater this year than last? Other questions are not as easily answered: will an increase in advertising expenditures lead to increased profits? Would a price cut be more appropriate? Would some combination of the two be best?

Spreadsheet programs are ideally suited to performing financial analyses, because they possess the capacity to hold and process complex formulas and functions while making modification and manipulation of one or more variables or functions an easy operation. With a microcomputer, software, and some training and practice, you can master rather complex financial analysis techniques.

FINANCIAL RATIO ANALYSIS

Financial ratio analysis is a means of determining how well the business is performing. Problem spots can be identified, and groundwork is established for predictions and projections of future performance. The types of questions addressed include

- How well is the business doing?
- Where are its strengths?
- What are its weaknesses?
- How does the firm rate vis-a-vis other similar firms in the industry?

Relevant factors for consideration in critiquing the performance of the firm are as listed below:

- Profitability ratios
- Liquidity ratios
- Valuation ratios
- Efficiency of asset use
- Growth ratios
- Use of debt capital

These ratios are not necessarily useful in and of themselves. To give them relevance, the financial manager should calculate these same ratios for several different periods so they can be compared and trends can be identified. They can also be compared to industry norms to see how the firm measures up.

The numbers with which these ratios are calculated come from the balance sheet and income statement for a given period. Simple formulas are entered onto the spreadsheet, which accesses the two financial statements (assuming that they, too, are on the spreadsheet) to obtain the pertinent figures, perform the necessary computations, and come up with the appropriate ratios. If the financial statements of the period for which ratios are being prepared are not contained on the spreadsheet, the pertinent figures can be manually entered into the appropriate spreadsheet cells with relative ease. If ratios are desired for a number of past periods for which only hard copies of their financial statements exist, the financial manager enters the figures for a period in the aforementioned manner, has the spreadsheet calculate the results, and then prints the results to obtain a hard copy for later comparison. You then move on to the financial statements of the next period to be analyzed, entering those figures to the spreadsheet for computation.

MAXIMUM VS. MINIMUM PROFITS

Accounting systems are the creations of men and, although they are usually thought of as cold and objective, they can be manipulated to arrive at different results for different purposes, and they can be based on different philosophies. The most obvious example is accounting used, on one hand, to increase and maximize profits to look good to outsiders. On the other hand, some accounting is used to minimize profits for tax purposes. It is not uncommon for a company to maintain two (sometimes even more) sets of accounting records—one for each purpose. Spreadsheets can perform many functions to assist in determination of the two different bottom lines. This includes the actual production of the two opposing income statements. Basically, any calculation you might perform on paper in arriving at the two figures can be set up and performed on the spreadsheet. Also, certain calculation routines on the spreadsheet can obtain required figures from cells on the spreadsheet that contain the results of other calculations, thus avoiding repetitive entries. All of these numbers and computations should interact and funnel down to their appropriate final position in the different income statements.

CHOICE OF DEPRECIATION METHOD

Whenever a company purchases a depreciable asset, it must decide which depreciation method will be used to write off the value of the asset over its useful life. The method chosen depends on the objective of management: is it the greatest possible tax relief in the current period or the largest bottom line profit possible? The lowest possible tax liability in the near term is the most common objective when choosing a depreciation method for tax purposes.

Depreciation Methods
Straight-line depreciation
Accelerated depreciation
Modified Accelerated Cost Recovery System (MACRS)
Production basis depreciation

It is up to the firm to determine its motives and establish objectives in deciding on a depreciation method. Whatever they are, the spreadsheet can play an important and useful role in the decision process—a role that will not be altered by the motives. The idea is to determine which method best produces the results. The following are required:

- Cost of the asset
- Estimation of the asset's post-useful-life salvage value
- IRS guidelines on the asset's useful life (found in IRS publication no. 534)
- IRS guidelines on MACRS

The spreadsheet is used to compute projections for certain elements of the income statement and income tax return. Based on these projections, the appropriate depreciation method can be determined.

Projection Results Desired
Depreciation expense
Income before taxes
Income tax
Net income

PLANNING AND FORECASTING

Once you enter the realm of the future of the business through forecasting and planning, the power of a spreadsheet or integrated program can really pay off. Performing repeated "what-if" calculations is the essence of forecasting—and the electronic worksheet's specialty.

Possible Planning and Forecasting Questions

What will the projected profit and cash flows be, based on current operational plans?

If the financial manager proceeds with present plans, how will it affect the company's current and fixed assets?

What levels of expenditures are needed to increase current and fixed assets?

What will be the additional cash requirements of the business if present plans are followed?

What is the break-even point?

In what areas is the firm strong and how can such strengths be maximized?

Where is the company weak and what can be done to improve?

What are "what-if" scenarios and their impact on profit, break-even point, cash flow, assets required, return on assets, funding required, working capital, etc.?

In performing ratio analysis, you scrutinize historical data to gain insight into things that have already occurred. In forecasting and planning, on the other hand, you are creating a picture of future events if present plans are followed; you predict how future financial statements will appear.

Before embarking on this process, work with the staff to develop the best possible guesses about future market conditions, market share, net sales, and so forth. These predictions are combined with present conditions to create a model on the spreadsheet for future company performance. The methods are rather straightforward and easy to master. For example, one part of the spreadsheet would multiply current net sales by the estimated percentage of market sales increase (or decrease) to arrive at next year's projected net sales. Running the program again at this point would yield projected net sales for year two of the forecast (or perhaps the formula could be set up to automatically provide projected net sales in year five immediately, etc.). Changes in the firm's market share would also be programmed in if they were anticipated. You can continue from this modest beginning until you have created a forecast tool that can be saved on diskette for the future. But for now, once all the data have been entered, the program can be run and the results obtained. It is at this point that the fun begins—the experimentation with "what-if" scenarios. If you change one or more figures, percentages, and so forth, the spreadsheet will provide new results for all items affected.

SHORT-TERM DECISIONS

The short-term decisions that businesses make are usually more or less involved with working capital. The types of issues addressed include the following:

- What is a safe minimum cash balance for the firm?
- How much does the cash flow fluctuate seasonally?
- When do these seasonal fluctuations occur?
- What are the temporary seasonal, working-capital borrowing requirements versus borrowing for more permanent items?
- The need to increase inventory: how much should your company borrow?
- When is the best time for this borrowing to occur?
- When would it benefit most to pay it back?
- What is the cost of capital?
- What would be the effect on revenues and profit of a change in the firm's credit terms?
- What is the amount lost if the company does not avail itself of all discounts offered by suppliers for expeditious payment?

The following financial ratios are useful in determining the status of the firm and in rating the financial manager's working capital decisions:

- Current ratio
- Quick ratio
- Net working capital
- Accounts receivable turnover
- Inventory turnover
- Sales to working capital
- Sales to fixed assets

The computations for these ratios are easily set up and performed on a spreadsheet program. A spreadsheet can also be used to generate a cash budget for determining the requirements, timing, and character of cash sought and for analyzing the effects of credit terms as a component of the marketing mix through analysis of the following factors:

- Present sales
- Change in sales attributable to changes in credit terms
- Gross margin
- Potential effect on bad debts
- Credit terms on increase in sales
- Cost of short-term borrowing

Spreadsheets are also ideal for calculating interest received or extended in any of various credit situations, such as past due accounts receivable and missed discounts.

LONG-TERM ASSET DECISIONS

Long-term asset decisions by their very nature are encountered less frequently than the types of working capital decisions previously discussed. Issues encountered include the following:

- Does this particular fixed-asset purchase decision make sense and seem appropriate?
- Which of several proposals seems the most advantageous?
- Should the firm buy this item at all, or would it be better to make it?
- Based on several proposals, which should be the priority purchase if funds are limited?

Spreadsheet programs can be very helpful in answering these types of questions. One of their most useful abilities in this particular area is that of calculating present values (or the time value of money). They all have the net present value (NPV) function built in for convenience and efficiency. By calculating the NPV of two or more long-term fixed-asset options, the more advantageous option becomes evident: the highest NPV is the most profitable. Thus, use of a spreadsheet program for calculating NPV can render fixed-asset decision making a more straightforward and less difficult process.

LONG-TERM FINANCING DECISIONS

The third major financial decision type is that of long-term financing. The types of issues addressed include

- The lease or buy decision
- Debt versus equity as a means of raising capital
- Safe debt limitations and sources of financing

The lease-or-buy decision can involve the following:

- Production equipment
- Motor vehicles
- Buildings
- Office equipment
- Computers
- Tools

A spreadsheet can be used to determine the net cash outflow associated with leasing versus buying a given item. This can help in making the best decision, since the lower present value of net cash outflow of the two given options is the cheaper one. When deciding on the use of debt versus equity financing, the financial manager can set up formulas in the spreadsheet to show the effects of each option on the following:

- Cash flow
- Net income
- Degree of company solvency
- Company value
- Debt capacity

This is accomplished by projecting certain elements of the balance sheet and income statement, as well as certain financial ratios for each alternative. By analyzing the results and determining which alternative yields the highest earnings per share—and considering other factors, such as if the debt ratio is acceptable—you arrive at the optimum alternative.

OTHER FINANCIAL MANAGEMENT SOFTWARE

More and more financial software—client/server and Windows-based—are clouding the market. A few popular ones are summarized below.

COMMANDER FDC AND COMMANDER BUDGET

Comshare's integrated suite of Windows-based, client/server financial and managerial applications for statutory consolidations, enterprise budgeting, and management reporting are built around a central financial database and share the same core technology. Commander FDC and Commander Budget provide specialized application interfaces to the financial database, which holds historic, actual, budget, and forecast data. Commander FDC is designed for use by finance professionals involved in the monthly closing process. Commander Budget is designed to meet the needs of all business professionals involved in the budgeting process, from cost center managers to budget administrators. With either application, anyone familiar with Excel or Lotus 1-2-3 can easily do reporting and data entry. Additional modules for "what-if" analysis, exception detection, and executive reporting from the financial database round out Comshare's financial managerial applications.

CASHE

Cashe™, by Business Matters Incorporated, is a new approach to financial forecasting and business modeling for people who make decisions that affect the overall financial position of their organizations. Cashe gives you a disciplined way of capturing and modifying your business assumptions so that financial forecasts can be reviewed, updated, and compared easily. Cashe's power comes from its built-in content and knowledge, which allow you to forecast your business's financial performance accurately without having to worry about formulas or accounting rules. Working on the business information you provide, Cashe's self-adjusting model ensures accuracy by automatically reflecting any changes you make throughout the entire model. Cashe is not intended to replace your spreadsheet but to work with it, allowing you to import and export all your financial models. The result is that, with Cashe, you forecast more accurately, more comprehensively, and more often.

QL FINANCIALS

QL Financials, by Microcompass Systems, Ltd., delivers true client/server financial management with many advanced features in a full Windows environment. It is a fully integrated suite of functionally rich modules, including general ledger, budget management, cash book/treasury management, accounts payable, accounts receivable, sales ordering/invoicing, fixed assets, requisitioning/purchase ordering, inventory management, and system integration. QL is written in Uniface Version 6, the world's leading 4GL development environment, and it has been designed to meet the needs of both public and private sectors at departmental and corporate levels. Written to full TICKIT standards, QL offers multicurrency and multilingual functionality in a complete desktop environment.

POPULAR BUDGETING AND PLANNING SOFTWARE

In addition to specialized budgeting and financial modeling software discussed previously, there are a variety of computer software designed specifically for budgeting and decision support systems (DSS) software. Some are stand-alone packages, others are templates, and still others are spreadsheet add-ins.

BUDGET EXPRESS

Budget Express "understands" the structure of financial worksheets and concepts such as months, quarters, years, totals, and subtotals, speeding up budget and forecast preparation. The program creates column headers for months, automatically totals columns and rows, and calculates quarterly and yearly summaries. And for sophisticated what-if analyses, just specify your goal, and Budget Express displays your current and target values as you make changes. (Add-in.)

PROPLANS

It creates your financial plan automatically and accurately—and slices months from your annual planning and reporting process. You just enter your forecast data and assumptions into easy-to-follow, comprehensive data-entry screens, and ProPlans automatically creates the detailed financials you need to run your business for the next year— your income statement, balance sheet, cash flow statement, receipts and disbursements cash flow statements, and ratio reports. (Template.)

PROFIT PLANNER

It provides titles and amounts for revenues, cost of sales, expenses, assets, liabilities, and equity in a ready-to-use 1-2-3 template. Financial tables are automatically generated on screen. It presents results in 13 different table formats, including a pro forma earnings statement, balance sheet, and cash flow statements. Profit Planner even compares your earnings statement, balance sheet, and ratios against industry averages, so you're not working in a vacuum. (Template.)

UP YOUR CASH FLOW

The program generates cash flow and profit and loss forecasts, detailed sales by product/product line and payroll by employee forecasts, monthly balance sheets, bar graphs, ratio and break-even analyses, and more. (Stand-alone.)

Cash Collector

It assists you in reviewing and aging receivables. You always know who owes what; nothing "falls through the cracks." What happens when collection action is required? Simply click through menu-driven screens to automatically generate letters and other professionally written collection documents (all included) that are proven to pull in the payments. (Stand-alone.)

Cash Flow Analysis

This software provides projections of cash inflow and cash outflow. You input data into eight categories: sales, cost of sales, general and administrative expense, long-term debt, other cash receipts, inventory build-up/reduction, capital expenditures (acquisition of long-term assets such as store furniture), and income tax. The program allows changes in assumptions and scenarios and provides a complete array of reports. (Stand-alone.)

Quicken

This program is a fast, easy to use, inexpensive accounting and budgeting program that can help you manage your business, particularly your cash flow. You record bills as postdated transactions when they arrive; the program's Billminder feature automatically reminds you when bills are due. Then, you can print checks for due bills with a few keystrokes. Similarly, you can record invoices and track aged receivables. Together, these features help you maximize cash on hand. (Stand-alone.)

CapPLANS

It evaluates profitability based on net preset value (NPV), internal rate of return (IRR), and payout period. Choose among five depreciation methods, including modified accelerated cost recovery system (MACRS). Run up to four sensitivity analyses. Project profitability over a 15-year horizon. In addition to a complete report of your analysis, CapPLANS generates a concise, four-page executive summary—great for expediting approval. Add ready-made graphs to illustrate profitability clearly, at a glance. (Template.)

Project Evaluation Toolkit

It calculates the dollar value of your project based on six valuation methods, including discounted cash flow and impact on the corporate balance sheet. Assess intangibles such as impact on corporate strategy, investors, or labor relations. Use scenario planning to show the effects of changing start dates, sales forecasts, and other critical variables. (Template.)

@Risk

How will a new competitor affect your market share? @RISK calculates the likelihood of changes and events that affect your bottom line. First, use @Risk's familiar

@ functions to define the risk in your worksheet. Then, let @Risk run thousands of what-if tests using one of two proven statistical sampling techniques—Monte Carlo or Latin Hypercube. You get a clear, colorful graph that tells you the likelihood of every possible bottom-line value. At a glance you'll know if your risk is acceptable, or if you need to make a contingency plan. (Add-in.)

CFO Spreadsheet Applications

These ready-to-use spreadsheet templates offer easy ways to make many financial decisions. They are divided into four modules: cash management, tax strategies, capital budgeting, and advanced topics. (Template.)

What's Best!

If you have limited resources—for example, people, inventory, materials, time, or cash—then What's Best! can tell you how to allocate these resources to maximize or minimize a given objective, such as profit or cost. What's Best! uses a proven method—linear programming (LP)—to help you achieve your goals. This product can solve a variety of business problems that cut across every industry at every level of decision-making. (Stand-alone.)

Inventory Analyst

Inventory Analyst tells precisely how much inventory to order and when to order it. Choose from four carefully explained ordering methods: economic order quantity (EOQ), fixed order quantity, fixed months requirements, and level load by work days. Inventory Analyst ensures that you'll always have enough stock to get you through your ordering period. Just load up to 48 months worth of inventory history, and Inventory Analyst makes the forecast based on one of three forecasting methods: time series, exponential smoothing, or moving averages. It explains which method is best for you. Inventory Analyst will adjust your forecast for seasonality. (Template.)

13 Manufacturing Information Systems and Packages

Manufacturing is a broad and complicated subject. With different products manufactured, the processes and operations may be totally different. The mission of a manufacturing information system is to apply computer technology to improve the process and the efficiency of a manufacturing system, thus raising quality of products and lowering the manufacturing costs. In other words, a manufacturing system is a system that takes material, equipment, data, management, and information systems technology as the input and uses manufacturing and information process to generate better final products as output (see Figure 13.1).

Manufacturing consists of many different disciplinary areas including product engineering, facility design and scheduling, Fabrication, and quality control management. Each of them can be dramatically improved by using information systems.

PRODUCT ENGINEERING

Product engineering is the starting point of the manufacturing process. It is the step in which the design and technical specifications for the product are finalized. Recently, product design and engineering are becoming more computerized through computer software packages such as computer aided design (CAD) and computer-

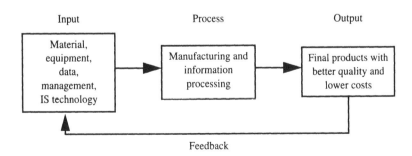

FIGURE 13.1 Model of a manufacturing information system.

aided manufacturing (CAM). With CAD, product designers use technologies to design a prototype of the product, test the product, and modify the design on the computer before the product goes into production. The initial design can be input to the CAD system in various ways, including drawing sketches on a digital tablet, using a digital camera, or even using a scanner to digitize photographs or pictures into the system. After the product is digitized, the design can then be simulated and tested under real-world conditions predefined by the designer. As changes are suggested, the original design can be modified—similar to editing a letter on a word processor. In addition, AI has also be used in CAD system. Artificial intelligence agents can help human designers make changes, offer suggestions, or perform tests based on different circumstances.

After the product has been designed, another important issue is how to produce this product efficiently and effectively. Designing products for easy and cheap assembly is critical, since assembly often accounts for over half of the total manufacturing costs. For example, by reducing the number of components by 30%, a manufacturer can drastically cut manual assembly times and manufacturing costs. Large corporations such as IBM, GM, Ford, HP, and GE have sophisticated product designs, which reflects how a product should be functioning as well as how it should be manufactured efficiently and economically.

FACILITY DESIGN AND SCHEDULING

After the product is designed, the facility or equipment used to produce the designed product should be arranged. This decision may be as simple as changing several tools or as complex as redesigning the entire plant. Some computer software packages can also arrange the plant layout based on the production information of the designed product. Many of the layout algorithms proposed use an improvement approach, a construction approach, or a simulation approach.

IMPROVEMENT APPROACH

This approach requires users to specify initial conditions and parameters. A combinatorial-based approach will then be applied to improve the initial layout. This process is usually done by intelligent search techniques to try numerous alternatives to find the best possible solution. For example, machine A can switch with machine B, and we can see the effects on the manufacturing process.

CONSTRUCTION APPROACH

This approach builds one or more layout solutions from scratch with or without user's initial suggestions. The best one will then be selected.

SIMULATION APPROACH

Monte Carlo simulation has also been used to solve facility layout problems. This approach simulates the real production environment, based on the assumptions provided by the designer. This process requires considerable computer resources and time to generate good results.

FABRICATION

Fabrication, or manufacturing, is the process of making new products from raw materials. There are two types of production methods: (1) job shop production and (2) process production.

JOB-SHOP PRODUCTION

Each work order is considered to be a job. For processing, raw materials must be routed to various work centers, depending on the production step required. The job shop is more flexible in terms of the products that can be produced. Therefore, a variety of products can be produced at the same time. Today, many computer software packages are able to generate a job shop schedule using mathematical programming or artificial intelligence technologies.

FLOW-SHOP PRODUCTION

One or a few products travel through a set of fabrication activities specially arranged for the particular products. In this approach, we have repetitive manufacturing (e.g., an automobile assembly line) and process industries, such as oil refineries, in which no significant stoppage in the flow of materials is evidenced. In this case, flow rate becomes the critical factor. The layout of the assembly line and the flow rate can be determined by expert systems, with the rule base retrieved from many manufacturing experts.

QUALITY CONTROL

Quality control relates to activities that ensure that the final product is of satisfactory quality. The quality control function is concerned with detecting existing quality deficiencies and preventing future product quality problems. If the quantity produced is small and the final product is expensive, all products are inspected for quality control. However, if the units produced is in a large quantity and inexpensive, such as pencils and diskettes, a statistical sample will be used to deter if the quality of a particular lot of products is acceptable. Total quality management (TQM) is a quality revolution taking place in recent years. It consists of five principles.

1. *Customer focus.* All efforts should be based on customers, including external customers and internal customers such as the company's accounting department.
2. *Continuous improvement.* TQM presumes that quality can be improved further; quality can always be improved.
3. *Everything TQM.* TQM includes everything that the company produces, including products, services, and how a customer service call is answered.

4. *Accurate measurement.* TQM uses statistical techniques to measure all available critical variables and compares them against benchmarks to identify problems.

5. *Empowerment of employees.* TQM involves everyone in the company in the effort to improve quality. Teamwork is heavily emphasized in the TQM process.

TQM represents a counterpoint of traditional management theories that emphasizes cost reduction above all else. The American auto industry represents a classic case of what can go wrong when attention is focused on trying to keep costs down to improve productivity without good quality management. As the matter of fact, productivity goes down when defects, recalls, and expensive repairs of defective products are factored in.

MANUFACTURING INTELLIGENCE

Expert Systems in Manufacturing

Expert systems (discussed in detail in Chapter 16) use a rule base to generate decision suggestions. Users can input facts and preconditions so that the rules will be triggered to provide results. Expert systems have been applied in many aspects of manufacturing. Much factory work has shifted to knowledge work (such as planning, design, and quality assurance) from labor work (such as machining, assembly, and handling). As the matter of fact, knowledge work accounts for about two-thirds of total manufacturing cost.

Robotics, expert systems, and other information systems can improve the productivity of labor work. For example, an expert system implemented at Northrop Corporation, a major producer of jet fighter planes, is responsible for planning the manufacture and assembly of up to 20,000 parts that go into an aircraft. A parts designer is able to enter a description of the engineering drawing of a part, and the expert system will tell him what materials and processes are required to manufacture it. This particular system actually improves the productivity of part design by a factor of 12 to 18×. Without the help of an expert system, the same task would require several days instead of several hours. An expert system is a computer system, including computer hardware and software, that can perform reasoning operations using a knowledge base.

Expert systems are made up of a *user interface,* a *knowledge base,* and an *inference engine.* The user interface has the function of providing end users with interactive channels so that they can interact with the system. A knowledge base contains a set of rules or cases to provide an expert system with the data necessary to conduct reasoning. The inference engine is the brain of the expert system. It receives the request from the user interface and conducts reasoning based on the knowledge base. Different rules or cases can be triggered to conclude a solution. After several question-and-answer sessions, a conclusion or suggestion can be generated and provided to the end user through the user interface.

EXPERT SYSTEM KNOWLEDGE BASES

An expert system contains the subject knowledge of the human experts in the *knowledge base*. The knowledge consists of two types of knowledge representations: inductive knowledge (case base) and deductive knowledge (rule base).

Rule-Based Expert Systems

The rule base of an expert system contains a set of production rules. Each rule has a typical IF-THEN clause. Expert system users provide facts or statements so that production rules can be triggered, and the conclusion can be generated. Ford Motor Company uses an expert system to diagnose engine repair problems. Typically, Ford dealers will call the help line in Ford headquarters to receive a suggestion when a complicated engine problem can not be diagnosed. Today, dealers can access the company's expert systems and receive correct engine diagnosis within seconds. Expert systems can be used at any types of business domain and at any level in an organization. Examples include diagnosing illnesses, searching for oil, making soup, and analyzing computer systems. More applications and more users are expected in the future.

Case-Based Expert Systems

A case-based expert system uses an inductive method to conduct expert system reasoning. In this type of expert system, a case base is employed. A case base consists of many historical cases, which have different results. The expert inference engine will search through the case base and find an appropriate historical case that matches the characteristics of the current problem to be solved. After a match has been allocated, the solution of a matched historical case will be modified and used as the new suggestion for the current problem.

Lockheed uses an expert system to help speed the purchase of materials ranging from industrial coolant to satellite and rocket parts. The old MIS request for a purchase order included more than 100 different forms, which were seldom completed by purchaser. Much time was spent in making corrections and changes to complete a purchase order. Using an expert system, less information is asked of the initiator, and the time required to finish a purchasing order is reduced.

One important issue in expert systems is the knowledge acquisition. Traditionally, the knowledge base is built from interviews with human experts. More advanced technology allows intelligent software to "learn" from different problem domains. The knowledge learned by computer software is more accurate and reliable as compared with that from human experts.

BENEFITS AND LIMITATIONS OF EXPERT SYSTEMS

For the past few years, the technology of expert system has been successfully applied in thousands of organizations worldwide to problems ranging from cancer research to the analysis of computer configurations. The reasons why expert systems have become so popular in recent years are as follows:

- *Increased output and productivity.* Expert systems can work faster and more accurately than human experts. For example, a system called XCON, by Digital Equipment Corporation, is able to provide a computer system configuration to potential buyers. This expert system increases fourfold the production preparation for minicomputers, which are customized for their clients.
- *Improved quality.* Expert systems provide advice or suggestions based on preprogrammed logistics, which are consistent and accurate. This reduces human errors.
- *Availability of scarce expertise.* The scarcity of experience becomes evident in situations where there are not enough experts for a task, where the expert is about to retire or leave the job, or where expertise is required over a broad geographic location.
- *Ability to operate in hazardous environments.*
- *Reliability.*
- *Provision of training.* ES can be a very good training tool.
- *Enhancement of problem-solving capabilities.*

ROBOTICS IN MANUFACTURING

A robot with AI capability is an electromechanical manipulator that is able to respond to a change in its environment based on its perception of that environment. The sensory subsystem is programmed to "see" or "feel" its environment and respond to it. For example, an industrial robot can manufacture one of many parts in its repertoire and manipulate it to inspect it for defects, recognizing very small departures from established standards. Robots have been used extensively in Japan to improve the quality and reduce the product cost. They are reliable, consistent, accurate, and insensitive to hazardous environments. A robot mimics human actions and appears to function with some degree of intelligence. Robots are commonly used in manufacturing and in other situations where it would be unsafe or unhealthy for a human to perform the same task.

The major problem of controlling the physical actions of a mobile robot might not seem to require much intelligence. Even small children are able to navigate within their environment and to manipulate items, as in playing with toys, using spoons, and turning on a TV. Performed almost unconsciously by humans, these tasks, when performed by a machine, require many of the same abilities used in solving more intellectually demanding problems. Research on robots or robotics has helped to develop many AI applications. It has led to several techniques for modeling "state of the world" and for describing the process of change from one world state to another. It has led to a better understanding of how to generate *action plans* in sequence and how to monitor the execution of these plans. One challenge is to develop methods for planning at high levels of abstraction, ignoring details, and then planning at lower level when details become important.

NEURAL NETWORKS IN MANUFACTURING

The human is the most complex computing device known to human beings. The brain's powerful reasoning, creation, recall, and problem-solving capabilities have inspired many scientists to attempt computer modeling of the brain's operation. Some researchers have sought to create a computer model that matches the functionality of the brain in a very fundamental manner. The result has been *neural computing.*

The neuron is the fundamental cellular unit of the nervous system and the brain. Each neuron functions as a simple microprocessing unit, which receives and combines signals from many other neurons through input channels called *dendrites.* If the combined signal is strong enough, it activates the firing of the neuron, which produces an output signal; the path of the output signal is along a cell component called the *axon.* This simple transfer of information is chemical in nature, but it has electrical side effects that we can measure.

The brain consists of hundreds of billions of loosely interconnected neurons. The axon (output path) of a neuron splits up and connects to dendrites (input path) of other neurons through a junction referred to as a *synapse.* The transmission across this junction is chemical in nature, and the amount of signal transferred depends on the amount of chemicals (neurotransmitters) released by the axon and received by the dendrites. This synaptic efficiency is what is modified when the brain learns.

The synapse combined with the processing of information in the neuron form the basic memory mechanism of the brain. In an artificial neural network, the unit analogous to the biological neuron is referred to as a *processing element.* A processing element has many input paths and combines, usually by a simple summation, the values of these input paths. The result is an internal activity level for the processing element. The combined input is then modified by a transfer function, which can be a threshold function. This threshold function passes information only if the combined activity level reaches a certain level, or it can be a continuous function of the combined input.

The output path of a processing element can be connected to input paths of other processing elements through connection weights that correspond to the synaptic strength of neural connections. Since each connection has a corresponding weight, the signals on the input lines to a processing element are modified by these weights prior to being summed. Thus, the summation function is a weighted summation. In summation, a neural network consists of many processing elements joined together in the above manner. Processing elements are usually organized into groups called *layers* or *slabs.* A typical network consists of a sequence of layers or slabs with full or random connections between successive layers. There are typically two layers with connections the outside world: an input buffer where data is presented to the network, and an output buffer that holds the response of the network to a given input. Layers distinct from the input and output buffers are called *hidden layers.* Applications of neural networks are language processing (text and speech), image processing, character recognition (handwriting recognition and pattern recognition), and financial and economic modeling.

PRODUCTION PLANNING AND CONTROL

PRODUCTION PLANNING

Planning encompasses defining the organization's objectives or goals and establishing an overall strategy for achieving these goals. Planning can be classified into several categories, described below.

- *Strategic vs. operational.* Plans that apply to the entire organization to establish the organizational overall objectives are call *strategic plans.* Plans that specify the detailed process of how the strategic plan can be achieved are called *operational plans.*
- *Short-term vs. long-term.* Plans that cover a longer time period are call *long-term,* and vise versa. Long-term plans tend to be strategic, and short-term plans tend to be operational
- *Specific vs. directional.* Specific plans have clearly defined objectives, whereas directional plans identify general guidelines. They provide focus but do not lock management into following specific objectives or specific courses of action.

In many cases, computer software packages for master production scheduling are an integral part of a large manufacturing information system—cost analysis, inventory information, and scheduling. IBM's Communications Oriented Production and Control System (COPICS) is an example of such a system. The system integrates forecasting, scheduling, inventory, and purchasing decisions into one large information system for planning and controlling all facets of the production system. Many computer programs also perform "what-if" (or sensitivity) analysis, which allows a production planner to determine how the production schedule would change with different assumptions concerning demand forecasts or cost figures.

Some recent computerized scheduling systems are gaining in popularity. Noteworthy among those are Optimized Production Technology (OPT), Disaster, and Q-Control, all of which concentrate their scheduling efforts on bottleneck operations. Dr. Eli Goldratt, in Israel, developed the first two, and William E. Sandman developed the third one.

Production planning consists of four key decisions—capacity, location, process, and layout.

Capacity Planning

Capacity planning deals with determining the proper size of your plant to satisfy the demand of the market. Capacity planning begins with making a forecast of sale demand and converting it into capacity requirements. This model can be easily entered into a spreadsheet to generate results (Figure 13.2).

Location Planning

When you determine the need for a new facility, you must determine where this facility should be installed. The location of the facility depends on which variables

Product	Units/demand	Machine-hours/unit	Total hours
A	200	3	600
B	400	2	800
C	100	7	700

Total machine hours =	2100
Machine run time =	24
Machine breakdown rate =	5%
No. of machines needed =	93

FIGURE 13.2 Capacity planning spreadsheet.

have the greatest impact on total production and distribution costs. These include availability of labor skills, labor costs, energy costs, proximity to suppliers or customers, and the like. The number of possible layout designs, even with a small number of departments, is so large that evaluating a considerable number of possibilities requires the aid of a computer.

Process Planning

In process planning, management determines how a product or service will be produced. Process planning encompasses evaluating the available production methods and selecting the set that will best achieve the operating objectives.

Layout Planning

Layout planning deals with the access of and selection among alternative layout options for equipment and workstations. The objective of layout planning is to find the physical arrangement that will best facilitate production efficiency. There are three types of workflow layouts, as follows:

- *Process layout.* Arrange manufacturing components according to similarity of function.
- *Product layout.* Arrange manufacturing components according to the progressive steps by which a product is made.
- *Fixed-position layout.* This is a manufacturing layout in which the product stays in place while tools, equipment, and human skills are brought to it.

Several computer software are available for developing and analyzing process layouts, including the ALDEP (Automated Layout Design Program), CORELAP (COmputerized RElationship LAyout Planning) and CRAFT (Computerized Relative Allocation of Facilities Technique) programs. The first two programs employ the ranking of the desirability of closeness of departments to each other, whereas the CRAFT program uses the quantitative measure of minimizing the total transportation costs between them and material-handling costs.

PRODUCTION CONTROL

Control can be defined as the process of monitoring activities to ensure that they are being accomplished as planned, and of correcting any significant deviations. The control process consists of three steps.

1. Measuring actual performance
2. Comparing actual performance against a standard
3. Taking managerial action to correct deviations or inadequate standards

There are three types of controls: *feedforward* control, *concurrent* control, and *feedback* control. Feedforward control prevents anticipated problems. Concurrent control occurs while an activity is in progress. Feedback control is imposed after an action has occurred. All three types of control can be implemented by information systems.

INVENTORY PLANNING AND CONTROL

A manufacturing company has three types of inventory.

1. Raw material
2. Work in process
3. Final products

To reach the goals of inventory control, two objects must be achieved: (1) to minimize costs due to out-of-stock situations and (2) to minimize inventory carrying costs. At the finished-product level, out-of-stock situations can result in loss of sales and too much inventory, which increases the carrying cost. At raw-material and work-in-process levels, an out-of-stock condition means that the production line must be stopped, and too much inventory means a higher cost in final products. A mathematical model used to determine the optimal ordering point is called an economic order quantity (EOQ) model.

Inventory planning, control, and management is done routinely by computers. IBM's Inventory Management Program and Control Techniques (IMPACT) and Communications Oriented Production and Control System (COPICS) are two prime examples of management information systems with embedded inventory packages. IMPACT is based on *independent demand* and therefore uses traditional or classical inventory analysis. The goal of IMPACT is to provide operating rules to minimize cost. To do this, the following functions are performed:

1. Forecast demand using various forecasting models such as exponential smoothing, trend, and seasonal (or cyclical) models. Forecasts are monitored based on the mean absolute deviation (MAD) and the tracking signal.
2. Determine the amount of stock required for a specified level of service.
3. Determine the order quantity and time for reorder using the EOQ model and quantity discount models.

4. Consider the effects of freight rates and quantity discounts.
5. Estimate the expected results of the inventory plan.

MATERIAL REQUIREMENT PLANNING AND MANUFACTURING RESOURCES PLANNING

Material Requirement Planning (MRP) differs from its expanded version, Manufacturing Resources Planning II (MRP II). MRP II is designed to satisfy the requirements of supplying materials to shop operations. In MRP II, the MIS is used to sequence materials inputs in accordance with chronological need. The evolution of MRP II from MRP is the logical outgrowth of the maturing of the use of computer application in manufacturing.

COMPUTER-AIDED DESIGN AND COMPUTER-AIDED MANUFACTURING

CAD programs are software applications for product design. CAD programs can be found in all types of computers, from mainframe systems to microcomputers. They are developed to help engineers design products ranging from airplanes to pens. The advantages of CAD software are that the design can be drawn in three dimensions, the design can be simulated in the computer, and design changes can be made very efficiently. Good CAD packages include AutoCAD, TurboCAD, and EasyCAD2. Some CAD programs are developed for nonprogrammers. For example, a relatively unskilled person can use this type of software to design an office or even a home. Theses programs include libraries of options such as cabinetry, furniture, trees, and even shadows. Once the design is completed, users can "walk into the design" and view this structure from different point of view. This is similar to a virtual reality system.

CAM is an umbrella term that includes almost any use of computers in manufacturing operations. It consists of the functions described below.

Monitoring

Computers can be used to control and monitor manufacturing operations in a dangerous environment. For example, an oil refinery facility uses CAM to open and shut valves when a certain temperature is reached in a tank.

Numeric Control

This involves using computer technology to control the manufacturing operations. For example, CAM can help manufacturing workers produce parts that require a high degree of precision, because computers are used to improve the accuracy of manufacturing process.

Optimization

Many manufacturing operations involve determining the best solution among many. For example, an oil refinery seeks the cheapest way to mix crude oils to achieve a finished gasoline that meets certain specifications. Auto assembly plants try to arrange the best schedule so that operating costs can be minimized. By using CAM techniques, optimization can be achieve, and the operation can be more economical and efficient.

Robotics

Robotics is the use of computer-controlled machines to perform physical activities previously done by humans such as welding a joint, painting, and fitting parts together. The automobile industry uses robotic to improve productivity and quality.

JUST-IN-TIME

Just-in-time (JIT) is fast becoming as familiar and identifiable in the lexicon of manufacturing terminology as *mass production*. Although the term is familiar to many people, the true meaning and definition remains clouded. The most common misunderstanding of just-in-time is that it means to deliver inventory when it is needed, with the aim of reducing inventory while the operation is maintained. However, this not the true meaning of just-in-time. The true definition is "an awareness that true optimum manufacturing performance revolves about the dictate to eliminate waste in all of its many manifestations." The goal of JIT is to eliminate all manufacturing waste in the following ways:

- By producing the product the customer wants
- By producing the product when the customer wants it
- By producing a good quality product
- By producing it instantly, with no lead time
- By producing it with no waste of labor, material, or equipment

Using electronic data exchange (EDI) can greatly enhance JIT implementation, especially when internal business partners are involved. Notable computer software for JIT includes the following:

- HP Manufacturing Management II, which supports multilocation tracking and JIT component ordering, extensive MRP and inventory control, and interactions with budgeting, costing, and CDA/CAM applications
- Control Manufacturing by Cincom Systems, which supports multiple location JIT inventory control, MRP, financial management, and production scheduling

QUALITY CONTROL AND TOTAL QUALITY MANAGEMENT

Quality control relates to activities that ensure that the final products is satisfactory. Major functions of quality control are twofold.

- Detection of existing quality deficiencies
- Prevention of future product quality problems

Due to the large quantity of units produced, quality control is usually conducted by statistical sampling of final products. The whole lot of final products can be either rejected or accepted on the basis of a small sample collected. However, if the manufacturer passes a production lot on a statistical basis that should have been rejected, the consequence is that customers will purchase defected merchandise. This can ruin the reputation of a manufacturer. Conversely, if statistically the manufacturer rejects a production lot on a statistical basis, but it should have been accepted, good products will be discarded and manufacturing resources wasted. Quality control is an important area both in terms of expense and opportunities. Regarding expense, a typical factory spends about one-fourth of its production budget just fixing and finding mistakes—and this cost does not reflect the true cost associated with this problem.

A new quality concept is called *total quality management (TQM)*. It has been touted as one of the few new management practices that will make companies competitive, particularly against the onslaught of Japanese competition. TQM has come to be seen as a powerful solution to all that ails modern North American Industry. It implies that, if we will only pay supreme attention to the needs and desires of our customers, and we deliver on those aspirations, we are bound to be successful. TQM focuses on awareness techniques for making products to the best of the organization's abilities. TQM theory can be described as a triangle, as shown below.

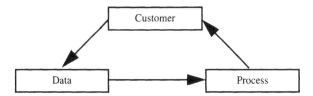

The focus is on the customer's requirements at the apex of the triangle. This, in turn, generates a process for achieving the requirements. The process is implemented, and data are generated from which the effectiveness of the plan is evaluated. The results are then compared with the customer's requirements, and the process is modified to improve results. TQM emphasizes a continuous improvement at all times. The modifications are implemented, and the results are analyzed to see if they are in compliance with the customer's needs. In other words, TQM is *continuous improvements until perfection is achieved.*

Computer Software for Quality Control

Computer software can relieve most of the tedious calculations formerly required to install and maintain a quality control system. Some popular packages, developed by TIME/WARE Corp., are listed below, with a brief description of each.

1. ML105$. Determines sampling plan to fit combinations of acceptable quality level (AQL), lot size, etc., and randomly determines which parts to sample according to military standards.
2. MLBIN$. Evaluates multiple-level sampling plans where users inspect a number of parts from a large lot and accept, reject, or resample based on the number of defectives found (binomial distribution).
3. OCBIN$. Plots the operating characteristic (OC) curve. User supplies the sampling size and number of defectives required to reject the lot.
4. CONLM$. Determines confidence limits and sample statistics on a process average.

FLEXIBLE MANUFACTURING SYSTEMS

The flexible manufacturing system (FMS) was introduced to provide shorter life cycle manufacturing process and responsive manufacturing facilities to improve competition. For example, A VCR factory can use FMS to produce different models using similar facility, which can be rescheduled and rearranged to fit into different manufacturing pattern.

SUMMARY

This chapter has described how MIS can be used in manufacturing systems to improve quality and productivity. Generally speaking, MIS can be applied to all four major manufacturing activities, which include product engineering, facility design and scheduling, fabrication, and quality control. Recently, an important new technology, artificial intelligence, has been used to design, perform, and schedule production activities more intelligently. As a result, the manufacturing process can be made more automated and efficient by using current information technologies.

14 Marketing Management Information Systems and Packages

The internal accounting information system is the primary source of marketing information in most business organizations and provides two basic types of information to management: information generated from processing of sales orders and cost report and analyses. Profitability analysis is generated from sales data records along with product cost data. Sales data processing also includes analysis of sales trends. In addition to the accounting and marketing departments, other departments within the company may contribute to the flow of information to marketing personnel. For example, the production or engineering department may provide information relating to product quality or design, which is useful to product planning or to salesmen. The economics department may provide useful analysis of the economy or of the particular field within which the firm operates. The personnel department may provide information relating to potential marketing department employees. While information from all the sources may be important, it is generally not as regular or as voluminous as the information provided by the accounting department. The information needs for marketers are listed in Figure 14.1.

	Main Information Needs
1.	Improving new product development
2.	Improving the use of market information
3.	Measuring and managing brand equity
4.	Market orientation and bottom line
5.	Market segmentation and implementation
6.	Identifying, anticipating, and responding to competitors
7.	Studying buyer behavior
8.	Strategic new product issues
9.	Integrating marketing mix
10.	Service quality/performance links

FIGURE 14.1 Information needs of marketing managers.

A marketing MIS supports managerial activity in the areas of product development, marketing mix, distribution, pricing decisions, promotional effectiveness, and sales forecasting. Recall that an MIS is made up of three sets of activities: information collection, information analysis, and information dissemination. A marketing MIS is certainly no exception. Figure 14.2 shows the inputs, subsystems, and outputs of a typical marketing MIS.

Among the other functional areas, the marketing MIS relies more heavily on external sources of data. These sources include commercial intelligence, competition, customers, trade shows, trade journals and magazines, and other publications. There are also important internal company information sources. An overview of these inputs is presented below.

1. *The corporate strategic plan or policies.* Marketing depends on the company's strategic plan for sales goals and projections. For instance, a strategic plan might show sales are expected to grow by a stable 5% for the next three years. A marketing MIS report for this company might detail current sales performance in terms of this strategic target. In addition to sales projections, the strategic plan can spell out detailed information about anticipated needs for the sales force, pricing, distribution channels, promotion, and new product features. The strategic plan can provide a framework in which to integrate marketing information and make appropriate marketing decisions.

2a. *The transaction processing system (TPS).* The TPS encompasses a huge amount of sales and marketing data on products or services, customers, and the sales force. Technology is revolutionizing the selling process. Most firms regularly collect an abundance of information that can also be used in making marketing decisions. Sales data on products can expose which products are selling at high volumes, which ones are slow sellers, and how much they are contributing to profits. The marketing MIS might synthesize this information in such a way as to be useful in formulating promotional plans. It can also be used to activate product development decisions. Analysis of sales by customers may display which customers

Inputs	Subsystems	Outputs
Strategic plan	Product development	Product development
Transaction processing	Marketing research	reports
system	Promotion and advertising	Marketing research reports
Internal sources	system	Locational analysis
External sources:	Pricing system	Supply and demand
Competition	Place planning system	analysis
The market		Sales by product
		Sales by salesperson
		Sales by customer

FIGURE 14.2 Overview of a marketing MIS.

are contributing to profits. This data can also be disseminated to determine the products specific customers are buying to help the sales force with their promotional efforts. The performance of the sales force can also be monitored from data captured in the TPS, which can help develop bonus and incentive programs to reward high-performing salespeople.

2b. *Internal company information.* Internal company information includes routinely collected accounting records such as daily sales receipts, weekly expense records and profit statements, production and shipment schedules, inventory records, orders, monthly credit statements, and quarterly and biennial reports. Field salespeople are increasingly likely to have portable personal computers, pagers, and personal digital assistants (PDAs) to log in data for immediate transmission back to the company or customers, and to receive information from the company and customers. Technology is revolutionizing the selling process. Most companies collect an abundance of information on a regular basis that can also be used in making marketing decisions.

3. *External sources: the competition and the market.* In most marketing decisions, it is important to determine what is happening in the business's external environment, particularly anything that involves the competition, the economy, the market, and consumers. External information can be obtained from many sources. Some of the most commonly used sources are commercial intelligence, trade shows, trade journals, the government, private publications, commercial data suppliers, and the popular press. Many companies purchase their competition's products and then perform "autopsies" to find out what makes them tick so they can improve on them. Marketing managers attend trade shows and read trade journals to keep an eye on the competition.

Figure 14.3 lists some trade journals and publications. Information can be purchased from information brokers—individuals and companies who help businesses by electronically searching information bases for useful data. Valuable information can be obtained by training salespeople to listen to and observe customers, suppliers, members of the distribution system, and the competition, and then contributing this intelligence to the MIS. The intent should be to obtain usable *marketing intelligence* (information that is available to the public) and not to conduct *industrial espionage* (stealing information not available to the public). The latter is unethical and illegal. Marketers should be savvy enough to realize that as they are collecting information about their competition, the competition is probably collecting information about them.

An additional external source of important information for the marketing MIS is the market for a company's products. A large amount of useful data can be obtained from the TPS for markets already being served by the company, but insights into buyer behaviors and preferences in new markets can be obtained only from sources outside the firm.

The Internet may become the ultimate information source for both the competition and the market. It already provides access to information provided by govern-

Air Conditioning, Heating & Refrigeration	*Industry Week*
News	*Iron Age*
Airline Executive	*Leather and Shoes*
American Banker	*Modern plastics*
American Druggist	*Paper Trade Journal*
American Gas Association Monthly	*Journal of Retailing*
Automotive Industries	*Labor Law Journal*
Aviation Week & Space Technology	*Merchandising*
The Banker	*Modern Plastics*
Best's Industry Report	*National Petroleum News*
Broadcasting	*Oil and Gas Journal*
Brewers Digest	*Paper Trade Journal*
Chain Store Age Executive	*PC World*
Chemical Week	*Personnel*
Computer Decisions	*Pipeline & Gas Journal*
Computers and People	*Polk's National New Car Sales*
Credit and Financial Management	*Printer's Ink*
Datamation	*Progressive Grocer*
Drug & Cosmetic Industry	*Public Utilities Fortnightly*
Electronic News	*Pulp & Paper*
Fleet Owner	*Quick Frozen Foods*
Food Management	*Television Digest*
Food Processing	*Textile World*
Forest Industries	*Transportation Journal*
Fuel Oil & Oil Heat and Solar Systems	*Ward's Auto World*
Housing	*World Oil*

FIGURE 14.3 Trade journals and publications.

ment (.gov), for-profit business (.com), nonprofits (.org), universities (.edu), and individuals.

MARKETING MIS SUBSYSTEMS AND OUTPUTS

Subsystems for the marketing MIS include forecasting, marketing research, product, place, promotion, and price subsystems. These subsystems and their outputs help marketing managers and executives increase sales, reduce marketing expenses, and develop plans for future products and services to meet the changing needs of customers.

FORECASTING

Forecasts are needed for marketing, production, purchasing, manpower, and financial planning. Furthermore, top management needs forecasts for planning and implementing long-term strategic objectives and planning for capital expenditures. Based on the firm's projected sales, the production function determines the machine, personnel, and material resources needed to produce its products or services. Marketing managers use sales forecasts to determine (1) optimal sales force allocations, (2) set sales goals, and (3) plan promotions and advertising. Other information, such as market share, prices, and trends in new product development, are required.

As soon as the company makes sure that it has enough capacity, the production plan is developed. If the company does not have enough capacity, it will require planning and budgeting decisions for capital spending for capacity expansion. Production planners need forecasts to schedule production activities, order materials, establish inventory levels, and plan shipments.

Some other areas that need forecasts include material requirements (purchasing and procurement), labor scheduling, equipment purchases, maintenance requirements, and plant capacity planning. The personnel department requires a number of forecasts in planning for human resources in the business. Workers must be hired and trained, and for these personnel there must be benefits provided that are competitive with those available in the firm's labor market. Also, trends that affect such variables as labor turnover, retirement age, absenteeism, and tardiness need to be forecast as input for planning and decision making in this function. On this basis, the financial manager must estimate the future cash inflow and outflow and must plan cash and borrowing needs for the company's future operations. Forecasts of cash flows and the rates of expenses and revenues are needed to maintain corporate liquidity and operating efficiency. In planning for capital investments, predictions about future economic activity are required so that returns or cash inflows accruing from the investment may be estimated. There are many forecasting methods in use, one of which is regression analysis. It is illustrated in Table 14.1, using Excel.

EXAMPLE 1

A firm wishes to develop a sales forecasting model by relating sales to price and advertising.

Using Regression on *Excel*

To utilize Excel for regression analysis, the following procedure needs to be followed:

1. Click the *Tools* menu.
2. Click *Add-Ins*.
3. Click *Analysis ToolPak*. (If Analysis ToolPak is not listed among your available add-ins, exit *Excel*, double-click the MS Excel Setup icon, click Add/Remove, double-click Add-Ins, and select Analysis ToolPak. Then restart Excel and repeat the above instruction.)

After ensuring that the Analysis ToolPak is available, you can access the regression tool by completing the following steps:

1. Click the *Tools* menu.
2. Click *Data Analysis*.
3. Click *Regression*.

TABLE 14.1

Month	Sales (Y)	Advertising (X1)	Price (X2)
1	25	4	75
2	26	5	82
3	32	6	94
4	30	6	95
5	32	7	98
6	37	7	110
7	38	8	110
8	41	8	99
9	46	9	95
10	48	10	97

Summary Output

Regression Statistics	
Multiple R	0.97366474
R Square	0.94802302
Adjusted R Square	0.93317246
Standard Error	2.0400664
Observations	10

ANOVA

	df	SS	MS
Regression	2	531.3669036	265.6835
Residual	7	29.13309639	4.161871
Total	9	560.5	

	Coefficients	Standard Error	t Stat
Intercept	10.1734656	6.251683507	1.627316
X Variable 1	4.41923505	0.480669674	9.193913
X Variable 2	–0.0587237	0.081383757	–0.72157

MARKETING RESEARCH

Marketing research is essentially a twofold activity. It involves (1) collecting current data describing all phases of the marketing operations and (2) presenting the findings to marketing managers in a form suitable for decision making. The focus is on the timeliness of the information. The goal of marketing research is to conduct a systematic, objective, bias-free inquiry of the market and customer preferences. A variety of tools, such as surveys, questionnaires, pilot studies, and in-depth interviews, are used for marketing research. Marketing research can identify the features that customers really want in a product or from a service. Important attributes of products or services—style, color, size, appearance, and general fit—can be investigated through the use of marketing research.

Marketing research broadly encompasses *advertising research* and *consumer behavior research.* Advertising research is research on such advertising issues as ad and copy effectiveness, recall, and media choice. Consumer behavior research answers questions about consumers and their brand selection behaviors and preferences in the marketplace. Research results are used to make marketing mix decisions and for pricing, distribution channels, guarantees and warranties, and customer service. Inexpensive software and statistical analysis software are used to analyze the data collected from marketing research endeavors. These software packages can determine trends, test hypotheses, compute statistical values, and more. These data are then often input into the marketing MIS so that marketing managers can be better informed and can better make their planning and resource allocation decisions.

PRODUCT DEVELOPMENT

Product development is one of "the four Ps" in the marketing mix—product, place, promotion, and price. Each is explained later. Product development involves the transformation of raw materials into finished goods and services, and it primarily focuses on the physical attributes of the product. Many factors, including materials, labor skills, plant capacity, and technical factors, are important in product development decisions. In many cases, a computer program for mathematical programming and simulations can be used to analyze these various factors and to select the appropriate mix of labor, materials, plant and equipment, and engineering designs. Make-or-outsource decisions can also be made with the assistance of computer software. A framework, called the *product life cycle,* guides the manager in making product development decisions. It takes into account four stages in the life cycle—introduction, growth, maturity, and decline.

PLACE PLANNING

Place planning involves planning about the means of physically distributing the product to the customer. It includes production, transportation, storage, and distribution on both the wholesale and retail levels. Where to deliver the product to the customer and how to get the product to this location are the principal concerns of place analysis subsystems. Typically, a distribution chain starts at the manufacturing plant and ends at the final consumer. In the middle is a network of wholesale and retail outlets employed to efficiently and effectively bring goods and services to the final consumer. But where are the best places to locate manufacturing facilities, wholesale outlets, and retail distribution points?

Factors such as manufacturing costs, transportation costs, labor costs, and localized demand levels become factors critical to answering this issue. Today, marketing MIS subsystems can analyze these factors and determine the least-cost placement of manufacturing facilities, wholesale operations, and retail outlets. The purpose of these locational analysis programs is to minimize total costs while satisfying product demand. Digital maps combined with customer database information in computer mapping software can be used to pinpoint locations for new retail outlets. For example, Yamaha Motor Corporation, USA, has made decisions as to where to locate the dealership by blending computer graphics with behavioral demographics. Behavioral demographics links psychological, lifestyle, and family expenditure data to geographic locations, often by zip code.

PROMOTION PLANNING

One of the most important functions of any marketing effort is *promotion*. Promotion is concerned with all the means of marketing the sale of the product, including advertising and personal selling. Product success is a direct function of the types of advertising and sales promotion done. The size of the promotions budget and the allocation of this budget to various promotional mixes are important factors in deciding the type of campaigns that will be launched. Television coverage, newspaper ads and coverage, promotional brochures and literature, and training programs for salespeople are all components of these promotional and advertising mixes. Because of the time and scheduling savings they offer, computer software is widely used to establish the original budget and to monitor expenditures and the overall effectiveness of various promotional campaigns.

Promotional effectiveness can be monitored through the TPS, or it may be monitored through a specialized functional system focusing exclusively on sales activity. For example, a significant proportion of many marketing managers' compensation is determined by the results of their promotional campaigns through specialized sales activity subsystems. Such systems often use data from retail outlet bar-code scanners to compile information on how effective certain promotions were within the promotional period. Without such sales activity, the time delay between wholesale shipments and retail sales would prevent the promotion's effectiveness from being accurately measured.

The following example illustrates the use of linear programming to determine optimal media selection.

EXAMPLE 2

The management of an electric-products company decided to spend up to $1,000,000 on the advertising of the women's electric razors that it manufactures. The advertising budget is to be spent in 12 consumer magazines that full-page, full-color advertisements. Let Xi be the number of dollars spent on advertising in magazine i. Management is advised by an advertising agency that an appropriate goal is to *maximize* the number of effective exposures given the advertising budget. Management wants to ensure that no more than 12 insertions are made in any one magazine, and it wishes the number of insertions in *Mademoiselle* and *Ladies Home Journal* to be less than or equal to 7 and 2, respectively. Suppose also that management wishes to specify minimum expenditures in certain of the magazines, say, $X2 \geq 17,810$, $X3 \geq 67,200$, $X5 \geq 42,840$, and $X10 \geq 32,550$. Finally, management desires an expenditure of no more than $320,000 in four of the magazines, say, 3, 9, 10, 12. The following table presents the number of exposures and cost for each advertising media.

Medium	Effective readings per dollar spent	Cost of one full-page, full-color advertisement
1. *Cosmopolitan*	158	$5,500
2. *Mademoiselle*	263	5,950
3. *Family Circle*	106	33,600
4. *Good Housekeeping*	108	27,400
5. *McCall's*	65	42,840
6. *Modern Romance*	176	3,275
7. *Modern Screen*	285	3,415
8. *Motion Picture*	86	2,248
9. *True Confessions*	120	25,253
10. *Women's Day*	51	32,550
11. *Seventeen*	190	8,850
12. *Ladies Home Journal*	101	35,000

The LP model is:

Maximize:

$$158\ X1 + 263\ X2 + 106\ X3 + 108\ X4 + 65\ X5 + 176\ X6 + 285\ X7$$
$$+\ 86\ X8 + 120\ X9 + 51\ X10 + 190\ X11 + 101\ X12$$

Subject to:
(1) $0 \leq Xi \leq 12\ (i = 1,2,3,\ldots,12)$
(2) $X2 \leq 7, X12 \leq 2$
(3) $5950\ X2 \geq 17810, 33600\ X3 \geq 67200,$
    $42840\ X5 \geq 42840$
    $32550\ X10 \geq 32550$
(4) $33600\ X3 + 25253\ X9 + 32550\ X10 + 35000\ X12 \leq 320000$

The LINDO input and output are summarized below.

$$\text{MAX } 158\ X1 + 263\ X2 + 106\ X3 + 108\ X4 + 65\ X5 + 176\ X6$$
$$+\ 285\ X7 + 86\ X8 + 120\ X9 + 51\ X10 + 190\ X11 + 101\ X12$$

SUBJECT TO

2) $X1 <= 12$
3) $X2 <= 12$
4) $X3 <= 12$
5) $X4 <= 12$
6) $X5 <= 12$

7) $X6 <= 12$
8) $X7 <= 12$
9) $X8 <= 12$
10) $X9 <= 12$
11) $X10 <= 12$
12) $X11 <= 12$
13) $X12 <= 12$
14) $X2 <= 7$
15) $X12 <= 2$
16) $5950\ X2 >= 17810$
17) $33600\ X3 >= 67200$
18) $42480\ X5 >= 42480$
19) $32550\ X10 >= 32550$
20) $33600\ X3 + 25253\ X9 + 32550\ X10 + 35000\ X12 <= 320000$
END
LP OPTIMUM FOUND AT STEP 14

OBJECTIVE FUNCTION VALUE
1)   15966.6100

VARIABLE	VALUE	REDUCED COST
X1	12.000000	.000000
X2	7.000000	.000000
X3	2.000000	.000000
X4	12.000000	.000000
X5	12.000000	.000000
X6	12.000000	.000000
X7	12.000000	.000000
X8	12.000000	.000000
X9	8.721736	.000000
X10	1.000000	.000000
X11	12.000000	.000000
X12	0.000000	65.316860

PRICING

Pricing is an important managerial decision that has a long-term effect on the sales and profitability of the firm. In most instances, especially in the field of durable consumer goods (notably audio-video equipment, automobiles, etc.), the scope for product differentiation allows competing firms to have considerable leeway in setting the prices of their products. Three popular pricing approaches are: a *cost-based* pricing policy, a *return-on-investment (ROI) based* pricing policy, and a *demand-based* pricing policy. The MIS can support the manager in all three pricing policies. With the cost-based approach, the accounting system can provide accurate product cost data on which to base a decision. With the other approaches, the MIS enables the manager to engage in "what-if" modeling to determine the price level that maximizes contribution to profits yet retards competitive activity.

A major factor in determining pricing policy is an analysis of the demand curve, which attempts to determine the relationship between price and sales. Most companies try to develop pricing policies that will maximize total sales revenues. This is usually a function of price *elasticity*. If the product is highly price-sensitive, a reduction in price can generate a substantial increase in sales, which can result in higher revenues. A product that is relatively insensitive to price can have its price substantially increased without a large reduction in demand. Figure 14.4 shows the relationships between price elasticity (e_p) and sales revenue (S), which can aid a firm in setting its price.

Computer programs exist that help determine price elasticity and various pricing policies. Typically, the marketing managers, with the aid of computer software for spreadsheets and statistical packages, can develop "what-if" scenarios in which they can alter factors to see price changes on future demand and total revenues.

EXAMPLE 3

One of the widely used pricing methods, especially in large corporations, is pricing to achieve a targeted rate of return on investment (ROI). Furthermore, there is an increasing tendency among firms to adopt some form of target ROI pricing. This is mainly due to a growing awareness of the need to integrate pricing policy with the objective of achieving a satisfactory rate for return on capital invested. ROI pricing is certainly the most widely used pricing method today. The use of spreadsheet software and "what-if" analysis can be readily be applied to the area of product pricing.

The conventional ROI pricing technique is generally along the following lines.

1. A standard volume of production is estimated.
2. The variable cost per unit is calculated for this level of production.
3. Fixed factory overhead, selling and administrative expenses are allocated over the number of units at standard volume of production.
4. Depreciation on assets is included in the fixed costs. The rate of depreciation is either an estimated rate that, in the opinion of management, reflects the fall in the value of assets, or more likely, the depreciation rate allowed under the tax law is generally adopted.
5. The markup per unit is arrived at by calculating the desired dollar return (on the total capital invested, i.e. debt as well as equity) and dividing by the number of units at standard volume.

Price	$e_p > 1$	$e_p = 1$	$e_p < 1$
Price rises	S falls	No change	S rises
Price falls	S rises	No change	S falls

FIGURE 14.4 Relationship between price elasticity and sales revenue.

6. The return on investment rate expected is determined by management according to its expectations of what constitutes a fair return.

7. Tax aspects are generally ignored.

The outline of a ROI pricing model (with assumed figures) is presented below:

X = estimated sales (units)	100,000	
OI = opening inventory	10,000	value $45,000
CI = closing inventory (units)	20,000	value $100,000
	(valuation at variable cost & FIFO)	
Production (units)	110,000	
VC = variable cost (@ $5)	550,000	
FC = fixed cost (manufacturing, selling, administrative)	200,000	
RR = recoveries required:		
Interest (INT)	50,000	
Dividends	60,000	
Debt Recovery	100,000	
Equity Recovery	90,000	300,000
T = tax rate		40%
D = depreciation allowable under tax laws		30,000

The selling price can then be calculated by the following formula:

$$SP = \frac{RR + FC - (t)(FC + D + INT + OI - CI) + VC/\text{unit}}{(1 - t)(X)}$$

Substituting the assumed figures in the above formula gives

$$SP = \frac{300000 + 200000 - (0.40)(200000 + 30000 + 50000 + 45000 - 100000) + 5}{(1 - 0.40)(100000)}$$

$$= 11.83 \text{ per unit}$$

The spreadsheet contains parameters for "what-if" (sensitivity) analysis on three levels: normal, optimistic, and pessimistic. Consequently, the template generates product prices under optimistic, pessimistic, and normal expectations of the person making the pricing decision. A printout of the worksheet with assumed figures is shown in Figure 14.5.

Variation Type	Normal	Pessimistic	Optimistic
(%)	100	96	102
Desired level % of sales			20
Unit cost	$5.00	$5.60	$4.50
(%)	100	101	99
Tax rate			40%
Depreciation (allowable under tax laws)			$30,000

	Normal	Pessimistic	Optimistic
Sales (units)	100,000	96,000	102,000
Beginning inventory	10,000	10,000	10,000
Value @ $4.5	$45,000	$45,000	$45,000
Ending inventory	20,000	19,200	20,400
Value	$100,000	$107,520	$112,400
Production (units)	110,000	105,200	112,400
Costs			
Variable costs	$550,000	$589,120	$505,800
Fixed costs (manufacturing, selling, and admin.)	$200,000	$202,000	$198,000
Total costs	$750,000	$791,120	$703,800
Recoveries			
Interest	$50,000	$50,000	$50,000
Dividends	$60,000	$60,000	$60,000
Debt recovery	$100,000	$100,000	$100,000
Equity recovery	$90,000	$90,000	$90,000
	$300,000	$300,000	$300,000
Selling price	$11.83	$12.79	$11.13

FIGURE 14.5 Product pricing worksheet ("what-if") parameters.

SALES ANALYSIS

Sales analysis assists managers in identifying those products, sales personnel, and customers that are contributing to profits and those that are not. Several reports can be generated to help marketing managers make good sales decisions. The *sales-by-product* report lists all major products and their sales for a period of time, such as a month. This report shows which products are doing well and which ones need improvement or should be discarded altogether. The *sales-by-salesperson* report lists total sales for each salesperson for each week or month. This report can also be subdivided by product to show which products are being sold by each salesperson. The *sales-by-customer* report is a useful way to identify high-and low-volume customers.

POPULAR FORECASTING AND STATISTICAL
SOFTWARE

Many computer software programs are used for forecasting purposes. They are broadly divided into two major categories: forecasting software and general-purpose statistical software. Some programs are stand-alone, while others are spreadsheet add-ins. Still others are templates. A brief summary of some popular programs follows.

SALES & MARKET FORECASTING TOOLKIT

This is a Lotus 1-2-3 template that produces sales and market forecasts, even for new products with limited historical data. It features

- Eight powerful methods for more accurate forecasts
- Spreadsheet models, complete with graphs, ready-to-use with your numbers

The Sales & Market Forecasting Toolkit offers a variety of forecasting methods to help you generate accurate business forecasts—even in new or changing markets with limited historical data. The forecasting methods include

- Customer poll
- Whole market penetration
- Chain method
- Strategic modeling
- Moving averages, exponential smoothing, and linear regressions

The customer poll method helps build a forecast from the ground up by summing the individual components, such as products, stores, or customers. Whole market penetration, market share, and the chain method are top-down forecasting methods used to predict sales for new products and markets lacking sales data. The strategic modeling method develops a forecast by projecting the impact of changes to pricing and advertising expenditures. Statistical forecasting methods include exponential smoothing, moving averages, and linear regression.

You can use the built-in macros to enter data into your forecast automatically. For example, enter values for the first and last months of a 12-month forecast. The compounded-growth-rate macro will automatically compute and enter values for the other ten months.

FORECAST! GFX

Forecast! GFX is a stand-alone forecasting system that can perform five types of time-series analysis: seasonal adjustment, linear and nonlinear trend analysis, moving-average analysis, exponential smoothing, and decomposition. Trend analysis supports linear, exponential, hyperbolic, S-curve, and polynomial trends. Hyperbolic trend models are used to analyze data that indicate a decline toward a limit, such as the output of an oil well or the price of a particular model of personal computer.Forecast! GFX can perform multiple-regression analysis with up to ten independent variables.

FORECALC

ForeCalc, a Lotus add-in, features the following:

- It uses nine forecasting techniques and includes both automatic and manual modes.
- It eliminates the need to export or reenter data.

You can use it in either automatic or manual mode. In automatic mode, just highlight the historical data in your spreadsheet, such as sales, expenses, or net income; then ForeCalc tests several exponential-smoothing models and picks the one that best fits your data.

Forecast results can be transferred to your spreadsheet with upper and lower confidence limits. ForeCalc generates a line graph showing the original data, the forecast values, and confidence limits.

ForeCalc can automatically choose the most accurate forecasting technique among the following:

- Simple one-parameter smoothing
- Holt's two-parameter smoothing
- Winters' three-parameter smoothing
- Trendless seasonal models
- Dampened versions of Holt and Winters's smoothing

ForeCalc's manual mode lets you select the type of trend and seasonality, yielding nine possible model combinations. You can vary the type of trend (constant, linear, or dampened) as well as the seasonality (nonseasonal, additive, or multiplicative).

STATPLAN IV

StatPlan IV is a stand-alone program for those who understand how to apply statistics to business analysis. You can use it for market analysis, trend forecasting, and statistical modeling.

StatPlan IV lets you analyze data by range, mean, median, standard deviation, skewdness, kurtosis, correlation analysis, one- or two-way analysis of variance (ANOVA), cross tabulations, and t-test.

The forecasting methods include multiple regression, stepwise multiple regression, polynomial regression, bivariate curve fitting, autocorrelation analysis, trend and cycle analysis, and exponential smoothing. The data can be displayed in X-Y plots, histograms, time-series graphs, autocorrelation plots, actual vs. forecast plots, or frequency and percentile tables.

GENEVA STATISTICAL FORECASTING

Geneva Statistical Forecasting, which is stand-alone software, can batch process forecasts for thousands of data series, provided the series are all measured in the same time units (days, weeks, months, and so on). The software automatically tries out as many as nine different forecasting methods, including six linear and nonlinear regressions and three exponential-smoothing techniques, before picking the one that best fits your historical data.

The program incorporates provisions that simplify and accelerate the process of reforecasting data items. Once you complete the initial forecast, you can save a data file that records the forecasting method assigned to each line item. When it is time to update the data, simply retrieve the file and reforecast, using the same methods as before. Geneva Statistical Forecasting tries as many as nine forecasting methods for each line item.

SMARTFORECASTS

SmartForecasts, a stand-alone forecasting program, features the following:

- Automatically chooses the right statistical method
- Lets you manually adjust forecasts to reflect your business judgment
- Produces forecast results

SmartForecasts combines the benefits of statistical and judgmental forecasting. It can determine which statistical method will give you the most accurate forecast and handle all the math. Forecasts can be modified using the program's EYEBALL utility. You may need to adjust a sales forecast to reflect an anticipated increase in advertising or a decrease in price. SmartForecasts summarizes data with descriptive statistics, plots the distribution of data values with histograms, plots variables in a scattergram, and identifies leading indicators.

You can forecast using single- and double-exponential smoothing, and simple and linear moving averages. It even builds seasonality into your forecasts using Winters's exponential smoothing, or you can eliminate seasonality by using times series decomposition and seasonal adjustment.

In addition, SmartForecasts features simultaneous multiseries forecasting of up to 60 variables and 150 data points per variable, offers multivariate regression to let you relate business variables, and has an "undo" command for mistakes.

TOMORROW

Tomorrow, stand-alone forecasting software, uses an optimized combination of linear regression, single exponential smoothing, adaptive rate response single exponential smoothing, Brown's one-parameter double exponential smoothing, Holt's two-parameter exponential smoothing, Brown's one-parameter triple exponential smoothing, and Gardner's three-parameter damped trend. Some of the main features are listed below:

- There is no need to reformat your existing spreadsheets. Tomorrow recognizes and forecasts formula cells (containing totals and subtotals, for example). It handles both horizontally and vertically oriented spreadsheets. It accepts historical data in up to 30 separate ranges.
- It allows you to specify seasonality manually, or calculates seasonality automatically.
- It allows you to do several forecasts of different time series (for example, sales data from different regions) at once.
- it recognizes and forecasts time series headings (names of months, etc.).
- Forecast optionally becomes normal part of your spreadsheet.
- The undo command restores the original spreadsheet.
- A browse feature allows you to look at any part of the spreadsheet (including the forecast) without leaving Tomorrow.
- It checks for and prevents accidental overlaying of nonempty or protected cells.
- An optional annotation mode labels forecast cells, calculates MAPE, and, when seasonality is automatically determined, describes the seasonality.
- It offers comprehensive context-sensitive on-line help.

FORECAST PRO

Forecast Pro, a stand-alone forecasting program, is the business software that uses artificial intelligence. A built-in expert system examines your data, then it guides you to exponential smoothing, Box-Jenkins, or regression—whichever method suits the data best.

MICROTSP

MicroTSP is a stand-alone program that provides the tools most frequently used in practical econometric and forecasting work. It covers the following:

1. Descriptive statistics
2. A wide range of single equation estimation techniques, including ordinary least squares (multiple regression), two-stage least squares, nonlinear least squares, and probit and logit

Forecasting tools include the following:

1. Exponential smoothing, including single exponential, double exponential, and Winters smoothing
2. Box-Jenkins methodology

SIBYL/RUNNER

Sibyl/Runner is an interactive, stand-alone forecasting system. In addition to allowing the usage of all major forecasting methods, the package permits analysis of the data, suggests available forecasting methods, compares results, and provides several accuracy measures in such a way that it is easier for the user to select an appropriate method and forecast needed data under different economic and environmental conditions. For details, see Makridakis, S., Hodgsdon, and S. Wheelwright, "An Interactive Forecasting System," *American Statistician*, November 1974.

OTHER FORECASTING SOFTWARE

There are many other forecasting software packages, such as Autocast II and 4 Cast and Trendsetter Expert Version.

GENERAL-PURPOSE STATISTICAL SOFTWARE

There are numerous statistical programs widely in use that can be utilized to build a forecasting model. Some of the more popular ones include

1. Minitab
2. SAS Application System
3. Statgraphics
4. SPSS
5. PC-90
6. Systat
7. RATS
8. BMD

Today's managers have some powerful tools at hand to simplify the forecasting process and increase its accuracy. Several forecasting models are available, and the automated versions of these should be considered by any manager who is regularly called upon to provide forecasts. A personal computer with a spreadsheet is a good beginning, but the stand-alone packages currently available provide the most accurate forecasts and are the easiest to use. In addition, they make several forecasting models available and can automatically select the best one for a particular data set.

15 Decision Support Systems

As discussed in Chapter 1, information systems are distinguished by the type of decisions they support, the operator who uses the system, the management control level of the system, the function of the system, and the attributes of the system (see Table 15.1). There are information systems to support structured decisions, unstructured decisions and anything in between. At the strategic level of management, decisions are unstructured, and decision styles may differ significantly among managers. Furthermore, a specific decision problem may occur only once. Thus, information systems developed for this level often are decision specific. Once the decision is made, the information system used for it is no longer applicable in its current form. For subsequent decisions, the system must be modified or discarded, a development that has major implications for the design of information systems. Whereas executive information systems and decision support systems aid in decisions that are unstructured, transaction processing systems and expert systems aid in decisions that are structured.

TABLE 15.1
Characteristics of DSS

Graphical
Large database
Integrate many sources of data
Report and presentation flexibility
Geared toward individual decision-making styles
Modular format
Optimization and heuristic approach
"What-if" and simulation
Goal-seeking and impact analysis
Perform statistical and analytical analysis

The manager who uses the information systems helps distinguish the systems. Transaction processing systems (TPSs) are used at the operational level of an organization, such as by clerks or secretaries. Executive information systems (EISs) are used specifically by personnel at the senior management level, such as vice presidents or presidents of an organization. Decision support systems (DSSs) are used by middle management, such as managers of the accounting department. Expert systems (ESs) are used by personnel at all levels of an organization.

Another factor in distinguishing information systems is the function of the systems. Transaction processing systems were established to computerize manual systems. Executive information systems (EISs) were designed to aid senior mangers in decision making. Decision support systems were designed to aid middle managers in decision making. Expert systems (ESs) were designed to aid all personnel in decision making.

The final distinguishing factor of information systems is the attributes of the system. Transaction processing systems are used to handle day-to-day transactions, such as the accounts payable system of an organization. Executive information systems attributes include visual summaries of forecasts and budgets of an organization. Decision support system attributes include visual displays of the sales, income, or interest estimates for the day, month, or year. Expert system attributes include systems that assess bad debt or authorize credit.

DECISION SUPPORT SYSTEM

A decision support system (DSS) is a computer-based information system that assists managers in making many complex decisions, such as decisions needed to solve poorly defined or semistructured problems. Instead of replacing the manager in the decision process, the DSS supports the manager in the application of the decision process. In other words, it is an automated assistant that extends the mental capabilities of the manager. Most authorities view the DSS as an integral part of the MIS in that its primary purpose is to provide decision-making information to managerial decision makers. A DSS allows the manager to change assumptions concerning expected future conditions and to observe the effects on the relevant criteria. As a result of these direct benefits, a DSS enables the manager to gain a better understanding of the key factors affecting the decision. It enables the manager to evaluate a large number of alternative courses of action within a reasonably short time frame. A DSS summarizes or compares data from either or both internal and external sources. Internal sources include data from an organization's database such as sales, manufacturing, or financial data. Data from external sources include information on interest rates, population trends, new housing construction, or raw material pricing.

DSSs often include query languages, statistical analysis capabilities, spreadsheets, and graphics to help the user evaluate the decision data. More advanced decision support systems include capabilities that allow users to create a model of the variables affecting a decision. With a model, users can ask "what-if" questions by changing one or more of the variables and seeing what the projected results would be. A simple model for determining the best product price would include factors for the expected sales volume at each price level. Many people use electronic spreadsheets for simple modeling tasks. A DSS is sometimes combined with executive information systems (EISs). DSS applications used in business include systems that estimate profitability, plan monthly operations, determine the source and application of funds, and schedule staff.

DSS DEVELOPMENT TOOLS

DSS development tools include the following:

1. IFPS Plus (Interactive Financial Planning System), developed by Comshare, is a modeling language that allows model building for "what-if," impact, and goal-seeking analyses. The program contains spreadsheet analysis, word processing abilities, and a convenient report writer.

2. EIS Micro-Workstation, developed by Boeing computer services, is an integrated software package that includes database systems, modeling, statistical analysis, forecasting, graphics, and report writing.

3. ENCORE, developed by Ferox Microsystems, has good financial modeling abilities. It can assist with cash-flow analysis, financial planning, and budget development and analysis. Word processing capabilities, graphics features, and forecasting and investment analysis are also available with this package.

4. MICROFORESIGHT is a package that provides sophisticated modeling abilities. It can analyze risk and determine how sensitive results are to certain decision or model parameters. Forecasting and statistical analysis are also available. This package can support goal seeking, thus allowing a decision maker to determine what inputs are required to obtain certain goals, such as profitability levels, rate of return targets, or cost targets.

5. PRO*FAS, developed by Decision Support Technology, is a DSS package to assist with fixed asset management. It allows managers to compare various depreciation models, using "what-if" analysis capabilities.

6. CFO Advisor is a DSS software package that performs financial analysis and allows managers to analyze the impact of financial changes on future financial outcomes.

7. PRECALC, developed at INSEAD, in France, assists decision makers in choosing from various options in the presence of multiple criteria in the decision. It is an interactive, menu-driven package that has graphical capabilities.

8. Commander™ Decision, developed by Comshare, is enterprise decision support software that allows you and other decision makers in your organization flexible access to the information you need—when you need it. Decision is designed for line managers, middle managers, directors, executives, analysts, and everyone who needs to work hands-on with business information to make better-grounded business decisions. Decision is especially designed for analysis applications: you gain insight by investigating plans and results by product, by market, by version, by region, and so on.

9. FISCAL, developed by Lingo Computer Design Inc., is "groupware for decision support," moving your decision support a quantum leap beyond spreadsheets. FISCAL supplies a complete architecture for rapidly implementing and managing major decision support systems. FISCAL can be used to extend the functionality of any major client-server application or database by supplying full decision support functionality for that appli-

cation. Some industry uses include financial services, insurance, mutual funds, pension funds, telecommunications, management consulting, utilities, oil and gas, healthcare, and manufacturing. FISCAL's architecture is a top-down approach to decision support and data warehousing, which ensures that the system will meet the business needs of end users.

In what follows, we will discuss one of the most popular modeling languages—IFPS/Plus—with illustrations.

INTERACTIVE FINANCIAL PLANNING SYSTEM

Interactive Financial Planning System (IFPS/Plus) is a multipurpose, interactive financial modeling system, often called *a decision support system (DSS)*, that supports and facilitates the building, solving, and asking of "what-if" questions of financial models. It is a powerful modeling and analysis tool, designed to handle large, complicated problems with lots of data. It is unsurpassed for large corporatewide applications—especially those that get their data directly from the enterprise relational database.

The output from an IFPS model is in the format of a spreadsheet—that is, a matrix or table in which

- The rows representing user-specified variables such as market share, sales, growth in sales, unit price, gross margin, variable cost, contribution margin, fixed cost, net income, net present value, internal rate of return, and earnings per share.
- The column designates a sequence of user-specified time periods such as month, quarter, year, total, percentages, or divisions.
- The entries in the body of the table display the values taken by the model variable over time or by segments of the firm such as divisions, product lines, sales territories, and departments.

IFPS offers the following key features:

- Like other special-purpose modeling languages, IFPS is an English-like modeling language. That means that, without an extensive knowledge of computer programming, the financial officer can build custom financial models and use them for "what-if" scenarios and managerial decisions.
- IFPS has a collection of built-in financial functions that perform calculations such as net present value (NPV), internal rate of return (IRR), loan amortization schedules, and depreciation alternatives.
- IFPS has a collection of built-in mathematical and statistical functions such as linear regression, linear interpolation, polynomial autocorrelation, and moving average functions.
- IFPS supports use of leading and/or lagged variables that are commonly used in financial modeling. For example, cash collections lag behind credit sales of prior periods.

- IFPS supports deterministic and probabilistic modeling. It offers a variety of functions for sampling from probability distributions such as uniform, normal, bivariate normal, and user-described empirical distributions.
- IFPS is non-procedural in nature. This means that the relationships, logic, and data used to calculate the various values in the output do not have to be arranged in any particular top-to-bottom order in an IFPS model. IFPS automatically detects and solves a system of two or more linear or non-linear equations.
- IFPS has extensive editing capabilities that include adding statements to and deleting statements from a model, making changes in existing statements, and making copies of parts or all of a model.

In addition, IFPS supports sensitivity analysis by providing the following solution options:

WHAT-IF

The IFPS lets you specify one or more changes in the relationships, logic, data, and/or parameter values in the existing model and recalculates the model to show the impact of these changes on the performance measures.

GOAL SEEKING

In the goal-seeking mode, IFPS can determine what change would have to take place in the value of a specified variable in a particular time period to achieve a specified value for another variable. For example, the financial officer can ask the system to answer the question, "What would the unit sales price have to be for the project to achieve a target return on investment of 20%?"

SENSITIVITY

This particular command is employed to determine the effect of a specified variable on one or more other variables. The *sensitivity* command is similar to the *what-if* command, but it produces a convenient, model-produced tabular summary for each new alternative value of the specified variable.

ANALYZE

The *analyze* command examines in detail those variables and their values that have contributed to the value of a specified variable.

IMPACT

The *impact* command is used to determine the effect on a specified variable of a series of percentage changes in one or more variables.

IFPS/OPTIMUM

The IFPS/OPTIMUM routine is employed to answer questions of a "what is the best?" type rather than "what-if" type.

OTHER FEATURES

- Routine graphic output
- Interactive color graphics
- Data files that contain both data and relationships
- A consolidation capability that lets the financial officer produce composite reports from two or more models
- Extraction of data from existing non-IFPS data files and placement of them in IFPS-compatible data files
- Operation on all major computer mainframes and microcomputers

Prospective users of IFPS/Plus are encouraged to refer to the following sources from Comshare, 3001 S. State St., P.O. Box 1588, Ann Arbor, Michigan 48106:

- *IFPS Cases and Models,* 1979
- *IFPS Tutorial,* 1980
- *IFPS User's Manual,* 1984
- *IFPS/Personal User's Manual,* 1984
- *IFPS University Seminar,* 1984
- *Comprehensive Fundamentals of IFPS,* 1984
- Papers Available from the Comshare University Support Programs

PALISADE'S DECISIONTOOLS SUITE

Palisade's *DecisionTools Suite* is a DSS tool in the area of risk and decision analysis. It includes such programs as @RISK, @RISK for Project, TopRank, PrecisionTree, BestFit, and RISKview. These programs analyze risk, run Monte Carlo simulations, perform sensitivity analyses, and fit data to distributions.

- *@RISK* is a risk analysis and simulation add-in for Microsoft Excel and Lotus 1-2-3. It is the risk analysis tool. Replace values in your spreadsheet with @RISK distributions to represent uncertainty, then simulate your model using powerful Monte Carlo simulation methods. @RISK recalculates your spreadsheet hundreds (or thousands) of times. The results: distributions of possible outcome values! Results are displayed graphically and through detailed statistical reports.
- *@RISK for Project* adds the same powerful Monte Carlo techniques to your Microsoft Project models, allowing users to answer questions such as, "What is the chance the project will be completed on schedule?"
- *TopRank* is a "what-if" analysis add-in for either Microsoft Excel or Lotus 1-2-3 for Windows. Take any spreadsheet model and select the cells that hold your results, and TopRank automatically determines which spreadsheet values affect your results the most. TopRank then ranks the values in order of importance. Your results can be displayed in Tornado, Spider, and Sensitivity high-resolution graphs, allowing the user to easily under-

stand the outcome at a glance. TopRank works easily and effectively with @RISK by identifying the critical cells users should concentrate on when running Monte Carlo simulations.

- *PrecisionTree* is a powerful, innovative decision analysis tool. Enter decision trees and influence diagrams directly in your spreadsheet models. Detail all available decision options and identify the optimal decision. Your decision analysis factors in your attitudes toward risk and the uncertainty present in your model. Sensitivity analysis identifies the critical factors that affect the decision you'll make. It is a real plus for outlining all available options for a decision or identifying and presenting the best course of action.
- *BestFit* is the distribution fitting solution for Windows. BestFit takes data sets (up to 30,000 data points or pairs) and finds the distribution that best fits the data. BestFit accepts three types of data from text files: direct entry, cut-and-paste, or direct link to data within Excel or Lotus 1-2-3 spreadsheets. BestFit tests up to 26 distributions types using advanced optimization algorithms. Results are displayed graphically and through an expanded report, which includes goodness-of-fit statistics. BestFit distributions can be used directly in @RISK for Excel, Lotus 1-2-3, and Microsoft Project models.
- *RISKview* is the distribution viewing companion to @RISK, @RISK for Project, or BestFit. It is a powerful tool for viewing, assessing, and creating probability distributions.

DSS APPLICATIONS

There are many DSS practical applications, as follows:

1. Hewlett-Packard developed *Quality Decision Management* to perform production and quality-control functions. It can help with raw material inspection, product testing, and statistical analysis.
2. *Manufacturing Decision Support System (MDSS)*, developed at Purdue University to support decisions in automated manufacturing facilities, is especially useful for CAD/CAM operations.
3. RCA has developed a DSS to deal with personnel problems and issues. The system, called *Industrial Relations Information Systems (IRIS)*, can handle problems that may not be anticipated or that may occur once, and it can assist in difficult labor negotiations.
4. The Great Eastern Bank Trust Division developed a DSS called *On-line Portfolio Management (OPM)* that can be used for portfolio and investment management. The DSS permits display and analysis of various investments and securities.
5. *RealPlan*, a DSS to assist with commercial real estate decisions, is useful for various decision aspects of purchasing, renovating, and selling property.
6. *EPLAN (Energy Plan) is* a DSS being developed by the National Audubon Society to analyze the impact of U.S. energy policy on the environment.

7. *The Transportation Evacuation Decision Support System (TEDSS)* is a DSS used in nuclear plants in Virginia. It analyzes and develops evacuation plans to assist managers in crisis management decisions regarding evaluation times and routes and the allocation of shelter resources.

8. The U.S. Army has developed an enlisted-manpower DSS to help with recruitment, training, education, reclassification, and promotion decisions. It encompasses simulation and optimization to model personnel needs and requirements. It interacts with an on-line database and other statistical analysis software packages.

9. *Voyage Profitability Estimator.* This DSS has been utilized by a shipping firm to compute the income from decisions affecting charter rates to be charged for particular trips. The system saves time and makes it possible to evaluate trade-offs between speed and fuel usage. The analysis involves ship and voyage characteristics such as tonnage, rate of fuel consumption, and port cost.

10. *Monthly Plan Calculations.* This DSS serves as a corporate budgeting tool to measure the levels of manpower needed to perform various functions, to calculate costs, and in general to evaluate the adequately of proposed operational plans. Using simple formulas, this system calculates the cost of materials, inventory, among other items, based on input that consists of monthly production and shipment plans. Typically, the system is used iteratively in an attempt to generate a plan that is sufficiently profitable and that meets the company's goal of maintaining reasonable level production in spite of the seasonal nature of the product.

11. *Source and Application of Funds.* An on-line budget of source and applications of funds has been used for operational decision making and financial planning in an insurance company to provide monthly cash flow figures. The DSS "output" is used at weekly meetings of an investment committee to help in allocating funds across investment areas and to minimize the amount of cash that is left idle in banks.

12. *Interactive Audit Staff Scheduling Systems.* An integer programming model has been designed by Balachandran and Zoltners to assist public accounting firms in scheduling their audit staff in an optimal and effective manner. The computerized management support system for scheduling staff to an audit can include the basic model along with a judgmental scheduling system and a scheduling information database. Motivation, morale, turnover, and productivity of the audit staff can all be affected by scheduling. In the scheduling process, the audit firm needs to consider its audit philosophy, objectives, staff size, rotational plans, and auditor evaluation. Many feasible audit staff schedules may fill these needs, but the firm needs to select the schedule that best meets its own objectives.

EXECUTIVE INFORMATION SYSTEMS

An executive information system (EIS) is a DSS made specially for top managers. It specifically supports strategic decision making. An EIS is also called *an executive support system (ESS).* It draws on data not only from systems internal to the organization but also from those outside, such as news services and market research databases. The EIS user interface often uses a mouse or a touch screen to help executives who are unfamiliar with using a keyboard. One leading system uses a remote control device similar to those used to control a television set. An EIS might allow senior executives to call up predefined reports for their personal computers, whether desktops or laptops. They might, for instance, call up sales figures in many forms—by region, by week, by fiscal year, by projected increases. The EIS includes capabilities for analyzing data and doing "what-if" scenarios.

Because top managers may not be familiar with (or comfortable with) computer systems, the EIS features make them easier for executives to use. Another aspect of the EIS user interface is the graphic presentation of user information. The EIS relies heavily on graphic presentation of both the processing options and data. Again, this is designed to make the system easier to use.

Because executives focus on strategic issues, the EIS often has access to external databases such as the Dow Jones News/Retrieval service. Such external sources of information can provide current information on interest rates, commodity prices, and other leading economic indicators. Table 15.2 presents the attributes of an executive information system.

TABLE 15.2
Characteristics of Executive Information Systems

Graphical
Easy-to-use interface
Broad, aggregated perspective
Accesses different data sources
Optionally expands to detail level
Provides context
Timeliness a crucial factor

A popular EIS software is Xecurive Pulse, developed by Megatrend Systems, Inc. It is a Windows-based executive information system. The software interfaces with many popular LAN-based accounting applications. It provides decision makers with easy access to financial and sales information, including trend analysis using drill-down and drill-across technology. Hundreds of charts, graphs, and views are available with a mouse click. The system extracts data from accounting history files, builds a database, and stores up to three years of information for each accounting period. Users can drill down through five organizational levels, compare actual vs. history and actual vs. budget, and display report or graphic results. Xecutive Pulse features extensive sales, cash flow, and human resource analysis, plus daily trends for accounts receivable, accounts payable, margins, sales, and inventory.

Comshare's Commander OLAP is another popular client/server software product for EIS and DSS applications like sales reporting and analysis, product profitability reporting, P&L analysis and reporting, enterprise budget reporting, critical success factor and key performance indicator reporting, and performance analysis and reporting. It transforms existing corporate data into usable information for management decision making.

LIMITATIONS OF CURRENT EIS

Although they offer great promise, many EISs have not been successfully implemented, and many executives have stopped using them. A common reason cited in several failed attempts is the mistake of not modifying the system to the specific needs of the individual executives who will use the system. For example, many executives prefer to have information presented in a particular sequence with the option of seeing different levels of supporting detailed information, such as cost data on a spreadsheet. The desired sequence and level of detail varies for each executive. It appears that an EIS must be tailored to the executives' requirements, or the executives will continue to manage with information they have obtained through previously established methods. This limitation can be corrected by tailoring the software based on the particular needs of the managers within the specific company. After the software has been appropriately modified, it will have significant practical applications.

EIS APPLICATIONS

There are many EIS applications for managers, including

1. *EIS in measuring productivity.* This application bears on management's concern over productivity. Management may use both internal and external information extracted from the EIS to show how productivity in an organization has declined in recent years. Financial data can be retrieved from the EIS database to demonstrate how increases in unit labor costs over time have been primarily responsible for significant increases in the product's unit cost and have been damaging to the company's competitiveness by forcing increases in the product's selling price. Executives can also compare company sales (internal data) to industry sales trends (external data) from the EIS to project market share changes in response to changes in selling price.

   External information may also be extracted from the EIS database to indicate how competitors achieve greater efficiency by using less labor and more advanced technology to manufacture a quality product at a materially lower unit cost. As a result, management may demonstrate that the competition is able to sell greater quantities of their products at lower prices. This information may provide justification for closing the unprofitable plant and opening a modern facility that will enable a company to be more competitive in the industry.

2. *EIS in product costing decisions.* Resolving the conflict between profitability in the short run and increasing market share in the long run requires a mix of both external and internal data for a rational decision. Executives

need information on product demand and elasticity, competing products and strategies, the economy, and other factors, such as the cost of manufacturing the product and trade-offs that exist relative to different product quality levels under different cost assumptions. Some questions executives may raise are as follows:

- What is the current level of quality, and how does the level differ from the desired level?
- What is the current full cost of producing a unit, and how does the amount differ from the full cost at the desired level of quality?
- What costs are variable over different levels of product quality?
- What costs are controllable relative to producing and selling the products?

EIS can provide data for solutions to some of these questions by computation. Many internal decisions depend on assumptions and measurements that require judgment and may be subject to different interpretations. In product costing decisions, issues involving appropriate cost and product quality trade-offs are equally subjective and unlikely to have a unique interpretation.

16 Artificial Intelligence and Expert Systems

Artificial intelligence (AI) is the application of human reasoning techniques to machines. Artificial intelligence systems use sophisticated computer hardware and software to simulate the functions of the human mind. Expert systems (ESs) are the most promising applications of artificial intelligence and have received the most attention. Expert systems are computer programs exhibiting behavior characteristics of experts. Expert systems involve the creation of computer software that emulates the way people solve problems. Like a human expert, an expert system gives advice by drawing on its own store of knowledge and by requesting information specific to the problem at hand. An expert systems is not exactly the same thing as a decision support system (DSS).

A DSS is computer-based software that assists decision makers by providing data and models. It performs primarily semistructured tasks, whereas an expert system is more appropriate for unstructured tasks. A decision support system can be interactive, just like an expert system. But, because of the way decision support systems process information, they typically cannot be used for unstructured decisions that involve nonquantitative data. Unlike expert systems, decision support systems do not make decisions but merely attempt to improve and enhance decisions by providing indirect support without automating the whole decision process.

Some general characteristics indicate whether a given business application is likely to be a good candidate for the development of an expert system. For example, its application requires the use of expert knowledge, judgment, and experience. The business problem must have a heuristic nature and must be defined clearly. The area of expertise required for the application must be well defined and recognized professionally, and the organization developing the expert system must be able to recruit an expert who is willing to cooperate with the expert system's development team. The size and complexity of the application must be manageable in the context of organizational resources, available technical skills, and management support.

EXPERT SYSTEMS

An expert system (ES), sometimes called *knowledge system*, is a set of computer programs that perform a task at the level of a human expert. Expert systems are created on the basis of knowledge collected on specific topics from human experts, and they initiate the reasoning process of a human being. Expert systems have emerged from the field of artificial intelligence, which is the branch of computer science that is attempting to create computer systems that simulate human reasoning and sensation. Artificial intelligence is covered in more detail later in this chapter.

Expert systems are used by management and nonmanagement personnel to solve specific problems, such as how to reduce production costs, improve workers' productivity, or reduce environmental impact. An ES is a computer program that, based on methodically using a narrowly defined domain of knowledge that is built into the program, comes up with a solution to a problem much the same way an expert would. The key to the definition is that the domain must be narrowly defined. An expert system cannot (at this point) be developed to give useful answers about all questions—it is limited as a human expert is limited to a particular field. For example, one expert system would not tell the controller both whether to lease or buy a piece of equipment based on the tax differences and also whether a pending business combination needs to be treated as a pooling or as a purchase.

HOW EXPERT SYSTEMS WORK

Expert systems are usually considered to have six major components as described below. The relationships of these components are illustrated in Figure 16.1. Based on the relationships illustrated in the figure, it is apparent that expert systems must work interactively with system users in assisting them in making better decisions. The system interacts with the user by continuously asking for information until it is ready to make a decision. Once the system has sufficient information, an answer or result is returned to the user. It is essential to note that not only must the system assist in making the decision itself, it must also provide the user with logic it employed to reach its decision.

1. *Knowledge database.* The knowledge database contains the rules and cases used when making decisions.
2. *Domain database.* This is the set of facts and information relevant to the domain (area of interest).
3. *Database management system.* This provides control input and management of both the knowledge and domain databases.
4. *Inference engine.* The inference engine contains the inference strategies and controls used by experts to manipulate knowledge and domain databases. It is the brain of the expert system. It receives the request from the user interface and conducts reasoning in the knowledge base.
5. *User interface.* The user interface provides the explanatory features, on-line help facilities, debugging tools modifications systems, and other tools designed to assist the user in effectively utilizing the system.
6. *Knowledge acquisition facility.* This allows for interactive processing between the system and the user; how the system acquires "knowledge" from human experts in the form of rules and facts. More advance technology allow intelligent software to "learn" knowledge from different

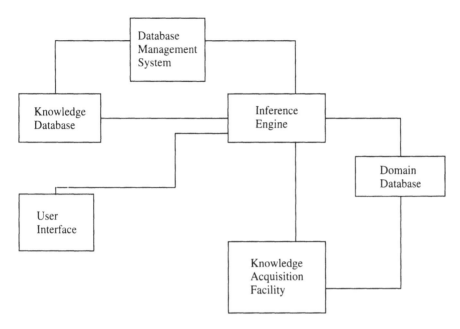

FIGURE 16.1 Expert system relationships.

problem domains. The knowledge learned by computer software is more accurate and reliable as compared with that of human experts.

The inference engine processes the data that the user inputs to find matches with the knowledge base. The knowledge base is where the expert's information is stored. The user interface is what allows the user to communicate with the program. The explanation facility shows the user how each decision was derived. Expert systems are only as good as their programming. If the information in the knowledge base is incorrect, or if the inference engine is not designed properly, the results will be useless. GIGO holds true: garbage in, garbage out.

The knowledge database consists of two types of knowledge representations; inductive knowledge (case base) and deductive knowledge (rule base).

RULE-BASED EXPERT SYSTEMS

The rule base of an expert system contains a set of production rules. Each rule has a typical IF-THEN clause. Expert system users provide facts or statements so that production rules can be triggered, and the conclusion can be generated. Ford Motor Company uses an expert system to diagnose engine repair problems. Typically, Ford dealers will call the help line at the Ford headquarters to receive a suggestion when a complicated engine problem cannot be diagnosed. Today, by using an expert system, dealers can access company's expert systems and receive a correct engine diagnosis within seconds. Expert systems can be used at any types of business domains and at any level in an organization. Examples are diagnosing illness, searching for oil, making soup, and analyzing computer systems. More applications and more users are expected in the future.

CASE-BASED EXPERT SYSTEMS

A case-based expert system uses an inductive method to conduct expert system reasoning. In this type of expert system, a case base is employed. A case base consists of many historical cases that have different results. The expert inference engine will search through the case base and find the appropriate historical case, which matches the characteristics of the current problem to be solved. After a match has been allocated, the solution of a matched historical case will be modified and used as the new suggestion for this current problem.

Lockheed uses an expert system to help speed the purchase of materials ranging from industrial coolant to satellite and rocket parts. The old MIS request for a purchase order included more than 100 different forms, which were seldom completed by the purchaser. Much time was spent in making corrections and changes to make a purchase order complete. By using an expert system, less information is asked, and the time required to finish a purchasing order is reduced.

EXPERT SYSTEM SHELLS AND PRODUCTS

An ES shell is a collection of software packages and tools used to design, develop, implement, and maintain expert systems. Expert system shells exist in many different forms. There are a number of off-the-shelf expert system shells that are complete and ready to run. The user enters the appropriate data or parameters, and the expert system provides output to the problem or situation. Some of the expert system shells include Level 5 and VP-Expert. Other shells are described in Table 16.1.

TABLE 16.1
Popular ES Shells

1st-Class Fusion offers a direct, easy-to-use link to the knowledge base. It also offers a visual rule tree, which graphically shows how rules are related.

Financial Advisor is an ES shell that can analyze capital investments in fixed assets such as equipment and facilities.

Knowledgepro is a high-level language that combines functions of expert systems and hypertext. It allows the setup of classic if-then rules, and it can read database and spreadsheet files.

Leonardo is an ES shell that employs an object-oriented language used to develop an expert system, called COMSTRAT, that can be used by marketing managers to help analyze the position of their companies and products relative to their competition.

Personal Consultant (PC) Easy is a shell used to route vehicles in warehouses and manufacturing plants.

Furthermore, a number of other expert system development tools make the development of expert systems easier and faster. These products help capture if-then rules for the rule base, assist in using tools such as spreadsheets and programming languages, interface with traditional database packages, and generate the inference engine.

Once developed, an expert system can be run by people who have virtually no computer experience. The expert system asks the user a series of questions. Subsequent questions are often based on answers to previous questions. After the user answers the system-generated questions, the expert system generates conclusions. Many expert systems have word-processing capabilities that can generate letters asking users for additional information.

APPLICATIONS OF EXPERT SYSTEMS

The use of expert systems is on the rise. Sales of expert system shells are increasing at about 20% per year, with about 60% of the sales for use on IBM PCs or compatibles. One of the main challenges to the development and use of expert systems is to integrate expert system concepts and functions into existing applications, including transaction processing. The applications of expert systems are many and varied, including security, capacity planning for information systems, military analysis, the construction of maps, and law enforcement.

A number of expert systems have been in existence for several years or more. A few of these systems are briefly described below:

1. *CoverStory* is an expert system that extracts marketing information from a database and automatically writes marketing reports.
2. Westinghouse Electric has an expert system, called *Intelligent Scheduling and Information System (ISIS-11)*, for scheduling complex factory orders.
3. *CARGEX-Cargo Expert System* is used by Lufthansa, a German airline, to help determine the best shipping routes.
4. NCR Corporation has an expert system for communications. The system allows the collection and encoding of an expert's knowledge into a form that can be used by a personal computer. The overall emphasis of the product is to allow more efficient analysis of difficulties regarding data communications.
5. ACE is an expert system used by AT&T to analyze the maintenance of telephone networks.
6. General Electric has an expert system called DELTA that assists in engine repair.
7. *XCON (Expert VAX System Configuration)* is an expert system developed by Digital Equipment Corporation (DEC) to help in configuring and organizing minicomputer systems. The system uses thousands of rules and helps DEC get the correct minicomputer system to customers.
8. *Authorizer's Assistant (AA)* is an ES developed by American Express for credit authorization. It is used to weed out bad credit risks and reduce losses.
9. *Watchdog Investment Monitoring System* is an ES developed by Washington Square Advisors, the investment management subsidiary of North-

western National Life Insurance Company. It is used to analyze potential and existing corporate bonds to enhance clients' revenue. The analysis includes a change in financial ratios as an indicator of past performance and predictor of future financial directions.

10. *Escape* is an expert system by Ford Motor Company for claim authorization and processing.

11. *Auditor,* developed by C. Duncan (University of Illinois), is an expert system to aid internal auditors in analyzing a company's allowance for bad debts.

12. TICOM, developed by A. Baily and M. Gagle (University of Minnesota), is an expert system to evaluate internal control systems.

13. *Financial Advisor,* developed by MIT Sloan School of Management, provides expert advice on projects, products, and mergers and acquisitions.

14. *Plan Power,* developed by Applied Expert Systems, is an expert system that takes into account a company's financial situation and then matches needs with the most appropriate financial products and services. The system will run scenario spreadsheets showing the income tax situation, cash flows, net worth, and other critical factors based on alternative decisions.

15. GURU, developed by Micro Data Base Systems, is an expert system shell and spreadsheet providing management advice and financial analysis.

16. Peat Marwick is using the advice of an expert system to bring more consistency and precision to the auditing of commercial bank loans. This allows the company to assess a company's provision for bad debts.

FUZZY LOGIC

Fuzzy logic deals with uncertainty. This technique, which uses the mathematical theory of fuzzy sets, simulates the process of normal human reasoning by allowing the computer to behave less precisely and logically than do conventional computers. Fuzzy logic is a type of mathematics. It deals with non-precise values with a certain degree of uncertainty. This technology allows logistics to be utilized by non-precise information.

Fuzzy logic can be advantageous for the following reasons:

- It provides flexibility; it gives you options.
- It gives you imagination.
- It is more forgiving.
- It allows for observation.

One example where fuzzy logic is being used extensively is in consumer products where the input is provided by sensors rather than by people. It is believed that fuzzy logic will become a valuable component in the next generation of computer systems. In such a system, each of the central technology building blocks can be used in series or in parallel.

AUTOMATIC PROGRAMMING

Automatic programming is described as a *super-compiler*, or a program that could take in a very high-level description of what the program is to accomplish and produce a program in a specific programming language. One of the important contributions of research in automatic programming has been the notion of debugging as a problem-solving strategy. It has been found that it is often much more efficient to produce an inexpensive, error-filled solution to a programming or robot control problem and then modify it than to insist on a first solution that is completely free of defects.

FUNCTIONAL AREA APPLICATIONS

In addition to the applications described above, expert systems are used in accounting-related systems, capital resource planning, loan applications, strategic marketing, and developing strategic objectives for the organization.

ACCOUNTING SYSTEMS

Internal accounting systems are an ideal area for expert systems applications. Expert systems can be developed to analyze cash flows, accounts payable, accounts receivable, and the appropriate use of general ledger entries. The knowledge base can include information from accounting organizations such as the American Institute of Certified Public Accountants (AICPA). Current tax laws, Securities and Exchange Commission requirements, and generally accepted accounting practices can also be entered into the knowledge base. The inference engine for the accounting expert system can assist in many important decisions, including financial accounting approaches, the management of cash flows, and other related accounting practices.

Four areas of accounting in which expert systems can be used are accounting standards, taxation, management and control, and auditing.

In the area of accounting standards, an expert system would apply standards in a consistent manner when preparing accounts or performing audits. This task would probably be performed more often by external auditors than by internal auditors.

Taxation is an area restricted by a complex set of rules and procedures. Expert systems make compliance with these rules much easier, since all rules can be programmed into the computer. Tax planning is an area that has also benefited. More on this is explained later.

In the area of management and control, expert systems are used to supplement management information systems. Expert systems provide decision models used for planning and control. As with any new management system, the internal auditor should evaluate the potential benefits and control areas. Furthermore, the auditor must periodically evaluate established expert systems to determine whether the systems continue to meet the objectives they were designed to meet.

Auditing is the final area of accounting where expert systems can be very useful. Expert systems can choose an audit program, choose test sample, determine the level of error, perform an analytical review, and then make a judgment based on the findings. Expert systems can also assist with the following:

- Preparing working papers
- Maintaining the ledger
- Preparing financial statements
- Planning budgets and forecasts
- Payroll preparation and analysis
- Revenue analysis by volume, price, and product-service mix
- Analyzing expenses
- Costs specified in terms of volume, price, and category
- Converting from cash to accrual basis
- Aging accounts receivable
- Financial statements analysis
- Financial aspects of the business

Currently, there are only a few tax expert systems available. This is due to two primary factors. First, if the information in the knowledge base is incorrect, and bad decisions are made based on the system, the developer could be sued. Second, many expert systems are developed by large firms that want to protect their investment. It is not difficult to develop an expert system using a shell. The reasons may include (a) the tax code is under constant revision (more change implies higher cost to maintain the expert system), (b) tax practitioners do not believe in the benefits of expert systems, (c) existing CD-ROM tax databases provide a lot of information, and (d) tax-only expert systems are not sufficient to do business planning—more support is needed to make planning decisions.

The following are examples of programs used in tax planning. *ExpeTAX*, developed by Coopers and Lybrand, is used in tax planning and tax accrual. It uses a question-and-answer format to run a maze of 3000 rules and outlines a client's best tax options. It will, for example, identify the differences between book and tax values. *Taxadvisor* is used for estate planning. *Corptax* examines the tax consequences for stock redemptions. CCH Inc. has introduced *CCH Tax Assistant*. This software, while not termed an *expert system* by CCH, performs in many ways like an expert system. Tax Assistant uses user-entered information while making decisions. The software can reduce the time spent by accountants calculating and generating reports. In addition, lower-level accountants can complete more difficult research tasks using the software.

Some believe that expert systems are the future of tax accounting. Expert systems could be used for *compliance* work, for example, to determine whether an activity is passive. In addition, they could be used for identifying problems and for planning purposes, for example, to determine whether a company is a personal holding company and how to avoid the associated penalty.

CAPITAL EXPENDITURE PLANNING

Capital investment planning involves making long-term planning decisions for alternative investment opportunities. There are many investment decisions that the company may have to make to allow it to grow. Examples of capital budgeting applications are product line selection, keeping or selling a business segment, leasing or buying, and the best asset in which to invest. Resource commitments may also be evaluated in the form of new product development, market research, acquisition of a computer, refunding of long-term debt, and so on. Expert systems may also be used in mergers and acquisitions analysis in the form of buying another company to add a new product line. *CashValue* is a commercially available expert system in capital projects planning.

ANALYSIS OF CREDIT AND LOAN APPLICATIONS

A major part of any lending institution is making sound, profitable loans to businesses. A large number of risky loans can result in large financial losses and potential bankruptcy for the institution. Reliable loans to companies with little chance of default can substantially increase a bank's overall profitability. Due to the high degree of analytical skills and experience involved, the analysis of loan applications is quite appropriate for computerized expert systems. Extending loans and lines of credit to businesses involve several key considerations, one of which is *management attitudes and style.* Does the management have the ability to grow in adverse as well as good times? How will management use the proceeds of the loan? Are there any potential problems with the company or management? The loan analysis expert system can either accept or reject the application for loans and credit. The acceptance can also be conditioned on some criteria. For example, the loan can be made only if the company receiving the funds agrees to make certain changes in their operation, management style, marketing strategy, and so forth. The expert system can also identify questionable loans in terms of default risk. The result could be a higher interest rate, a lower loan amount, an altered repayment structure, or higher collateral requirements.

MARKETING APPLICATIONS

Marketing expert systems can be developed to allow marketing managers to make strategic marketing-related decision making and planning activities. Establishing sales and profit goals, products and services on which to focus, and prospective customer profiles are examples. The marketing expert system requires a knowledge base covering relevant data on customers, the overall market structure, diverse internal and external factors, and the competition. Once the overall strategic marketing plan has been mapped out, the expert system can explore specific goals. The types of marketing mix (that is, what products and services to be produced), promotional efforts, pricing considerations, and the distribution system are resolved at this level. The product quality, style, packaging, warranties, customer services offered, features and options, and return policies are analyzed. Pricing policy decisions are equally important. The list price, discounts, and credit terms are determined as a part of price analysis. Advertising, the role of sales representatives, direct marketing, publicity, the use of marketing research firms, and using professional marketing companies are important decisions for promotion. Finally, the distribution channel of delivering products and services to customers is examined.

APPLICATIONS IN FINANCE

INSURANCE

Underwriting. Expert systems will increase the consistency of applying company standards in evaluating various risks (fire, flood, theft, and so on).

Claims processing. Fraud detection is particularly difficult in medical insurance due to the complexity of claims. Expert systems will substantially reduce labor cost by quickly evaluating claims and improving the detection of suspicious information.

Reserving. Deciding how much reserves to set aside for future claims and ongoing payout is similar to factory inventory schedules in many ways. ESs will provide the means to consistently allocate resources to meet uncertain demands.

PORTFOLIO MANAGEMENT

Security selection. With more than 100,000 stocks and bonds to choose from, selecting the right securities is a substantial challenge. Too much information is available than can be intelligently digested. ESs will analyze data and provide recommendations. For example, Unitek Technologies' *Expert Strategist* performs financial statement analysis.

Consistent application of constraints. Managers of multiple portfolios must consistently apply multiple constraints on different portfolios. The constraints include compliance with legal SEC rules, clients' guidelines, consistency across related accounts, etc. ESs will help financial professionals in applying different portfolio designs under the multiple constraints.

Hedge advisor. The number of financial instruments available, and the complexity of their relationship, is increasing rapidly. These instruments vary in margin, liquidity, and price. They can be combined to create "synthetic securities," thereby hedging against market risk. ES will help the process of creating *synthetic securities.*

TRADING ADVISOR

Real-time data feed. Timely information is critical in any trading application. Expert systems will integrate real-time multiple external/internal data sources and provide timely information.

Trading rules and rule generators. The conventional knowledge-engineering approach to rule writing will be replaced by rule generators. A rule generator ES will recognize data patterns and generate immediate hypotheses (trading rules) that lead to trading recommendations.

Critics and neural nets. Critic ESs will review and evaluate system-recommended trades, process explanations of those trades, and find culprits and heroes.

ES in The Global Financial Market

Financial statement advice for multinational companies. Multinational firms have unique problems with regard to reporting and legal requirements. These firms must deal with inconsistencies such as varying reporting formats, regulatory requirements, and account types. These problems will be solved by ESs.

24-hour trading programs. Individual human traders cannot work 24 hours a day. However, ESs can. With traderless expert systems, smaller companies will have a better chance of entering global markets and foreign exchange trading.

Hedges. In the international securities markets, many different types of hedges are possible, including interest-rate swaps, currency swaps, options, and futures. ESs can take advantage of those hedges.

Arbitrage. ESs will quickly identify and evaluate arbitrage opportunities and trigger transactions.

BENEFITS AND DISADVANTAGES OF EXPERT SYSTEMS

The following are benefits expert systems offer:

- Increased output and productivity as well as better accuracy and reliability
- The ability to function as tutors, distilling expertise into clearly defined rules
- Capture of scarce expertise
- Knowledge sharing (The system will be available to provide second opinions within the domain, as well as provide "what-if" analysis where results are sought on variable changes.)
- A shorter decision time (Routine decisions are rapidly made by the systems.)
- Enhancement of problem-solving capabilities
- Greater security (more secure than an expert employee, who may be hired by a competitor)

The drawbacks to expert systems are as follows:

- They fail to adapt to a continually changing environment.
- They are usually confined to a vary narrow domain and may have difficulty coping with broad discipline knowledge decisions.

NEURAL NETWORKS

Expert systems typically require huge databases of information gathered from recognized experts in a given field. This system will then ask questions of the user and deduce an answer based on the responses given and the information in the database.

These answers are not necessarily correct but should be a logical conclusion based on the information provided. Neural networks are a developing technology in which computers actually try to learn from the database and operator what the right answer is to a question. The system gets positive or negative response to output from the operator and stores that data so that it will make a better decision the next time. While still in its infancy, this technology shows promise for use in fraud detection, economic forecasting, and risk appraisals.

The idea behind this software is to convert the order-taking computer into a "thinking" problem solver. This would allow computers to take over some of the more mundane decision-making jobs of accountants, such as determining if a lease is operating or capital. Neural networks are software programs that simulate human intelligence. They are designed to learn from experience. For example, each time a neural network program makes the right decision (which is predetermined by a human instructor) on recognizing a number or sequence-of-action pattern, the programmer reinforces the program with a confirmation message that is stored. In the event of a wrong decision, a negative message is reinforced. Thus, it gradually builds experimental knowledge in that subject.

Today, most neural networks take the form of mathematical simulations embedded in software that runs on ordinary microprocessors. Future developments will include the emergence of network chips that will dramatically increase both the speed of operations and their work applications. These chips will be used to mimic decision operations and carry them out the way humans do.

NEURAL NETWORK APPLICATIONS IN BUSINESS

Currently, a neural computer network is being employed at the Mellon Bank's Visa and Master Card operation in Wilmington, Delaware, which keeps a daily track of 1.2 million accounts. One of the functions of this operation's computer is to scan customer purchases and look for spending patterns that may indicate stolen credit cards. The neural network compares purchases with customer behaviors. It also generates data without being told to do so, because the system has been programmed to take the initiative and think like a human.

One way in which neural networks will help accountants is in internal audits. Ernst & Young, in Dallas, is working on this application, which would allow financial managers to improve their handling of working capital.

Neural networks are beginning to be helpful in many business problems when information is not easy to quantify. In addition to bankruptcy applications, they are being used in management of portfolios. A portfolio manager must continuously scan for nonperforming stocks while, on the other side, stock analysts are looking for undervalued stocks. Neural networks are particularly good for problems when deductive reasoning gives mixed results. The inductive reasoning of neural networks can do a better job. There is a large store of historical information about good and bad investments that can be analyzed for relationships that may be quite subtle. Shearson-Lehman is using neural networks to predict stock patterns.

Furthermore, neural networks appear to be useful tools in bankruptcy prediction. They can use some of the tools already in place to improve prediction. If the ratios chosen for the Z model (discussed in Chapter 11) are used, but the neural network is allowed to form its own functions, the predictive abilities of the Z formula can be much improved. This is of significant value to managers, creditors, and investors, since misclassification, particularly of a firm that is going bankrupt, has huge monetary implications.

Applications of neural networks are language processing (text and speech), image processing, character recognition (handwriting recognition and pattern recognition), and modeling.

The following is a list of popular neural network software.

Al Ware Inc.
11000 Cedar Avenue
Cleveland, Ohio 44106
(216) 421-2380
Products: Unix computer system
                       VMS computer system

California Scientific Software
10024 Newtown Road
Nevada City, California 95959
(800) 284-8112
Products: BrainMaker
                       BrainMaker Plus
                       Condensed Version

HNC, Inc.
5501 Oberlin Drive
San Diego, CA 92121-1718
(619) 546-8877
Products: Explore Net 3000
                       Knowledge Net

Neural Systems, Inc.
2827 West 43rd Ave.
Vancouver, British Columbia V6N3HG
(604) 263-3667
Product: Genesis

Neural Ware, Inc.
Penn Center West
Building IV, suite 227
Pittsburgh, Pennsylvania 15276
(412) 787-8222
Products: Neural Works Professional, II/Plus
                       Neural Works Explorer

Scientific Consultant Services, Inc.
20 Stagecoach Road
Selden, NY 11784
(516) 696-3333
Product: N-Train

Teranet
1615 Bowen Road
Manaio, British Columbia V9F 1G5
Canada
(604) 754-4223
Products: ModelWare
                           ModelWare Professional

17 Computer Security and Auditing

Every day, there are news stories about computer-related data errors, thefts, burglaries, fires, and sabotage. Although considerable efforts have been made to reduce vulnerability to such events, much more effort is needed. Weak computer security and lack of internal controls tremendously increase an organization's vulnerability to the following:

- Commission of fraud
- Theft of electronic information
- Theft of physical information, such as printed outputs or computer disks/tapes
- Invasion of privacy
- Damage to computers and peripherals
- Interception of communications
- Illegal recording of electromagnetic emanations from computers and peripherals
- Unintentional data errors due to carelessness or negligence
- Loss of information integrity through unauthorized alterations and modifications to data
- Sabotage by disgruntled employees or competitors
- Power failure

Crime insurance policies should be taken out to cover such areas as theft, fraud, intentional destruction, and forgery. Business interruption insurance covers lost profits during downtime. Insurance should also cover computer equipment in transit.

A risk analysis should be performed in planning computer security policies and financial support. Computer security risks fall into one of three major categories: destruction, modification, and disclosure. Each of these may be further classified into intentional, unintentional, and environmental attacks. The threat comes from computer criminals and disgruntled employees who intend to defraud, sabotage, and "hack." It also comes from computer users who are careless or negligent. Lastly, the threat comes from the environment; an organization must protect itself from disasters such as fire, flood, and earthquakes. An effective security plan must consider all three types of threats: intentional attacks, unintentional attacks, and environmental attacks. What is the company's degree of risk exposure?

FINANCIAL LOSS AND THE COST-BENEFIT CRITERION

The danger of financial loss to a company can be greatly reduced by increasing computer security. In all likelihood, not investing in appropriate security measures will prove to be far more expensive for a company than investing in the appropriate security measures. It would even be appropriate for a company to consider the cost of investing in computer security as a form of insurance.

The cost of security measures must always be compared with the benefits received. As Figure 17.1 illustrates, the optimal level of security expenditure is when the combined cost of security measures and financial loss is minimized. The law of diminishing returns clearly applies here. Additional expenditures on security measures, beyond a certain point, are not likely to be cost effective. While appropriate security measures can greatly reduce the likelihood of a financial loss, security measures by themselves cannot guarantee against every kind of damage and accident: a certain degree of risk will always have to he accepted.

The cost-benefit criterion dictates that a company formally assess the risks it faces. The following three questions must be answered by the organization:

- What type of threats may affect our organization?
- What is the probability that a threat will occur?
- What is the potential liability for each threat?

For each type of threat, expected loss may be calculated as follows:

$$\text{Loss expectancy} = \text{Probability of Loss} \times \text{Amount of Loss}$$

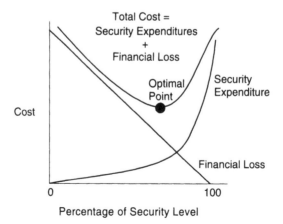

FIGURE 17.1 Optimal security expenditure as a function of financial loss and security expenditure.

Using the above formula, expected losses may be classified into three categories. As shown in Figure 17.2, loss expectancy is highest for category A and lowest for category C. Clearly, considerable attention must be directed toward category A, since there is both a high amount and a high probability of loss. In contrast, little attention needs to tie given to category C items, which seldom occur and for which the associated loss is small. Professional judgment will be required to determine which items in category B require attention and which do not.

While the above model is theoretically appealing, it does have serious practical limitations. The model relies heavily on estimating future probabilities and costs; it is extremely difficult to make such estimates with reasonable accuracy. When implementing the model, it is also possible for the user to overlook many serious indirect consequences of the threat.

PHYSICAL AND DATA SECURITY

Physical security is the first line of defense in protecting a computer system. It encompasses the plant, equipment, and personnel. Data security is also of vital concern to an organization; data integrity, data accuracy, and data privacy are of paramount importance. Physical and data security considerations are equally important. An effective security system will prevent a security breach. However, if, in spite of proper protection, a system is successfully attacked, the system should create an audit trail to allow prompt investigation.

The computer room is the structure that houses the computer facilities. Unauthorized access to the computer room should be restricted. Sensing and surveillance devices may be installed. The plant should also be designed to protect the computer environment, including heating, cooling, dehumidifying, ventilating, lighting, and power. Air ducts of air-conditioning units should also be secured against access with heavy-gauge screens. Appropriate care must also be taken to protect the plant from harm from accidents and disasters such as fire and floods. Adequate emergency lighting should be available for safe evacuation in case of fire or other disaster.

Consideration must also be given to loss or damage to computer equipment and peripherals. Media, such as disks, tapes, and output, should be protected. User manuals for equipment and software must be protected to maintain continuity of proper operations. Surge protectors should be used to protect the computer system against power line disturbances. Finally, the organization must consider loss of or injury to its personnel. Not only must the organization be concerned about the physical safety of its employees, it must also consider the threat of psychological

	High	Low
High	A	B
Low	B	C

Amount of Loss

FIGURE 17.2 Loss expectancy.

dissatisfaction. Disgruntled employees may do intentional damage. Moreover, job turnover associated with dissatisfied employees disrupts the routine operation and maintenance of computer systems.

The integrity, accuracy, and privacy of data must be protected. Data integrity is essential to computer security. Data lacks integrity if it is missing, incomplete, inconsistent, or stored in a poorly designed database environment. The concept of *accuracy* is distinct from that of *integrity*. Data is accurate if it is reliable and the data is what it purports to be. Privacy means that only authorized individuals have access to data. Programmers should not have free access to the computer area or library due to possible data manipulation. Important diskettes should be locked up.

CONTROLLING PHYSICAL ACCESS

Access controls guard against improper use of equipment, data files, and software. To limit physical access, a security system must be able to discriminate between authorized and unauthorized individuals. Physical access can be limited using three general methods.

Identification. Identification is based on comparing the physical characteristics of the individual with previously stored information. For example, an individual's signature, personnel number, code, voice print, palm print, fingerprint, teeth print, or other personal trait could be verified before allowing access. Secondary authentication, such as the user's place of birth, may be required for highly sensitive information.

User's name and passwords. Passwords are based on some memorized combination of letters or numbers. There should be no logic to the password, so it cannot be easily guessed. Individuals are authorized based on what they know. Passwords should be changed regularly. Inactive passwords (e.g., more than four months old) should be deleted. Passwords should be changed and confidential data withdrawn from terminated employees. If a user changes a password, controls must exist to ensure that the user cannot use the old password. Passwords should not be shared. Access control software may be used that provides a minimum password time period in which a new password cannot be changed or a new password matching an old one will be rejected.

Cards or keys. Access can also be limited through the use of cards, keys, or badges; individuals are authorized based on what they possess. Improper access may be signaled by an alarm, and unauthorized access patterns should be investigated. Smart cards may be used in which the user enters both the identification number and a random generated code, which changes each time the card is used or over a stated time period.

Within the plant, areas containing sensitive data should be accessible only to authorized personnel. These areas, including the computer room, should have only a single entry door, which can be operated by an appropriate encoded magnetic-strip ID card. Physical controls might include having a librarian keep a log. A lockout should occur with repeated errors. Logs should automatically be kept of the ID number, time of access, and function performed. Furthermore, data dictionary software provides an automated log of access to software and file information. Intrusion detection devices such as cameras and motion detectors should be used to monitor sensitive and high-risk areas to protect against unauthorized individuals.

Are controls being diligently followed over processing, maintaining records, and file or software modification? Each individual function (e.g., accounts receivable or payroll) may have its own password so that users have access to limited areas of the database. The computer can keep an internal record of the date and time each file was last updated, and this internal record is compared against the log. The hours to access "key" microcomputer files can be limited to prevent unauthorized access after normal working hours. Files should be displayed in terms of different levels of confidentiality and security, such as *top secret, confidential, internal use only,* and *unrestricted.* Confidential information should not be displayed on the screen. To control access to sensitive data, there should be a mapping of access requirements to the system components. Access rights should he based on job function, and there should exist an appropriate segregation of duties. Temporary employees should be restricted to specific project, activity, system, and time period.

FIRE SECURITY

According to insurance companies, fire is the most frequent cause of damage to computer centers. Simple steps can reduce the damage caused by fire and, in the process, reduce insurance premiums.

- Safes for document storage should have a minimum four-hour fire rating.
- Walls, floors, and ceilings of computer facilities should have a minimum two-hour fire rating.
- Fire alarm should ring simultaneously at the computer facility and the nearest fire department. In addition, fire alarm signals should be located where prompt response is assured.
- Vaults used for storing backup tapes and records should be located in a separate building, at sufficient distance.
- Smoke and ionization detection systems should be installed throughout the ceiling of the computer facilities. Water detection systems should also be installed under the floor of computer facilities.
- Halon or a similar fire extinguishing system should he installed throughout computer facilities. Automatic sprinkler systems can be used in the supply and support areas. In case of destruction, there should be a disaster recovery plan.
- Adherence to building codes and fire marshal regulations is a must.

SABOTEUR'S TOOLS

In recent years, ingenious procedures have been developed to preserve computer security, and yet many computer systems are still astonishingly insecure. Saboteurs may use a wide variety of tools and techniques to overcome security. Some of the methods are as follows:

Trojan horse. The saboteur places a hidden program within the normal programs of the business. The computer continues to function normally while the hidden program is free to collect data make secret modifications to programs and files, erase or destroy data, and even cause a complete shutdown of operations. Trojan horses can be programmed to destroy all traces of their existence after execution.

Salami techniques. The perpetrator can make secret changes to the computer program that cause very small changes that are unlikely to be discovered, but whose cumulative effect can be very substantial. For example, the perpetrator may steal ten cents from the paycheck of each individual and transfer it to his own account.

Back door or trap door. During the development of a computer program, programmers sometimes insert a code to allow them to bypass the standard security procedures. Once the programming is complete, such a code may remain in the program either accidentally or intentionally. Attackers rely on their knowledge of this extra code to bypass security.

Time bomb/logic bomb. A code may be inserted into a computer program that causes damages when a predefined condition occurs, such as a date or time.

Masquerade. A computer program is written that masquerades or simulates the real program. For example, a program may be written to simulate the log-in screen and related dialog. When a user attempts to log in, the program captures the user's ID and password and displays some error message, prompting the user to log-in again. The second time, the program allows the user to log in, and the user may never know that the first log-in was fake.

Scavenging. A computer normally does not erase data that is no longer needed. When the user "deletes" some data, that information is not actually destroyed; instead, that space is made available for the computer to write on later. A scavenger may thus be able to steal sensitive data, which the user thought had been deleted but was actually still available on the computer.

Viruses. Viruses are similar to Trojan horses, except the illegal code is capable of replicating itself. A virus can rapidly spread throughout the system, and eradicating it can be expensive and cumbersome. To guard against viruses, there should be care in using programs on diskettes or in copying software from bulletin boards or other sources outside the company. Disks should only be used from verified sources. The best precaution is to use a commercial virus scanner on all downloaded files before using them. An example is McAfee's virus scan. Virus protection and detection is crucial.

Data manipulation. The most common and easiest way of committing fraud is to add or alter the data before or during input. The best way to detect this type of computer crime is the use of audit software to scrutinize transactions and review audit trails that indicate additions, changes, and deletions were made to data files. The use of batch totals, hash totals, and check digits can also help prevent this type of crime. A hash total is a reconciliation between the total daily transactions processed by the micro and manually determined totals by an individual other than the computer operator. Material deviations must be investigated. A hash total is generated by adding values that would not typically be added together, so the total has no meaning other than for control purposes. Examples are employee and product numbers. A check digit is used to ascertain whether an identification number (e.g., account number or employee number) has been correctly entered by adding a calculation to the identification number and comparing the outcome to the check digit.

Piggybacking. Piggybacking is frequently used to gain access to controlled areas. Physical piggybacking occurs when an authorized employee goes through a door using his magnetic ID card, and an unauthorized employee behind him also enters the premises. The unauthorized employee is then in a position to commit a crime. Electronic piggybacking may also occur. For example, an authorized employee leaves his terminal or desktop, and an authorized individual uses that to gain access.

COMMUNICATIONS SECURITY

Attacks on computer security that do not require physical access fall under the domain of *communications security.* The increased use of computer technology has also increased dependence on telecommunications. All types of data, including sound, video, and traditional text data, are transferred between computers over networks. Communications security means ensuring that the physical links between the computer networks function at all times. This also means that, during data transmission, breakdowns, delays, and disturbances are prevented. Care must be taken to prevent unauthorized individuals from tapping, modifying, or otherwise intercepting data transmission. Six considerations in communications security are as follows:

Line security. Line security is concerned with restricting unauthorized access to the communication lines that connect the various parts of the computer systems.

Transmission security. Transmission security is concerned with preventing unauthorized interception of communications.

Digital signature. This is used to authenticate the sender or message integrity to the receiver. A secure digital signature process is a method of signing a document making forgery infeasible and then validating that the signature belongs to the authorized individual.

Cryptographic security. Cryptography is the science of secret writing. The purpose of cryptographic security is to render the information unintelligible if transmission is intercepted by unauthorized individuals. When the information is to be used, it can be decoded. Security coding (encryption) of sensitive data is necessary. A common method is the Data Encryption

Standard (DES). For even greater security, double encryption may be used in which encryption is processed twice using two different keys. (One may also encrypt files on a hard disk to prevent an intruder from reading the data.) IBM announced in May 1997 that it developed a new encryption system generating hundreds of codes at random, each being extremely difficult to crack.

Emission security. Electronic devices emit electromagnetic radiation that can be intercepted without wires by unauthorized individuals. Emission security is concerned with containing the emission of such radiation.

Technical security. Technical security is concerned with preventing the use of devices, such as microphones, transmitters, or wiretaps, to intercept data transmission. Security modems may be used that allow only authorized users to access confidential data. A modem may have graduated levels of security, and different users may be assigned different security codes. There can be password and call back features. There may be built-in audit trail capabilities allowing you to monitor who is accessing private files.

CONTROLS

Controls are used to reduce the probability of attack on computer security. As additional controls are placed, the overall operating costs are likely to increase. As discussed earlier, cost-benefit considerations require a careful balance of controls. There are four main classes of controls, discussed below.

Deterrent controls. The aim of deterrent controls is to create an atmosphere conducive to control compliance. For example, the organization could impose penalties whenever a control is disregarded, regardless of the actual damage. Deterrent controls are inexpensive to implement. However, their effectiveness is difficult to measure. These controls complement other controls and are not sufficient by themselves.

Preventive controls. Preventive controls are designed to reduce the probability of an attack. They serve as the first line of defense. Effective preventive controls will thwart a perpetrator who is attempting to obtain access to the computer system.

Detective controls. Once a system has been violated, detective controls help identify the occurrence of harm. These controls do nothing to insulate the system from harm; they only serve to focus attention on the problem. For example, a bait file will identify unauthorized use. Here, a "dummy" non-existent record is put into processing. There may be a comparison between standard run time and actual run time for an application to spot possible misuse.

Corrective controls. After a loss has occurred, corrective controls serve to reduce the impact of the threat. Their purpose is to aid in recovering from damage or in reducing the effect of damage. For instance, lost information on floppies may be restored with utility programs.

APPLICATION CONTROLS

Application controls are built into software to deter crime and minimize errors. Application controls typically include: input controls, processing controls, change controls, testing controls, output controls, and procedural controls.

Input controls. The purpose of input controls is to ensure that each transaction is authorized, processed correctly, and processed only once. An *edit program* substantiates input by comparing fields to expected values and by testing logical relationships. A *missing-data check* assures that all data fields have been used. A *valid-character check* verifies that only alphabetical, numeric, or other special characters are present in data fields. *Dual read* is an input control in which duplicate entry or key verification verifies the accuracy of some critical field in a record by requiring a data item to be entered twice. A *valid-code check* compares a classification (e.g., asset account number) or transaction code (e.g., credit sale entry) to a master list of account or transaction codes (master file reference). Input controls include rejecting, correcting, and resubmitting data that were initially wrong. Is input information properly authorized? Character validation tests may also be programmed to check input data fields to see if they contain alphanumerics when the are supposed to have numerics. A preprocessing edit check verifies a key entry by a second one or a visual examination. There may be a limit test check of input data fields to make sure that some predetermined limit has not been exceeded (e.g., employee weekly hours should not be automatically processed if the sum of regular and overtime hours per individual exceeds 60).

Processing controls. Processing controls are used to ensure that transactions entered in to the system are valid and accurate, that external data are not lost or altered, and that invalid transactions are reprocessed correctly. Sequence tests may be performed to note missing items. In batch or sequential processing, batch totals are used to ensure that the counted and totaled number and value of similar data items are the same before and after processing. In a parity check, because data are processed in arrays of bits (binary digits of 1 or 0), we add a parity bit, if needed, so as to make the total of all the "1" bits even or odd. The parity bit assures that bits are not lost during computer processing. Parity checks prevent data corruption. External and internal file identification labels may be used. The program may check to see if an item in a record is within the correct range. Crossfooting tests apply to logical tests for information consistency (e.g., sum totals to column totals). Application reruns ensure that the initial run was correct.

Change controls. Change controls safeguard the integrity of the system by establishing standard procedures for making modifications. For example, a log file can be maintained to document all changes. A report may be prepared showing the master file before and after each update.

Testing controls. Testing controls ensure that a system is reliable before the system becomes operational. For example, limited test data could be processed and tested using the new system. Utility programs can be used to diagnose problems in application software.

Output controls. The purpose of output controls is to authenticate the previous controls; this is used to ensure that authorized transactions are processed correctly. Random comparisons can be made of output to input to verify correct processing. For example, an echo check involves transmitting data received by an output device back to its source. Output controls presume that information is not lost or improperly distributed. Errors by receivers of output, such as customers, should be investigated.

Procedural controls. Procedural controls safeguard computer operations, reduce the chance of processing mistakes, and ensure continued functioning if a computer failure occurs. Processing errors must be thoroughly evaluated. Output should be distributed to authorized users of such information. A record retention and recovery plan must also exist.

ELECTRONIC DATA INTERCHANGE

Electronic data interchange (EDI) is the electronic transfer of business information among trading partners. Thousands of businesses use EDI to exchange information with suppliers and customers. The benefits of EDI are clear. The paperwork is greatly reduced, and the efficiency in accounting and processing functions is greatly enhanced.

The risk inherent in EDI is much greater than in standard computer processing systems. An EDI security system is only as strong as the weakest link among the trading partners. Some risks of EDI include the following:

- Data could be lost in the interchange.
- Unauthorized changes may be made to the data.
- The lack of paperwork means a greater likelihood that an audit trail may not be maintained.
- Authorized individuals can initiate unauthorized transactions.
- Unauthorized individuals can gain access to the system through the weakest link among the trading partners.

PERSONNEL SECURITY

Each employee should sign a nondisclosure agreement not to reveal computer security information to anyone outside the business or to unauthorized staff within the firm. If a staff member leaves the company, certain control procedures are required, including returning all badges, keys, and company materials. Access codes, passwords, and locks may need to be changed.

Specific procedures should be established for recruiting and hiring computer data processing professionals. A security investigation should include contacting the applicant's work references, checking the applicant's background with appropriate authorities, and verifying the applicant's school references. New employees should be educated about the importance of computer security with respect to every phase of computer data processing. For example, to indoctrinate new employees, educational seminars can be scheduled in which security professionals communicate the company's rules and procedures to new employees.

In addition, formal performance evaluation systems should be in place to ensure that employees' performances and skills are routinely reviewed. An effective review procedure can help prevent job frustration and stress. It can also help maintain employee morale. Discontent often acts as a catalyst for computer crime. Possible indicators of discontent include excessive absenteeism, late arrival, low quality or low production output, complaints, putting off vacations, and excessive unwarranted overtime. Quick action such as communicating with the employee on a one-to-one basis can minimize, if not eliminate, job discontentment.

Segregation of duties among staff is needed. For example, a programmer should not also serve as an operator. Rotation of assignments should also exist, such as programmers doing different assignments and operators working different shifts. A function may be designed to require more than one operator to make it more difficult for an individual to perpetrate an improper act, since others are involved. The development and testing of software should also be separate.

ENVIRONMENTAL SECURITY

Computer areas should be properly cleaned and dusted. Facilities should be protected against adverse effects of the weather.

AUDIT TRAILS

Audit trails contain information regarding any additions, deletions, or modifications to the system, providing evidence concerning transactions. An effective audit trail allows the data to be retrieved and certified. Audit trails will give information regarding the date and time of the transaction, who processed it, and at which terminal it was processed.

To establish an adequate audit trail, you must analyze transactions related to the physical custody of assets, evaluate unusual transactions, and keep track of the sequential numbering of negotiable computer forms. Controls should be periodically tested. For example, the audit trail requires the tracing of transactions to control totals and from the control total to supporting transactions. Computer-related risks affect the company's internal control structure and thereby affect the company's audibility.

Electronic data interchange (EDI) systems are online systems in which computers automatically perform transactions such as order processing and invoice generation. Although this can reduce costs, it can adversely affect a company's auditability because of the lessened audit trail.

The American Institute of Certified Public Accountants (AICPA) has issued control techniques to ensure the integrity of an EDI system. The AICPA recommends controls over accuracy and completeness at the application level of an EDI system to include checks on performance to determine compliance with industry standards, checks on sequence numbering for transactions, reporting irregularities on a timely basis, verifying adequacy of audit trails, and checking of embedded headers and trailers at interchange, functional group, and transaction set level. Control techniques at the environmental level include reviewing quality assurance of vendor software, segregation of duties, ensuring that software is virus-free, procuring an audit report from the vendor's auditors, and evidence of testing. To ensure that all the EDI transactions are authorized, the AICPA provides these authorization controls: operator identification code, operator profile, trading partner identifier, maintenance of user access variables, and regular changing of passwords.

NETWORK SECURITY

Network security is needed for both local area networks (LANs) and wide area networks (WANs). There must be positive authentication before a user can gain knowledge of the online applications, network environment, nature of applications, terminal identification, and so on. Information should be provided on a *need to know* basis only.

Access controls should exist to enable a specific terminal or application. Date and time constraints, along with restricted file use, may be employed. Unauthorized use may deactivate or lock a terminal. "Diskless" workstations may result in a safer network environment.

There must be a secure communication link of data transmission between interconnected host computer systems of the network. A major form of communication security on the network is the use of cryptography to safeguard transmitted data confidentiality. Cryptographic algorithms may be either symmetric (private key) or asymmetric (public key). The two popular encryption methods are *link-level* security and *end-to-end* security. The former safeguards traffic independently on every communication link, whereas the latter safeguards messages from the source to the ultimate destination. Link-level enciphers the communications line at the bit level; data is deciphered upon entering the nodes. End-to-end security enciphers information at the entry point to the network and deciphers at the exit point. Unlike link-level security, protection exists over information inside the nodes.

Security should be provided in different layers. Security must exist over networking facilities and telecommunication elements. Controls must be placed over both host computers and subnetworks.

Network traffic may travel over many subnetworks, each having its own security levels that depend on confidentiality and importance. Therefore, different security services and controls may be required. Security aspects of each subnetwork have to be distributed to the gateways so as to incorporate security and controls in routing decisions.

The architecture of a network includes hardware, software, information link controls, standards, topologies, and protocols. A protocol relates to how computers communicate and transfer information. Security controls must exist over each component within the architecture to ensure reliable and correct data exchanges. Otherwise, the integrity of the system may be compromised.

Communication security may be in the following forms:

- *Access control.* These guard against improper use of the network. For example, KERBEROS is commercial authentication software that is added to an existing security system to verify a user's existence and prevent access by an imposter. KERBEROS does this by encrypting passwords transmitted around networks. Password control and user authentication devices may be used such as Security Dynamics' SecurID (800-SECU-RID) and Vasco Data Security's Access Key 11 (800-238-2726). Do not accept a prepaid call if it is not from a network user. Hackers do not typically spend their own funds. Review data communications billings and verify each host-to-host connection. Review all dial-up terminal users. Are the telephone numbers unlisted and changed periodically? Control specialists should try to make unauthorized access to the network to test whether the security is properly working.
- *Identification.* This identifies the origin of a communication within the network through digital signals or notarization.
- *Data confidentiality.* This maintains confidentiality over unauthorized disclosure of information within the communication process.
- *Data integrity.* This security form guards against unauthorized changes (e.g., adding or deleting) of data at both the receiving and sending points, such as through cryptographic methods. Antivirus software should be installed at both the network server and workstations. Detection programs are available to alert users when viruses enter the system.
- *Authentication.* This substantiates the identity of an originating or user entity within the network. The authenticator verifies that the entity is actually the authorized individual and that the information being transmitted is appropriate. Examples of security controls are passwords, time stamping, synchronized checks, nonrepudiation, and multiple-way handshakes. Biometric authentication methods measure body characteristics with the use of equipment attached to the workstation. Retinal laser beams may also be used. Keystroke dynamics is another possibility for identification.
- *Digital signature.* With this method, messages are signed with a private key.
- *Routing control.* This inhibits data flow to insecure network elements such as identified unsecure relays, links, or subnetworks.
- *Traffic padding.* This is traffic analysis of data for reasonableness.
- *Interference minimization.* Radar/radio transmission interference must be eliminated or curtailed. There are various ways to backup data in networks. For a small network, one workstation may be used as the backup and restore unit for other nodes. In a large network, backup may be done by several servers, since the failure of one could have disastrous effects on the entire system. Access to backup files must be strictly controlled.

An example of a network security package is Intrusion Detection Incorporated's Kane Security Analyst, which assesses existing security.

THE SECURITY ADMINISTRATOR

The size and needs of the company will dictate the size of the security administration department. This department is responsible for the planning and execution of a computer security system. They ensure that the information system's data is reliable and accurate. The security administrator should possess a high level of computer technical knowledge as well as having management skills and a general understanding of the organization's internal control structure.

A security administrator should interact with other departments to learn about the organization's changing needs and to be able to maintain and update the security system efficiently The security administrator is responsible for enacting and customizing policies and standards for the organization based on specific needs. Checks on performance and monitoring of staff should be done to ensure compliance with these policies and standards. In developing these policies and procedures, as well as the overall information computer security system, the security administrator must perform a risk assessment (see Figure 17.3).

THE LAW

The Computer Fraud and Abuse Act is a federal law making it a crime to engage in any unauthorized use (copying, damaging, obtaining database information, etc.) of computer hardware or software across state lines. Offenders can be sentenced to up to 20 years in prison and fined up to $100,000.

SUMMARY

Computer security is intended to safeguard software, data, hardware, and personnel. Monitoring and control measures and devices are needed. Duties should be segregated, and proper training should exist. Computer equipment, including peripherals, should be properly maintained. Someone should be in charge of monitoring computer security in the entire company. Periodic and surprise computer security audits should be undertaken. Employees who do not follow computer security guidelines should be identified and disciplined.

Insurance coverage should not be inadequate or excessive. If inadequate, there is a great risk of loss. If excessive, insurance costs are exorbitant. Insurance coverage depends on numerous factors including risk level, loss exposure, cost, time period, and policy provisions.

Microcomputer Security Checklist

(A "no" response indicates a potential vulnerability.)

Organizational

1. Is management's attitude toward microcomputer security, as reflected by its actions, appropriate?
2. Has the organization prepared a coordinated plan of implementation for microcomputers, addressing such factors as
   - ❏ Hardware compatibility within and between departments?
   - ❏ Software compatibility within and between departments?
   - ❏ Future expansion?
   - ❏ A manual of standard practices?
3. Is rotation of duties utilized to increase the chance of exposure of errors and irregularities and to give depth to microcomputer operations?
4. Are vacations mandatory to reduce the likelihood of fraud or embezzlement resulting from increased chance of exposure?
5. Do personnel policies include background checks to reduce the likelihood of hiring dishonest employees?
6. Have employees who have access to sensitive data been bonded?
7. Is there a quality control program in existence?
8. Are exception reports to procedures and policies prepared?

Hardware

1. Is theft and hazard insurance covering microcomputers adequate?
2. Which of the following theft deterrence techniques are in operation:
   - ❏ Limiting computer access to employees with a defined need?
   - ❏ Installing computers only in areas that are locked and kept under surveillance when not in use?
   - ❏ Bolting computers to desks or tables?
   - ❏ Placing lockable covers on computers?
   - ❏ Installing alarms and motion detectors in areas with a high concentration of computer equipment?
   - ❏ Placing internal trip alarms inside computers?
3. Which of the following factors for the physical protection of hardware are present:
   - ❏ Elementary surge suppressors or noise filtering devices to protect against surges and spikes?
   - ❏ Line conditioners to smooth out power?
   - ❏ Uninterruptible power supply units to supply power during power outages?
   - ❏ Antistatic mats and pads to neutralize static electricity?
   - ❏ Halon fire extinguishers to reduce losses from fire?
   - ❏ Placement away from the sprinkler system to avoid water damage?
   - ❏ Waterproof covers to avoid water damage?
   - ❏ Implementation of a smoking ban, or the use of a small fan around the computer to blow any smoke away from the system?
   - ❏ Avoidance of other potential pollutants (e.g., dust, food, and coffee) around the computer?
4. In the event of equipment breakdown, is substitute equipment available?

FIGURE 17.3 Microcomputer security checklist *(continues next page).*

Software

1. Does present insurance cover software?
2. Is insurance carried to cover the cost of a business interruption resulting from a computer mishap?
3. Are backups and working copies maintained on site?
4. Do software backups, like originals, have write-protect tabs in place?
5. Are originals placed in off-site storage (e.g., a safe-deposit box or the home of the owner or chief executive officer)?
6. Are steps taken to avoid unauthorized copying of licensed software?
7. Are steps taken to avoid the use of bootleg software?
8. Is software tested before use?

Data and Data Integrity

1. Are backups in data files routinely prepared?
2. Is documentation duplicated?
3. Are backups placed in off-site storage, e.g., a safe-deposit box or the home of the owner or chief executive officer? (For particularly important files, a third copy may be kept.)
4. Are backups of sensitive data that are stored off site encrypted to reduce the chance of unauthorized exposure?
5. Do hard disks include an external hard disk or a cassette tape as a backup?
6. Is a program such as *Ship* or *Park* used when removing the read/write head from the hard disk to reduce tire likelihood of a crash?
7. Has the FORMAT command been left off the hard disk?
8. Have DEBUG and other utilities that provide a means of accessing restricted software or data been left off the disk?
9. Has data encryption been considered for sensitive data (e.g., payroll)?
10. Is work on sensitive data limited to private offices to reduce the likelihood of exposure?
11. Is sensitive data only placed on distinctly marked diskettes or removable hard disks?
12. Are diskettes or cartridges removed from unattended computers?
13. Does the organization have a designated custodian for sensitive data disks?
14. Are unattended microcomputers turned off when data is removed from the system?
15. Is reformatting of the disk or overwriting of the file required for destruction of sensitive data?
16. Have legally binding confidentiality agreements been drafted by the employer and signed by microcomputers users with access to sensitive data (e.g., customer lists)?
17. Are diskettes or cartridges stored or fire-rated safe?
18. Which of the following are required before decision are made based on microcomputer-generated reports:
    ❏ Validating the accuracy of customized microcomputer programs and imbedded formulas?
    ❏ Dating changes to databases?
    ❏ Dating reports with the date of production and the date of the database?
    ❏ Independent validation of the data input?
19. In the event of downtime, are there alternative processing arrangements with service bureaus?
20. Does a preventive maintenance program exist?
21. Have data been processed out of sequence or priority?
22. Do transactions not fit a trend (e.g., too little, too much, too often, too late, illogical)?
23. Are compiled data in conformity with legal and regulatory dictates?
24. Did any individuals attempt access above their authorization level?

FIGURE 17.3 Microcomputer security checklist *(continued)*.

Glossary

Application program. Computer software written specifically to process data in an information system. It performs tasks and solves problems applicable to a manager's work. Business applications include word processors, spreadsheets, and financial applications.

Artificial intelligence (AI). Thinking and reasoning software based on information input into it by a human expert. The reasoning process involves self-correction. Significant data are evaluated, and relevant relationships are uncovered. The computer learns which kind of answers are reasonable and which are not. Artificial intelligence performs complicated strategies that determine the best or worst way to accomplish a task or avoid an undesirable result. Examples of applications of AI are tax planning and capital budgeting analysis.

Audit software. Computer programs designed to examine and test a company's accounting records. Some packages aid in gathering evidence, performing analytical tests, sampling data, appraising internal control, audit scheduling, and printing exception reports. The software is used by internal auditors.

Automatic programming. The process of using one program to prepare another program.

Automatic recovery program. A program enabling a system to continue functioning even though equipment has failed.

Background processing. Lower-priority programs are executed when the system is not being used by higher-priority programs.

Baud rate. Serial information transfer speed with which a modem receives and sends data.

Beta. Work-in-progress version of a program. Typically two or three betas are released to testers before the application is sent to manufacturing, or *goes* gold.

Block diagram. A diagram using symbols to explain the interconnections and information flow between hardware and software.

Budgeting models. Computer-based mathematical models generating all kinds of corporate budgets (e.g., cash flow or profitability). The models help managers look at a variety of "what-if" questions. The resultant calculations provide a basis for choice among alternatives under conditions of uncertainty.

Buffer. The area of a computer's memory used to hold information temporarily.

Catalog. Directory of locations of files.

Chain links. A series of linked data items.

Client. A personal computer that is connected via a network to a server, which stores data and applications and manages communications among the clients.

Corporate planning model. A computer-based integrated business planning model in which production and marketing models are linked to the financial model. It is a description, explanation, and interrelation of functional areas of a business (accounting, finance and investments, marketing production, management, economics), expressed in terms of mathematical and logical equations so as to generate a variety of reports, including financial forecasts. Corporate planning models may also be used for risk analysis and "what-if" experimentation. The goals of the model include improving the quality of planning and decision making, reducing the decision risk, and favorably influencing the future corporate environment.

Cyber investing. Investing, such as on-line trading, on the Internet.

Cyberspace. Originally used in *Neuromancer,* William Gibson's novel of direct brain-computer networking, it refers to the collective realms of computer-aided communication.

Data interchange format (DIF). A file system used to transfer computer files from one program to another.

Database management software. Computer programs used to manage data in a data base. It consists of a set of programs that provide for defining, controlling, and accessing the data base. The software allows managers to enter, manipulate, retrieve, display, select, sort, edit, and index data.

Debug. The process of tracing and correcting flaws in a software program or hardware device. Computerized routines may be used to find bugs.

Decision support system. A branch of a management information system that provides answers to management problems and integrates the decision maker into the system as a component. DSS software provides support to the manager in the decision-making process. It analyzes a specific situation and can be modified as the manager desires. Examples of applications include planning and forecasting.

Expert systems. Computer software involving stored reasoning schemes and containing decision-making processes of business experts in their specialized areas. The software mimics the way human experts make decisions. The expert system appraises and solves business problems requiring human intelligence and imagination that involve known and unknown information. The components of the expert system include a knowledge base, inference engine, user interface, and knowledge acquisition facility.

Financial analysis software. Software capable of taking financial data (e.g., online information on the World Wide Web) and performing trend and ratio calculations. Investment and credit decisions are based on the analysis results.

Functional model. A functional branch of a general corporate planning model. It is essentially used to generate pro forma financial statements and financial ratios. A financial model is a mathematical model describing the interrelationships among financial variables of the firm. It is the basic tool for budgeting and budget planning. Also, it is used for risk analysis and "what-if" experiments. Many financial models of today are built using special modeling languages, such as IFPS or spreadsheet programs such as Excel.

Graphics software. A program showing business information in graphic form, including charts and diagrams. This enhances the understanding of the information including in terms of trends and relationships.

Hypertext. A database approach linking related data, programs, and pictures.

Integrated software. A software package that combines many applications in one program. Integrated packages can move data among several programs utilizing common commands and file structures. An integrated package is recommended when identical source information is used for varying managerial purposes and activities.

Interface. A means of interaction between two computer devices or systems that handle data (e.g., formats or codes) differently. An interface is a device that converts signals from one device into signals that the other device needs.

Internet. International network connecting smaller networks linking computers of different entities.

Intranet. Internal company web sites. An intranet is developed by the company itself.

Linux. Freeware variant of the UNIX operating system. Since the source code for Linux is freely distributed, problems can be fixed and updates developed very rapidly.

Local area network. The linking of computers and other devices for intersite and intercompany applications in a small geographic area.

Management information system. A computer-based or manual system that transforms data into information that is useful in the support of decision making.

Material requirement planning (MRP). A computer-based information system designed to handle ordering and scheduling of demand-dependent inventories (such as raw materials, component parts, and subassemblies that will be used in the production of a finished product).

Modeling languages. Usually, English-like programming languages that are used to solve a specific task and generate various reports based on the solution and analysis. For example, financial planning modeling languages such as IFPS (Integrated Financial Planning System) are computer software packages that help financial planners develop a financial model in English terms (not requiring any computer programming knowledge on the user's part), perform various analyses such as "what-if" analysis, and further generate pro forma financial reports.

Multitasking. Simultaneous execution of two or more computer functions.

Network. 1. interconnected nodes, i.e., points where working units interact (link) with others. 2. Connection of computers and devices.

Neural network. A technology in which computers actually try to learn the right answer to a question from the database and operator. The system receives a positive or negative response to output from the operator and stores that data so that it will make a better decision the next time. While still in its infancy, this technology shows promise for use in fraud detection, accounting, economic forecasting, and risk appraisals.

Online searching. Using a computer retrieval system to obtain information from a database such as on the Internet.

Optical character recognition (OCR). A computer software tool that recognizes typed or printed characters on paper so they can be recorded on disk.

Real-time processing. Computer processing of data in connection with another process outside the computer.

Relational database. A database consisting of relationships between data items.

Simulation. An attempt to represent a real-life system via a model to determine how a change in one or more variables affect the rest of the system. Also called "what-if" analysis.

Speech recognition software. A program in which verbal commands activate the computer to perform functions.

Spreadsheet. A table of numbers arranged in rows and columns to make accounting, finance, marketing, and other business calculations. Spreadsheets facilitate end-result summary numbers, "what-if" experimentations, and projections.

Statistical software. A computer program making quantitative calculations such as standard deviation, coefficient of variation, regression analysis, correlation, and variance analysis.

Tax software. Tax modules for preparing federal and state income tax returns. Tax planning modules exist to examine tax options and alternatives to minimize the company's tax liability in current and future years. "What-if" tax situation scenarios may be evaluated.

Template. A computer-based worksheet that includes the relevant formulas for a particular application but not the data. It is a blank worksheet on which data are saved and filled in as needed for a future business application and to solve problems. Templates are predefined files, including cell formulas and row and column labels, for specific spreadsheet applications. Templates allow for the referencing of cells and formulations of interrelated formulas and functions. They are reused to analyze similar transactions.

Terminal. An input-output device allowing a user to communicate directly with a computer.

Thinking software. Computer programs used by managers for preparing written reports, including specialized analyses of corporate operations. The software contains aids to improve writing skills and idea formulation so managers can better create an outline and written report. The information is labeled, organized, and structured.

Time software. A computer program that tracks hours worked by employees by function, operation, or activity. It prepares an analysis of the variance between budgeted and actual hours and prepares trends in actual hours over a stated time period (e.g., quarterly comparisons).

Utility program. A program supporting the processing of a computer such as diagnostic and tracing programs.

Wide area network (WAN). A network comprising a large geographic area.

World Wide Web (WWW). Internet system for worldwide hypertext linking of multimedia documents, making the relationship of information that is common between documents easily accessible and completely independent of physical location.

Index